PREFACE

This monograph arose from an attempt to write a paper that would unify the division theorems for matrix and operator functions which appear in different fields. In the course of our investigations we observed a general geometric principle that could be applied to rational matrices, matrix and operator polynomials and characteristic operator functions of various kinds. From our contacts with P. DeWilde and P. Van Dooren, we learned about applications to system and network theory and also about the importance of perturbation problems in connection with numerical computations. We also observed connections with the theory of Wiener Hopf factorization and with methods of solving singular integral equations. A lecture of C.G. Lekkerkerker drew our attention to possible applications to the energy transport equation. As the number of topics we were able to include in our approach grew, it became clear that the confines of one paper were too restrictive. On the other hand, because of the nice and strong connections between the different fields, we did not like to split the material into several parts, and therefore we decided to write this monograph. This also allowed us to make the presentation more selfcontained.

Jael Fried and Marja Verburg prepared very efficiently and with great care the typescript of the present monograph. We are grateful for their excellent work. Also we thank Betty Kuiper for secretarial assistance.

Amsterdam, July 1979 The authors

TABLE OF CONTENTS

Introduction 1

1. Divisibility of transfer functions 5
   1.1 Multiplication and divisibility of nodes 5
   1.2 Canonical spectral factorization (1) 11
   1.3 Finite dimensional nodes 17
   1.4 Characteristic operator functions and transfer functions 19
      1.4.1 Brodskii nodes 20
      1.4.2 Krein nodes 21
      1.4.3 Monic nodes 24
      1.4.4 Polynomial nodes 29
      1.4.5 Final remarks 31
   1.5 Möbius transformations of nodes 34

2. Realization and linearization 44
   2.1 Realization for rational matrix functions 44
   2.2 Realization for rational operator functions 52
   2.3 Realization for arbitrary holomorphic operator functions 53
   2.4 Linearization 56

3. Minimal nodes 62
   3.1 Minimality of nodes 62
   3.2 Minimality for finite dimensional nodes 65
   3.3 Minimality in special cases 71
      3.3.1 Brodskii nodes 71
      3.3.2 Krein nodes 72
      3.3.3 Monic nodes 73
      3.3.4 Polynomial nodes 73

4. Minimal factorizations of rational matrix functions 77
   4.1 Local degree and local minimality 77
   4.2 McMillan degree and minimality of nodes 82

4.3 Minimal factorization 84
4.4 Canonical spectral factorization (2) 91
4.5 Application to Wiener-Hopf integral equations 93
4.6 Application to block Toeplitz matrices 100
4.7 Application to singular integral equations 105

5. Divisibility and Riccati equation 110
5.1 Angular subspaces and angular operators 110
5.2 Angular operators and the division theorem 113
5.3 The Riccati equation 118

6. Application to transport equation 121
6.1 The transport equation 121
6.2 Wiener-Hopf equations with operator-valued L_1-kernels 123
6.3 Construction of the Wiener-Hopf factorization 125
6.4 The matching of the subspaces 136
6.5 Formulas for solutions 139

7. Stability of spectral divisors 142
7.1 Examples and first results for finite dimensional case 142
7.2 Opening between subspaces and angular operators 146
7.3 Stability of spectral divisors of nodes 153
7.4 Applications to transfer functions 161
7.5 Applications to Riccati equation 165

8. Stability of divisors 169
8.1 Stable invariant subspaces 169
8.2 Stable minimal factorizations of rational matrix functions 178
8.3 Stable factorization of monic matrix polynomials 182

8.4 Stable solutions of the operator Riccati equation 186
8.5 Stability of stable factorizations 187

9. Factorization of real matrix functions 191
9.1 Real rational matrix functions 191
9.2 Real monic matrix polynomials 195
9.3 Stable and isolated invariant subspaces 196
9.4 Stable and isolated real factorizations 207
9.5 Stability of stable real factorizations 212

References 217

Subject index 223

INTRODUCTION

In this monograph different types of factorization problems are studied from one general point of view. The treatment is based on a new geometric principle. Considerable attention is given to the matter of stability and to applications.

The matrix and operator functions considered here appear as transfer functions of certain systems of operators. In fact they are of the form

$$(0.1) \qquad W(\lambda) = D + C(\lambda - A)^{-1}B,$$

where λ is the complex parameter and A,B,C and D are matrices or bounded linear operators acting between appropriate spaces. When D is the identity operator I, by the geometric principle referred to above, the function $W(\lambda)$ admits a factorization $W(\lambda) = W_1(\lambda)W_2(\lambda)$ whenever there exists a pair of complementary subspaces M and $M^\times$ such that M is invariant under A and $M^\times$ is invariant under $A-BC$, and in that case the factors are given by

$$W_1(\lambda) = I + C(\lambda - A)^{-1}(I - \Pi)B,$$

$$W_2(\lambda) = I + C\Pi(\lambda - A)^{-1}B,$$

where Π is the projection along M onto $M^{\times}$. If in (0.1) the triple A,B,C is chosen in a minimal way, we obtain by the above procedure all so-called minimal factorizations of $W(\lambda)$. Furthermore, in that case there is a one-one correspondence between the admissible projections Π and the minimal factorizations of $W(\lambda)$.

Factorizations of matrix and operator functions of the type described above appear in many branches of analysis and applications. In network theory minimal factorizations of the transfer function are of interest in order to obtain a network with a prescribed transfer function by a cascade connection of elementary sections that have the simplest synthesis [6,14]. Factorization problems also appear in the theory of non-selfadjoint operators. Characteristic operator functions have the form (0.1), and it is important to know the regular factors of a given characteristic operator function or to have its continuous multiplicative representations [8,11,47]. For a Wiener-Hopf integral operator the Wiener-Hopf (or spectral) factorization of the symbol allows one to answer questions about the invertibility of the operator and to get explicit formulas for its inverse [19,23]. It turns out that in many cases the Wiener-Hopf factorization falls into the category described here. In particular this is true for the Wiener-Hopf integral equation associated with the energy transport equation. Also the division theory for monic matrix and operator polynomials, which has been developed in [24,25,26] recently, may be explained in terms of the geometric principle referred to above (cf. [3]).

Although from the point of view developed here all these factorizations are very much alike, the reasons to consider them differ from field to field and can be quite opposite indeed. For example, in network theory, because of finite dimensionality, the structure of the invariant subspaces M and $M^{\times}$ is well understood, and the geometric principle may be used to reduce the factorization problem to a construction of a direct sum of invariant subspaces. In the theory of characteristic operator functions the converse situation appears, because there in some cases the structure of the factors is known and the geometric principle can be employed to describe the invariant subspaces of some infinite dimensional operators.

The problem to compute numerically the factors of a given transfer function leads in a natural way to questions about the stability of divisors under small perturbations (see [5]). It turns out that in general the factors are unstable. Using the geometric principle all stable cases can be determined and estimates can be given for the measure of stability.

The description of divisors of characteristic operator functions in terms of invariant subspaces of a single operator (cf. [8]) may be viewed as a pre-version of the geometric principle we described above. Statements that are more close to it can be found in [3,38,45]. In the most general form it was considered for the finite dimensional case in [5], where also the numerical aspects of minimal factorizations were investigated from this point of view. In preparing the present monograph [5] was our starting point.

Now let us give a short description of the contents of the different chapters. In the first chapter multiplication and division of operator functions of the form (0.1) are described in terms of operations on the four operators appearing in (0.1). The connections with characteristic operator functions and the theory of matrix and operator polynomials are also explained in this chapter. The realization problem, that is, the problem to represent an operator function in the form $D+C(\lambda-A)^{-1}B$ is considered in Chapter 2. Also in this chapter we compare realization with the method of linearization by extension (cf. [20]). The special type of minimal factorization is studied in Chapters 3 and 4; its main properties are described and applications to Wiener-Hopf and singular integral equations and block Toeplitz matrices are given. In the fifth chapter another view on the divisibility theory is given using so-called angular operators. Here there is an important connection with the operator Riccati equation. Applications to the transport equation are given in Chapter 6. Stability problems are studied in Chapters 7 and 8.

First we consider mainly the stability of spectral factorizations while in Chapter 8 the general case of stable divisors is completely characterized in terms of spectral properties. In Chapter 9 the full theory is reviewed for the case of real matrices and operators acting on real spaces.

As it was our intention to make this monograph of interest for readers with different mathematical backgrounds, the exposition is made reasonably selfcontained. In particular we included some known material about characteristic operator functions, angular operators, minimal factorizations of rational matrices, the gap between subspaces et cetera.

Finally, a few words about notation and terminology. By an operator we shall mean any bounded linear operator acting between Banach spaces. The null space and range of an operator T are denoted by Ker T and Im T, respectively. The symbol $L(X,Y)$ will be used to denote the space of all operators acting between the Banach spaces X and Y. We assume that $L(X,Y)$ is endowed with the usual operator norm. Instead of $L(X,X)$ we write $L(X)$. The identity operator on a Banach space is denoted by I; we shall write I_X if we want to make clear that we mean the identity operator on the space X. The symbol I_n denotes the $n \times n$ identity matrix.

Chapter I

DIVISIBILITY OF TRANSFER FUNCTIONS

1.1 Multiplication and divisibility of nodes

A *node* is a system $\theta = (A,B,C,D;X,U,Y)$ of three complex Banach spaces X,U,Y and four (bounded linear) operators $A:X \to X$, $B:U \to X$, $C:X \to Y$ and $D:U \to Y$. The spaces U,X and Y are called the *input space*, *state space* and *output space*, respectively. Further the operator A is referred to as the *state space operator* or *main operator*. Two nodes $\theta_1 = (A_1,B_1,C_1,D_1;X_1,U,Y)$ and $\theta_2 = (A_2,B_2,C_2,D_2;X_2,U,Y)$ with the same input and output space are said to be *similar*, written $\theta_1 \simeq \theta_2$, if $D_1=D_2$ and there exists an invertible operator $S:X_1 \to X_2$, called a *node similarity*, such that

$$A_1 = S^{-1}A_2S \ , \ B_1 = S^{-1}B_2 \ , \ C_1 = C_2S. \tag{1.1}$$

Observe that the relation $\simeq$ is reflexive, symmetric and transitive.

Let $\theta = (A,B,C,D;X,U,Y)$ be a node. The *transfer function* $W_\theta(\lambda)$ of θ is defined by

$$W_\theta(\lambda) = D+C(\lambda-A)^{-1}B \ , \ \lambda\in\rho(A).$$

Here $\rho(A)$ is the resolvent set of A. Obviously similar nodes have the same transfer function. Note that

$$D = \lim_{\lambda\to\infty} W_\theta(\lambda). \tag{1.2}$$

We call D the *external operator* of θ. Instead of (1.2) we often write $W_\theta(\infty) = D$, and we consider the transfer function W_θ as an analytic operator function, defined on an open neighbourhood of ∞ on the Riemann sphere $\mathbb{C}_\infty = \mathbb{C}\cup\{\infty\}$.

If W is an operator function, analytic on an open subset

Ω of $\mathbb{C}_\infty$, we say that the node $\theta = (A,B,C,D;X,U,Y)$ is a <u>realization</u> for W on Ω if $\Omega \subset \rho(A) \cup \{\infty\}$ and $W(\lambda) = W_\theta(\lambda)$ for each $\lambda \in \Omega$. If there is no danger of ambiguity (e.g., if W is a rational matrix function), we shall simply speak about "realization" and omit the additional qualifiers. The term realization will also be used to denote any expression of the form $W(\lambda) = D + C(\lambda - A)^{-1}B$.

Part of our terminology is taken from system theory where the transfer function $W_\theta(\lambda) = D+C(\lambda-A)^{-1}B$ is used to describe the input/output behaviour of the linear dynamical system

$$\dot{x}(t) = Ax(t) + Bu(t) \ , \ y(t) = Cx(t) + Du(t).$$

The idea of introducing the concept of a node comes from the theory of characteristic operator functions as explained, for instance, in [8].

In the next paragraph we shall define the product of two nodes. This definition is motivated by the theory of characteristic operator functions. It is also related to the concept of series connection of two linear dynamical systems (cf.,e.g.,[41]).

Let $\theta_1 = (A_1,B_1,C_1,D_1;X_1,W,Y)$ and $\theta_2 = (A_2,B_2,C_2,D_2;X_2,U,W)$ be nodes such that the output space of θ_2 coincides with the input space of θ_1. Put $X = X_1 \oplus X_2$ and

$$A = \begin{bmatrix} A_1 & B_1C_2 \\ 0 & A_2 \end{bmatrix}, \ B = \begin{bmatrix} B_1D_2 \\ B_2 \end{bmatrix}, \ C = [C_1 \ \ D_1C_2], \ D=D_1D_2.$$

Then $(A,B,C,D;X,U,Y)$ is a node. It is called the <u>product</u> of θ_1 and θ_2 and denoted by $\theta_1\theta_2$. A straightforward calculation shows that

(1.3) $$W_{\theta_1\theta_2}(\lambda) = W_{\theta_1}(\lambda)W_{\theta_2}(\lambda) \ , \ \lambda \in \rho(A_1) \cap \rho(A_2) \subset \rho(A).$$

In general the inclusion in the second half of (1.3) is strict; equality occurs when, for instance, $\rho(A)$ is connected or $\sigma(A_1) \cap \sigma(A_2) = \phi$ (cf. Remark 1.2 below). Here $\sigma(A_i)$ denotes the spectrum $\mathbb{C} \setminus \rho(A_i)$ of A_i.

Let $\theta = (A,B,C,D;X,U,Y)$ be a node with invertible external operator D. Then

$$\theta^{\times} = (A-BD^{-1}C, BD^{-1}, -D^{-1}C, D^{-1} ; X, Y, U)$$

is again a node. We call $\theta^{\times}$ the <u>associate node</u> of θ. By abuse of notation we write $A^{\times}$ for $A-BD^{-1}C$, and we call $A^{\times}$ the <u>associate (main) operator</u> of θ. Note that $A^{\times}$ does not depend on A only, but also on the other operators appearing in the node θ. One can show that $W_{\theta}(\lambda)$ is invertible if and only if $\lambda \in \rho(A) \cap \rho(A^{\times})$ (see Corollary 2.7) and in that case $W_{\theta}(\lambda)^{-1} = W_{\theta^{\times}}(\lambda)$. Moreover $(\theta^{\times})^{\times} = \theta$ (in particular $(A^{\times})^{\times} = A$) and $(\theta_1\theta_2)^{\times} = \theta_2^{\times}\theta_1^{\times}$, the natural identification of $X_1 \oplus X_2$ and $X_2 \oplus X_1$ being a node similarity.

In the following we shall often deal with nodes having an invertible external operator. For such a node $\theta = (A,B,C,D;X,U,Y)$ the input space U and the output space Y are isomorphic. For simplicity we shall assume from now on that they are the same. Instead of $(A,B,C,D;X,Y,Y)$ we shall write $(A,B,C,D;X,Y)$.

The following theorem is a factorization theorem for nodes having an invertible external operator. A slightly more sophisticated result will be presented in Section 5.2. For a factorization theorem not dealing with the case when the external operators are invertible, we refer to Subsection 1.3.3 and Section 1.4 (cf. [3]).

THEOREM 1.1. <u>Let</u> $\theta = (A,B,C,D;X,Y)$ <u>be a node with invertible external operator</u> D, <u>let</u> Π <u>be a projection of</u> X, <u>and let</u>

$$A = \begin{pmatrix} A_{11} & A_{12} \\ A_{21} & A_{22} \end{pmatrix}, \quad B = \begin{pmatrix} B_1 \\ B_2 \end{pmatrix}, \quad C = [C_1 C_2] \tag{1.4}$$

<u>be the matrix representations of</u> A,B <u>and</u> C <u>with respect to the decomposition</u> $X = \operatorname{Ker}\Pi \oplus \operatorname{Im}\Pi$. <u>Assume</u> $D = D_1D_2$, <u>where</u> D_1 <u>and</u> D_2 <u>are invertible operators on</u> Y. <u>Write</u>

$$\theta_1 = (A_{11}, B_1D_2^{-1}, C_1, D_1; \operatorname{Ker}\Pi, Y), \tag{1.5}$$

$$(1.6) \qquad \theta_2 = (A_{22}, B_2, D_1^{-1}C_2, D_2; \operatorname{Im}\Pi, Y).$$

Then $\theta = \theta_1\theta_2$ *if and only if*

$$(1.7) \qquad A[\operatorname{Ker}\Pi] \subset \operatorname{Ker}\Pi \ , \ A^{\times}[\operatorname{Im}\Pi] \subset \operatorname{Im}\Pi .$$

PROOF. Assume $\theta = \theta_1\theta_2$. Then we know from the definition of the product that $\operatorname{Ker}\Pi$ is invariant under A. Identifying $\operatorname{Ker}\Pi \oplus \operatorname{Im}\Pi$ and $\operatorname{Im}\Pi \oplus \operatorname{Ker}\Pi$ we have $\theta^{\times} = \theta_2^{\times}\theta_1^{\times}$, and hence we conclude that $\operatorname{Im}\Pi$ is invariant under $A^{\times}$. So (1.7) is proved.

Conversely, assume (1.7) holds. The fact that $\operatorname{Ker}\Pi$ is invariant under A implies that $A_{21} = 0$. As

$$A^{\times} = A - BD^{-1}C = \begin{bmatrix} A_{11} - B_1D_2^{-1}D_1^{-1}C_1 & A_{12} - B_1D_2^{-1}D_1^{-1}C_2 \\ -B_2D_2^{-1}D_1^{-1}C_1 & A_{22} - B_2D_2^{-1}D_1^{-1}C_1 \end{bmatrix}$$

leaves the space $\operatorname{Im}\Pi$ invariant, we have $A_{12} = B_1D_2^{-1}D_1^{-1}C_2$. But then the conclusion $\theta = \theta_1\theta_2$ follows directly from the definition of the product of two nodes.

In view of formula (1.3) a factorization theorem for nodes implies a factorization theorem for transfer functions. So we have the following corollary.

COROLLARY. *Let* W *be the transfer function of a node* $\theta = (A,B,C,D;X,Y)$ *with invertible external operator* D, *and let* Π *be a projection of the state space* X *such that*

$$A[\operatorname{Ker}\Pi] \subset \operatorname{Ker}\Pi, \quad A^{\times}[\operatorname{Im}\Pi] \subset \operatorname{Im}\Pi .$$

Assume $D = D_1D_2$, *where* D_1 *and* D_2 *are invertible operators on* Y. *Then for* λ *in some open neighbourhood of* ∞ *we have* $W(\lambda) = W_1(\lambda)W_2(\lambda)$, *where*

$$W_1(\lambda) = D_1 + C(\lambda - A)^{-1}(I-\Pi)BD_2^{-1},$$

$$W_2(\lambda) = D_2^{-1}+D_1^{-1}C\Pi(\lambda-A)^{-1}B.$$

PROOF. Let θ_1 and θ_2 be defined as in formulas (1.5) and (1.6). Then $\theta = \theta_1\theta_2$, and hence by formula (1.3) we have $W_{\theta_1}(\lambda)W_{\theta_2}(\lambda) = W(\lambda)$ for λ in some open neighbourhood of ∞. To complete the proof observe that $W_1(\lambda) = W_{\theta_1}(\lambda)$ and $W_2(\lambda) = W_{\theta_2}(\lambda)$ for λ near ∞.

A projection Π of X satisfying (1.7) will be called a <u>supporting projection</u> for θ. If Π is a supporting projection for θ, then $I-\Pi$ is one for $\theta^{\times}$.

In a certain sense Theorem 1.1 gives a complete description of all possible factorizations of the node θ. Indeed, if $\theta \simeq \theta_1'\theta_2'$ for some nodes θ_1' and θ_2' having invertible external operators, then there exists a supporting projection Π for θ such that $\theta_1 \simeq \theta_1'$ and $\theta_2 \simeq \theta_2'$, where θ_1 and θ_2 are the nodes defined by (1.5) and (1.6).

It is interesting to consider the case when the input/output space Y is finite dimensional. Then the second part of (1.7) is equivalent to the rank condition

$$\text{rank}\begin{pmatrix} A_{12} & B_1 \\ C_2 & D \end{pmatrix} = \dim Y. \tag{1.8}$$

To see this we make the following general remark.

REMARK 1.2. Consider the operator

$$S = \begin{pmatrix} S_{11} & S_{12} \\ S_{21} & S_{22} \end{pmatrix} : Z_1 \oplus Z_2 \to Z_1 \oplus Z_2,$$

where $S_{ij} : Z_j \to Z_i$ $(i,j=1,2)$ are given linear operators. Assume that S_{22} is invertible. Then

$$S = \begin{pmatrix} I & S_{12}S_{22}^{-1} \\ 0 & I \end{pmatrix} \begin{pmatrix} S_{11} - S_{12}S_{22}^{-1}S_{21} & 0 \\ 0 & S_{22} \end{pmatrix} \begin{pmatrix} I & 0 \\ S_{22}^{-1}S_{21} & I \end{pmatrix}.$$

Since the first and third factor in the right hand side of this identity are invertible, it follows that

$$\text{(1.9)} \qquad \operatorname{rank} S = \operatorname{rank}(S_{11}-S_{12}S_{22}^{-1}S_{21}) + \operatorname{rank} S_{22}.$$

We also see that S is invertible if and only if $T = S_{11} - S_{12}S_{22}^{-1}S_{21}$ is invertible, and one computes easily that in that case

$$S^{-1} = \begin{pmatrix} T^{-1} & -T^{-1}S_{12}S_{22}^{-1} \\ -S_{22}^{-1}S_{21}T^{-1} & S_{22}^{-1}S_{21}T^{-1}S_{12}S_{22}^{-1} + S_{22}^{-1} \end{pmatrix}.$$

Of course a similar remark can be made when S_{11} is invertible.

Returning to (1.8), note that because of (1.9) the identity (1.8) is equivalent to $A_{12} - B_1D^{-1}C_2 = 0$. But this in turn is equivalent to the second part of (1.7).

Suppose $\theta = (A,B,C,D;X,Y)$ is a node for which the external operator D is equal to the identity operator on Y. In that case we write $\theta = (A,B,C;X,Y)$ instead of $\theta = (A,B,C,I;X,Y)$. Let Π be a projection of X. With respect to the decomposition $X = \operatorname{Ker}\Pi \oplus \operatorname{Im}\Pi$, we write A,B and C as in formula (1.4). The node

$$\text{(1.10)} \qquad \operatorname{pr}_\Pi(\theta) = (A_{22},B_2,C_2 \,;\, \operatorname{Im}\Pi, Y)$$

will be called the <u>projection</u> of θ associated with Π (cf. [8]). Observe that

$$\text{(1.11)} \qquad \operatorname{pr}_{I-\Pi}(\theta) = (A_{11},B_1,C_1;\operatorname{Ker}\Pi, Y)$$

One easily verifies that $pr_{\Pi}(\theta^{\times}) = pr_{\Pi}(\theta)^{\times}$. Note that (1.10) and (1.11) are defined for any projection Π of the state space X. By Theorem 1.1 the projection Π is a supporting projection for the node θ if and only if $\theta = pr_{I-\Pi}(\theta)pr_{\Pi}(\theta)$. In fact, the following slightly more general theorem holds true.

THEOREM 1.3. _Let_ $\theta = (A,B,C;X,Y)$ _be a node, and let_ $\Pi_1,\ldots,\Pi_n$ _be mutually disjoint projections of_ X _such that_ $\Pi_1+\ldots+\Pi_n$ _is the identity on_ X. _Then_

$$\theta = pr_{\Pi_1}(\theta)pr_{\Pi_2}(\theta)\ldots pr_{\Pi_n}(\theta)$$

if and only if for $j=1,\ldots,n-1$ _the projection_ $\Pi_{j+1}+\ldots+\Pi_n$ _is a supporting projection for_ θ.

PROOF. To prove the theorem one can employ the same arguments as in the proof of Theorem 1.1. Of course the decomposition $X = \text{Ker}\,\Pi \oplus \text{Im}\,\Pi$ has to be replaced by the decomposition $X = X_1\oplus\ldots\oplus X_n$, where $X_j = \text{Im}\,\Pi_j$, and with respect to the latter decomposition one writes A, B and C in block matrix form.

1.2 Canonical spectral factorization (1)

In this section we shall consider the factorization theorem of the previous section for the special case that the two factors have disjoint spectra. First we introduce some notation and terminology. By a _Cauchy contour_ Γ we shall mean the positively oriented boundary of a bounded Cauchy domain in $\mathbb{C}$. Such a contour consists of a finite number of non-intersecting closed rectifiable Jordan curves. We say that a Cauchy contour Γ _splits the spectrum_ $\sigma(S)$ of a bounded linear operator S if $\Gamma\cap\sigma(S) = \phi$. In that case $\sigma(S)$ decomposes into two disjoint compact sets σ_1 and σ_2 such that σ_1 is in the inner domain of Γ and σ_2 is in the outer domain of Γ. If Γ splits the spectrum of S, then we have a Riesz projection associated with S and Γ, namely the projection

$$P(S;\Gamma) = \frac{1}{2\pi i}\int_{\Gamma}(\lambda - S)^{-1}d\lambda.$$

The subspace $N = \operatorname{Im} P(S;\Gamma)$ will be called the _spectral subspace_ for S corresponding to the contour Γ (or to the spectral set σ_1).

In the following lemma Y_1 and Y_2 are complex Banach spaces.

LEMMA 1.4. _Let the operator_

$$S = \begin{bmatrix} S_{11} & S_{12} \\ 0 & S_{22} \end{bmatrix} : Y_1 \oplus Y_2 \to Y_1 \oplus Y_2$$

be given, and let Π _be a projection of_ $Y = Y_1 \oplus Y_2$ _such that_ $\operatorname{Ker} \Pi = Y_1$. _Then the compression_ $\Pi S|_{\operatorname{Im} \Pi}$ _and_ S_{22} _are similar. Further,_ Y_1 _is a spectral subspace for_ S _if and only if_ $\sigma(S_{11}) \cap \sigma(S_{22}) = \phi$, _and in that case_ $\sigma(S) = \sigma(S_{11}) \cup \sigma(S_{22})$ _and_

$$Y_1 = \operatorname{Im}\left(\frac{1}{2\pi i}\int_{\Gamma}(\lambda I - S)^{-1}d\lambda\right), \tag{1.12}$$

where Γ _is a Cauchy contour around_ $\sigma(S_{11})$ _separating_ $\sigma(S_{11})$ _from_ $\sigma(S_{22})$.

PROOF. Let P be the projection of $Y = Y_1 \oplus Y_2$ along Y_1 onto Y_2. As $\operatorname{Ker} P = \operatorname{Ker} \Pi$, we have $P = P\Pi$ and the map

$$E = P|_{\operatorname{Im} \Pi} : \operatorname{Im} \Pi \to Y_2$$

is an invertible operator. Write S_0 for the compression of S to $\operatorname{Im} \Pi$, and take $x = \Pi y$. Then

$$ES_0x = P\Pi S\Pi y = PS\Pi y = PSP\Pi y = S_{22}Ex,$$

and hence S_0 and S_{22} are similar.

Now suppose that $\sigma(S_{11})\cap\sigma(S_{22}) = \phi$. Then we can use Remark 1.2 to **show that** $\sigma(S) = \sigma(S_{11})\cup\sigma(S_{22})$. Let Γ be a Cauchy contour around $\sigma(S_{11})$ separating $\sigma(S_{11})$ from $\sigma(S_{22})$. Note that Γ splits the spectrum of S. For the corresponding Riesz projection we have

$$P(S;\Gamma) = \begin{pmatrix} I & * \\ 0 & 0 \end{pmatrix},$$

and it is clear that $Y_1 = \mathrm{Im}\, P(S;\Gamma)$. So Y_1 is a spectral subspace for S and (1.12) holds.

Next assume that $Y_1 = \mathrm{Im}\, Q$, where Q is a Riesz projection for S. Put $\Pi = I-Q$, and let S_0 be the restriction of S to $\mathrm{Im}\,\Pi$. Then $\sigma(S_{11})\cap\sigma(S_0) = \phi$. By the first part of the proof, the operators S_0 and S_{22} are similar. So $\sigma(S_0) = \sigma(S_{22})$, and hence we have shown that $\sigma(S_{11})\cap\sigma(S_{22}) = \phi$.

For a Cauchy contour Γ we let F_+ denote the interior domain of Γ and F_- will be the complement of $\bar{F}_+$ in $\mathbb{C}_\infty = \mathbb{C}\cup\{\infty\}$. Note that it is assumed that $\infty\in F_-$.

Let W be an operator function, analytic on a neighbourhood of Γ, whose values are invertible operators on Y. By a _right canonical (spectral) factorization_ (cf. [19]) of W with respect to Γ we mean a factorization

$$(1.13) \qquad W(\lambda) = W_-(\lambda)W_+(\lambda)\ ,\ \lambda\in\Gamma\ ,$$

where W_- and W_+ are Y-valued operator functions, analytic on $\bar{F}_-$ and $\bar{F}_+$, respectively, such that $W_-(\lambda)$ is invertible for each $\lambda\in\bar{F}_-$ and $W_+(\lambda)$ is invertible for each $\lambda\in\bar{F}_+$. If in (1.13) the factors W_- and W_+ are interchanged, then we speak of a _left canonical (spectral) factorization._

THEOREM 1.5. *Let* $W(\lambda)$ *be the transfer function of the node* $\theta = (A,B,C;X,Y)$, *and let* Γ *be a Cauchy contour that splits the spectra of* A *and* $A^{\times}$. *Assume*

$$X = \operatorname{Im} P(A;\Gamma) \oplus \operatorname{Ker} P(A^{\times};\Gamma).$$

Let Π *be the projection of* X *along* $\operatorname{Im} P(A;\Gamma)$ *onto* $\operatorname{Ker} P(A^{\times};\Gamma)$, *and define*

$$W_- = W_{pr_{I-\Pi}(\theta)}, \quad W_+ = W_{pr_{\Pi}(\theta)}.$$

Then $W(\lambda) = W_-(\lambda)W_+(\lambda)$ *for* $\lambda \in \rho(A)$ *and this factorization is a right canonical factorization of* W *with respect to* Γ.

Conversely, if $W = W_-W_+$ *is a right canonical factorization with respect to* Γ *and* $W_-(\infty)$ *is the identity operator on* Y, *then there exists a node* $\theta = (A,B,C;X,Y)$ *such that* θ *is a realization of* W *on a neighbourhood of* Γ, *the contour* Γ *splits the spectra of* A *and* $A^{\times}$,

$$X = \operatorname{Im} P(A;\Gamma) \oplus \operatorname{Ker} P(A^{\times};\Gamma)$$

and if Π *is the projection of* X *along* $\operatorname{Im} P(A;\Gamma)$ *onto* $\operatorname{Ker} P(A^{\times};\Gamma)$ *then*

$$W_-(\lambda) = W_{pr_{I-\Pi}(\theta)}(\lambda), \quad W_+(\lambda) = W_{pr_{\Pi}(\theta)}(\lambda)$$

for $\lambda \in \bar{F}_-$ *and* $\lambda \in \bar{F}_+$, *respectively.*

PROOF. Let θ be as in the first part of the theorem. Note that $X_1 = \operatorname{Im} P(A;\Gamma)$ is invariant for A and $X_2 = \operatorname{Ker} P(A^{\times};\Gamma)$ is invariant for $A^{\times}$. So, by definition, the projection Π is a supporting projection for θ. Let

$$A = \begin{pmatrix} A_{11} & A_{12} \\ 0 & A_{22} \end{pmatrix}, \quad B = \begin{pmatrix} B_1 \\ B_2 \end{pmatrix}, \quad C = [C_1 \ C_2]$$

be the matrix representations of A, B and C with respect to the decomposition $X = X_1 \oplus X_2$. Then

$$pr_{\Pi}(\theta) = (A_{22}, B_2, C_2; X_2, Y),$$

$$pr_{I-\Pi}(\theta) = (A_{11}, B_1, C_1; X_1, Y),$$

and we know that $\theta = pr_{I-\Pi}(\theta) pr_{\Pi}(\theta)$. It follows that

$$W(\lambda) = W_\theta(\lambda) = W_-(\lambda) W_+(\lambda) \tag{1.14}$$

for each $\lambda \in \rho(A_{11}) \cap \rho(A_{22})$.

As X_1 is a spectral subspace for A, we can apply Lemma 1.4 to show that $\sigma(A_{11}) \cap \sigma(A_{22}) = \phi$. But then $\rho(A) = \rho(A_{11}) \cap \rho(A_{22})$, and it follows that (1.14) holds for each $\lambda \in \rho(A)$. Also, we see from Lemma 1.4 that

$$\sigma(A_{11}) = \sigma(A) \cap F_+ \, , \quad \sigma(A_{22}) = \sigma(A) \cap F_- . \tag{1.15}$$

In a similar way one proves that

$$\sigma(A_{11}) = \sigma(A^\times) \cap F_+ \, , \quad \sigma(A_{22}^\times) = \sigma(A^\times) \cap F_- . \tag{1.16}$$

As $W_-(\lambda) = I + B_1(\lambda I - A_{11})^{-1} C_1$, we know that W_- is defined and analytic on the complement of $\sigma(A_{11})$ and $W_-(\lambda)$ is invertible for $\lambda \notin \sigma(A_{11}^\times)$. So using the first parts of (1.15) and (1.16), it follows that W_- is analytic and has invertible values on $\bar{F}_-$. In the same way, using the second parts of (1.15) and (1.16), one proves that W_+ is analytic and has invertible values on $\bar{F}_+$.

To prove the second part of the theorem, let us assume that $W(\lambda) = W_-(\lambda) W_+(\lambda)$ is a right canonical factorization with respect to Γ and $W_-(\infty) = I$. As W_- is analytic on a neighbourhood of $\bar{F}_-$ and as $W_-(\lambda)$ is invertible for each $\lambda \in \bar{F}_-$, one can find a realization $\theta_1 = (A_1, B_1, C_1; X_1, Y)$ for W_- on a neighbourhood of $\bar{F}_-$ such that $\sigma(A_1)$ and $\sigma(A_1^\times)$ are subsets of F_+. This follows from the realization theorems we shall prove in the next chapter. Also W_+ admits a realization $\theta_2 = (A_2,B_2,C_2;X_2,Y)$ such that $\sigma(A_2)$ and $\sigma(A_2^\times)$ are subsets of F_-. Put $\theta = \theta_1\theta_2$. Then $\theta = (A,B,C;X,Y)$, where $X = X_1 \oplus X_2$ and

$$A = \begin{bmatrix} A_1 & B_1C_2 \\ 0 & A_2 \end{bmatrix}.$$

As $\sigma(A_1)\cap\sigma(A_2) = \phi$, we have $\sigma(A) = \sigma(A_1)\cup\sigma(A_2)$. But then $\Gamma\subset\rho(A) = \rho(A_1)\cap\rho(A_2)$ and

$$W_\theta(\lambda) = W_{\theta_1}(\lambda)W_{\theta_2}(\lambda) = W_-(\lambda)W_+(\lambda) = W(\lambda) \ , \ \lambda\in\rho(A).$$

So θ is a realization for W on a neighbourhood of Γ. Observe that Γ splits $\sigma(A)$ and $X_1 = \operatorname{Im} P(A;\Gamma)$. Since

$$A^\times = \begin{bmatrix} A_1^\times & 0 \\ -B_2C_1 & A_2^\times \end{bmatrix},$$

the contour Γ splits the spectrum of $A^\times$ too and $X_2 = \operatorname{Ker} P(A^\times;\Gamma)$. It follows that

$$X = X_1\oplus X_2 = \operatorname{Im} P(A;\Gamma)\oplus\operatorname{Ker} P(A^\times;\Gamma).$$

If Π is the projection of X along $X_1 = \operatorname{Im} P(A;\Gamma)$ onto $X_2 = \operatorname{Ker} P(A^\times;\Gamma)$, then

$$\theta_1 = pr_{I-\Pi}(\theta) \ , \ \theta_2 = pr_\Pi(\theta).$$

Since $W_-(\lambda) = W_{\theta_1}(\lambda)$ for $\lambda\in\overline{F}_-$ and $W_+(\lambda) = W_{\theta_2}(\lambda)$ for $\lambda\in\overline{F}_+$, we have completed the proof of the second part of the theorem.

For left canonical factorizations an analogous theorem may

be proved. In fact, if in the first part of Theorem 1.5 we have $X=\operatorname{Ker}P(A;\Gamma)\oplus\operatorname{Im}P(A^{\times};\Gamma)$, then one obtains a left canonical spectral factorization with respect to Γ. With some minor modifications we could have worked in Theorem 1.5 with two curves, one splitting the spectrum of A and the other splitting the spectrum of $A^{\times}$ (cf. [38]). In Section 4.4 we shall resume the discussion of canonical factorizations.

1.3 Finite dimensional nodes

If the spaces X and Y are of finite dimension, then the node $\theta = (A,B,C,D;X,Y)$ is called a _finite dimensional_ node. The transfer function of a finite dimensional node is a rational operator function on the Riemann sphere, which is analytic at ∞, and whose values act on a finite dimensional linear space. In Chapter 2 we shall see that conversely any such function may be realized by a finite dimensional node.

The set of poles of the transfer function W_{θ} of a finite dimensional node $\theta= (A,B,C,D;X,Y)$ is contained in the spectrum of A. Similarly, if D is invertible, then the set of zeros of W_{θ} is a subset of the spectrum of $A^{\times}$. Here, by definition, a zero of W_{θ} is just a pole of W_{θ}^{-1}. Under certain minimality conditions these inclusions are actually equalities (see Section 3.2).

Let $\theta = (A,B,C,D;X,Y)$ be a finite dimensional node with invertible operator D. Assume $Ax_0 = \lambda_0 x_0$, $x_0 \neq 0$, and let M be the space spanned by the eigenvector x_0. Of course M is invariant under A. Now suppose that one can find a subspace $M^{\times}$ of X, invariant under $A^{\times}$, such that $X = M\oplus M^{\times}$. Then one can apply Corollary to Theorem 1.1 to show that from W_{θ} one can split off a linear factor of the form $I-(\lambda-\lambda_0)^{-1}R_0$, where R_0 has rank at most one. This is the main idea in the proof of the next theorem. Recall that A is said to have simple eigenvalues only whenever the Jordan matrix of A is diagonal.

THEOREM 1.6. _Let_ W _be the transfer function of the fin-_

<u>ite dimensional node</u> $\theta = (A,B,C;X,Y)$. <u>Assume that</u> A <u>has simple eigenvalues only</u>. <u>Then</u> W <u>admits a factorization of the following form</u>

$$W(\lambda) = (I - \frac{1}{\lambda-\lambda_1}R_1)\dots(I - \frac{1}{\lambda-\lambda_m}R_m),$$

<u>where</u> $\lambda_1,\dots,\lambda_m$ <u>are the eigenvalues of</u> A <u>counted according to multiplicity and</u> $R_1,\dots,R_m$ <u>are operators on</u> Y <u>of rank at most one</u>.

PROOF. Since A has simple eigenvalues only, we can find a basis $e_1,\dots,e_m$ of X such that the matrix of A with respect to this basis is diagonal, say

$$A = \begin{pmatrix} \lambda_1 & & \\ & \ddots & \\ & & \lambda_m \end{pmatrix}.$$

Here $\lambda_1,\dots,\lambda_m$ are the eigenvalues of A counted according to multiplicity. Next we choose a basis $f_1,\dots,f_m$ of X such that the corresponding matrix of $A^\times$ has lower triangular form. Then clearly f_m is an eigenvector of $A^\times$. We may assume that $e_1,\dots,e_m$ are ordered in such a way that

$$X = \mathrm{sp}\{e_1,\dots,e_{m-1}\}\oplus\mathrm{sp}\{f_m\}.$$

Here $\mathrm{sp}V$ denotes the linear hull of V. For convenience we put $X_o = \mathrm{sp}\{e_1,\dots,e_{m-1}\}$ and $X_m = \mathrm{sp}\{f_m\}$. Clearly $A[X_o]\subset X_o$ and $A^\times[X_m]\subset X_m$.

Let Π be the projection of X onto X_m along X_o. Then Π is a supporting projection for θ. Let $W = W_oW_m$ be the corresponding factorization of W. Then W_m is the transfer function of the node $\theta_m = \mathrm{pr}_\Pi(\theta)$. Write

$$\theta_m = (A_m,B_m,C_m;X_m,Y).$$

By Lemma 1.4, the operator A_m is similar to the restriction of A to $sp\{e_m\}$. Hence $\sigma(A_m) = \{\lambda_m\}$ and

$$W_m(\lambda) = I - \frac{1}{\lambda-\lambda_m}R_m,$$

where R_m has rank at most one.

Next consider the factor W_o which is the transfer function of the node $\theta_o = p_{I-\Pi}(\theta)$. Write

$$\theta_o = (A_o,B_o,C_o;X_o,Y).$$

Then A_o is the restriction of A to $X_o = sp\{e_1,\ldots,e_{m-1}\}$. Note that A_o has simple eigenvalues only. Therefore we can repeat the above argument with W_o and θ_o in place of W and θ. In a finite number of steps, we thus obtain the desired result.

We shall come back to a slightly stronger version of the above theorem in Section 3.2.

1.4 Characteristic operator functions and transfer functions

There exist several theories of characteristic operator functions. In most of them one studies a Hilbert space operator by means of an analytic operator function associated to it. Depending on the properties one wants to investigate, different types of characteristic operator functions may be employed. For instance the Livsic-Brodskii characteristic operator function has been designed to deal with operators that are close to selfadjoint (see [8]). Also there are characteristic operator functions that are particularly suitable for the study of almost unitary operators; see, e.g., [9,11,47]. Recently it has been shown that inverses of monic operator polynomials can also be considered as characteristic operator functions (see [2,3]).

It is known that there are several connections between characteristic operator functions and transfer functions. Among the first to observe this were P. Dewilde, P. Fuhrmann and W. Helton (see [36] and the references given there). In this section we shall describe how many of the known characteristic functions may be viewed as transfer functions of certain special types of nodes.

1.4.1 Brodskii nodes. In this subsection the underlying spaces are assumed to be Hilbert spaces. The adjoint of a Hilbert space operator T is denoted by T^*.

The Livsic-Brodskii characteristic operator function is of the form

$$I + 2iK^*(\lambda - A)^{-1}KJ \ , \ \lambda \in \rho(A), \tag{1.17}$$

where $A : H \to H$, $K : G \to H$ and $J : G \to G$ satisfy the following conditions

$$J^* = J \ , \ J^2 = I \ , \ KJK^* = \frac{1}{2i}(A - A^*).$$

This function, which is used to study operators that are close to selfadjoint ones, is the main subject of [8].

It is clear that (1.17) is the transfer function of the node $\theta = (A, KJ, 2iK^*; H, G)$. A node of this type for which the operators have the properties mentioned above will be called a Brodskii J-node. Observe that a node $\theta = (A,B,C;H,G)$ is a Brodskii J-node if and only if H and G are Hilbert spaces, J is a selfadjoint and unitary operator acting on G and

$$A - A^* = B - C \ , \ C = 2iJB^*.$$

Our notation and terminology differ slightly from those employed in [8]. The reason is that we want to stay within the framework described in Section 1.1.

The product of two Brodskii J-nodes is again a Brodskii J-node (cf. [8], page 6). A node which is similar to a Brodskii J-node need not be of this type, but it is a Brodskii J-node provided that the node similarity is a unitary operator (cf. [8], page 11). On the other hand, if two Brodskii J-nodes are similar, say with node similarity S, then one can prove that there exists a unitary operator U that provides the similarity too. In fact for U one may take the unitary operator appearing in the polar decomposition $S = U\sqrt{S^*S}$ of S.

Let $\theta = (A,B,C;H,G)$ be a Brodskii J-node. As the external operator is equal to the identity operator on G, the associate node $\theta^\times = (A^\times,B,-C;H,G)$ is well-defined. Note that $A^\times = A-BC = A^*$. So in this case the associate main operator of θ depends exclusively on A and coincides with the adjoint of A. From the relationships between the operator A, B and C in θ it follows that the associate node $\theta^\times$ is a Brodskii (-J)-node.

Suppose now that Π is an orthogonal projection of H and $A[\mathrm{Ker}\,\Pi] \subset \mathrm{Ker}\,\Pi$. Then automatically $A^*[\mathrm{Im}\,\Pi] \subset \mathrm{Im}\,\Pi$, and hence Π is a supporting projection for θ. So we can apply Theorem 1.3 to show that

$$\theta = \mathrm{pr}_{I-\Pi}(\theta)\mathrm{pr}_{\Pi}(\theta).$$

The nodes $\mathrm{pr}_{\Pi}(\theta)$ and $\mathrm{pr}_{I-\Pi}(\theta)$ are Brodskii J-nodes again (cf. [8], page 6). This result leads to an important multiplicative representation of the Livsic-Brodskii characteristic operator function (cf. [8], page 143).

It is possible to give an intrinsic characterization of the class of transfer functions of Brodskii J-nodes (see [8]).

<u>1.4.2 Krein nodes</u>. The Livsic-Brodskii characteristic operator function has been designed to study operators that are not far from being self-adjoint. There are also characteristic operator functions that have been introduced in order to deal with almost unitary operators. Among them are the characteristic operator function of Sz.-Nagy and Foias and that of Krein (see [11, 47] for references). Here we shall only discuss the characteristic operator function of Krein.

The Krein characteristic operator function has the form

$$J(K^*)^{-1}[J-R^*(I-\lambda A)^{-1}R]. \tag{1.18}$$

Here $A:H \to H$, $R:G \to H$, $J:G \to G$, $K:G \to G$ are operators, the underlying spaces G and H are complex Hilbert spaces,

$$(1.19) \qquad J^* = J\ ,\ J^2 = I\ ,\ I-AA^* = RJR^*\ ,\ J-R^*R = K^*JK,$$

and the operators A and K are invertible. Obviously, (1.18) does not fit into the framework developed in Section 1.1. However, replacing λ by λ^{-1} and using (1.19), one can transform (1.18) into

$$K - J(K^*)^{-1}R^*A(\lambda-A)^{-1}R.$$

This is the transfer function of the node

$$(1.20) \qquad \theta = (A,R,-J(K^*)^{-1}R^*A,K;H,G).$$

A node of this type for which the operators have the properties mentioned above will be called a <u>Krein J-node</u>. Observe that the external operator of a Krein J-node is invertible.

The product of two Krein J-nodes is again a Krein J-node. A node, similar to a Krein J-node, need not be of this type, but it is a Krein J-node provided the node similarity is a unitary operator. Also, if two Krein J-nodes are similar, say with node similarity S, then the unitary operator that appears in the polar decomposition of S also establishes the similarity.

Let θ, given by (1.20), be a Krein J-node. Carrying out the multiplication

$$(1.21) \qquad (I-RJR^*)(I+RK^{-1}J(K^*)^{-1}R^*)$$

and substituting $J-K^*JK$ for R^*R, one sees that (1.21) is equal to the identity operator on H. The same is true when we interchange the factors. Hence

$$(1.22) \qquad (AA^*)^{-1} = (I-RJR^*)^{-1} = I+RK^{-1}J(K^*)^{-1}R^*.$$

It follows that $\theta^\times = ((A^*)^{-1}, RK^{-1}, JR^*(A^*)^{-1}, K^{-1};H,G)$. From this we see that $\theta^\times$ is a Krein $(-J)$-node. Observe that here the associate main operator $A^\times$ depends again exclusively on A and coincides with $(A^*)^{-1}$.

Let Π be an orthogonal projection of H. With respect to the decomposition $H = \operatorname{Ker}\Pi \oplus \operatorname{Im}\Pi$, we write

$$A = \begin{pmatrix} A_{11} & A_{12} \\ A_{21} & A_{22} \end{pmatrix}, \quad R = \begin{pmatrix} R_1 \\ R_2 \end{pmatrix}.$$

Suppose now that $A_{21} = 0$ (i.e., $\operatorname{Ker}\Pi$ is an invariant subspace for A) and A_{11} is invertible. Then A_{22} is invertible too and $\operatorname{Im}\Pi$ is an invariant subspace for $A^{\times} = (A^*)^{-1}$. From $RJR^*=I-AA^*$ one easily deduces that

$$R_2JR_2^* = I-A_{22}A_{22}^*.$$

But this implies (see [11]) the existence of an invertible operator K_2 on G such that $J-R_2^*R_2 = K_2^*JK_2$. Put $K_1=KK_2^{-1}$. Then K_1 is also invertible and $K = K_1K_2$. We are now in a position to apply Theorem 1.1. The result is a factorization $\theta = \theta_1\theta_2$, where θ_1 and θ_2 can be described explicitly with the help of formulas (1.5) and (1.6). It can be shown that θ_1 and θ_2 are Krein J-nodes (cf. [10]).

It is possible to give an intrinsic characterization of the class of transfer functions of Krein J-nodes. See [11] for further details.

We conclude this subsection with an interesting characterization of Krein J-nodes. Let G and H be complex Hilbert spaces and let J be an operator on G such that $J = J^*$ and $J^2=I$. By definition a node $\theta = (A,B,C,D;H,G)$ is a Krein J-node if and only if A and D are invertible and

$$I-AA^* = BJB^*, \quad J-B^*B = D^*JD, \quad C =-J(D^*)^{-1}B^*A.$$

A straightforward calculation shows that these conditions are equivalent to the requirement that the external operator D of θ is invertible and the operator

(1.23)
$$\begin{bmatrix} A & B \\ C & D \end{bmatrix}$$

on $H \oplus G$ is $\mathfrak{J}$-unitary. Here $\mathfrak{J} = I \oplus J$. Observe that $\mathfrak{J}^* = \mathfrak{J}$ and $\mathfrak{J}^2 = I$. The class of nodes $\theta = (A,B,C,D;H,G)$ for which the operator (1.23) is $\mathfrak{J}$-unitary (but D not necessarily invertible) is closed under multiplication. Characteristic operator functions of the form

$$D + \lambda C(I-\lambda A)^{-1}B = D + C(\lambda^{-1}-A)^{-1}B,$$

where A,B,C and D are such that (1.23) is unitary, have been investigated (see [9]).

<u>1.4.3 Monic nodes</u>. The characteristic operator function introduced in [2,3] has the form

(1.24)
$$Q(\lambda-T)^{-1}R \ , \ \lambda \in \rho(T),$$

where $T : X \to X$, $R : Y \to X$ and $Q : X \to Y$ are operators, the underlying spaces are complex Banach spaces, and there exists a positive integer ℓ such that the operator

$$\operatorname{col}(QT^{i-1})_{i=1}^{\ell} = \begin{bmatrix} Q \\ QT \\ \vdots \\ QT^{\ell-1} \end{bmatrix} : X \to Y^{\ell}$$

is invertible and its inverse is of the form

$$\operatorname{row}(U_{i-1})_{i=1}^{\ell} = [U_0 \dots U_{\ell-1}] : Y^{\ell} \to X$$

with $U_{\ell-1} = R$. The integer ℓ is unique. Clearly (1.24) is the transfer function of the node $\theta = (T,R,Q,0;X,Y)$. We emphasize the fact that the external operator of this node is equal to the zero operator; so $\theta^{\times}$ is not defined. A node $\theta = (T,R,Q,0;X,Y)$ for which the operators have the properties mentioned above will be called a monic node of degree ℓ.

To justify our terminology we make the following remark. Suppose $\theta = (T,R,Q,0;X,Y)$ is a monic node of degree ℓ, and let $U_0,\dots,U_{\ell-1}$ be as above. Then the transfer function (1.24) of θ coincides with the inverse L^{-1} of the monic operator polynomial L given by

$$L(\lambda) = \lambda^{\ell}I - \sum_{i=0}^{\ell-1} \lambda^{i}QT^{\ell}U_{i}.$$

It can be shown that L can also be written as

$$L(\lambda) = \lambda^{\ell}I - \sum_{i=0}^{\ell-1} \lambda^{i}V_{i}T^{\ell}R,$$

where $\mathrm{col}(V_{\ell-i})_{i=1}^{\ell}$ is the inverse of the invertible operator $\mathrm{row}(T^{\ell-i}R)_{i=1}^{\ell}$. For details we refer to [2,3].

Suppose now, conversely, that L is a given monic operator polynomial whose coefficients are operators on Y. Then it is easy to find a monic node θ for which $W_{\theta} = L^{-1}$. Indeed, if $L(\lambda) = \lambda^{\ell}I + \sum_{j=0}^{\ell-1}\lambda^{j}A_{j}$ and

$$C_{1,L} = \begin{bmatrix} 0 & I & & 0 \\ \vdots & & \ddots & \vdots \\ 0 & 0 & & I \\ -A_0 & -A_1 & \cdots & -A_{\ell-1} \end{bmatrix},$$

then

$$\theta = (C_{1,L}, \mathrm{col}(\delta_{i\ell}I)_{i=1}^{\ell}, \mathrm{row}(\delta_{i1}I)_{i=1}^{\ell}, 0; Y^{\ell}, Y) \tag{1.25}$$

has the desired properties. The operator $C_{1,L}$ is known as the first companion operator associated with L, and for that reason the node (1.25) will be called the first companion node corresponding to L. When Y is finite dimensional it is possible to construct a node θ with $W_\theta = L^{-1}$ from the spectral data (eigenvalues, eigenvectors and associated eigenvectors) of L. The construction may be found in [25] (see also Section 2.1). The concept of a node does not appear in [24,25]. Its role is played by the notion of a standard triple. We note that a triple (Q,T,R) of operators is a standard triple for a monic operator polynomial L if and only if $\theta = (T,R,Q,0;X,Y)$ is a monic node and $W_\theta = L^{-1}$.

If θ_1 and θ_2 are monic nodes of degree ℓ_1 and ℓ_2, respectively, then $\theta_1\theta_2$ is a monic node of degree $\ell_1+\ell_2$. A node which is similar to a monic node of degree ℓ is again a monic node of degree ℓ.

In Section 1.1 we introduced the notion of a supporting projection for nodes having invertible external operator. This notion does not apply to monic nodes because of the fact that the external operator of a monic node, being the zero operator, is not invertible. Still, a similar concept has been introduced in [2,3]. We shall recall some of the material presented there.

Let $\Theta = (T,R,Q,0;X,Y)$ be a monic node of degree ℓ, and let Π be a projection of X. We say that Π is a <u>monic supporting projection</u> for Θ if $\operatorname{Ker}\Pi$ is a non-trivial invariant subspace for T and there exists a positive integer m (necessarily unique and less than ℓ) such that

$$\operatorname{col}(QT^{i-1})_{i=1}^{m}\Big|_{\operatorname{Ker}\Pi} : \operatorname{Ker}\Pi \to Y^m \tag{1.26}$$

is invertible. We call m the <u>degree</u> of the monic supporting projection. The operator (1.26) is invertible if and only if this is the case for the operator

$$\Pi\operatorname{row}(T^{k-i}R)_{i=1}^{k} : Y^k \to \operatorname{Im}\Pi. \tag{1.27}$$

Here $k = \ell - m$.

Let Π be a monic supporting projection for the monic node $\theta = (T,R,Q,0;X,Y)$, and let m be the degree of Π.

Put $X_1 = \text{Ker}\, \Pi$, and define $T_1 : X_1 \to X_1$ and $Q_1 : X_1 \to Y$ by $T_1 x = Tx$ and $Q_1 x = Qx$ for each $x \in X_1$. The invertibility of (1.26) now implies that $\text{col}(Q_1 T_1^{i=1})_{i=1}^m$ is invertible. Hence there exists a unique $R_1 : Y \to X_1$ such that $\theta_1 = (T_1, R_1, Q_1, 0; X_1, Y)$ is a monic node. This node, which has degree m, is called the left projection of θ associated with Π.

Put $X_2 = \text{Im}\, \Pi$, $k = \ell - m$, and define $T_2 : X_2 \to X_2$ and $R_2 : Y \to X_2$ by $T_2 x = \Pi T x$ and $R_2 y = \Pi R y$. Since $\text{Ker}\, \Pi$ is invariant under T, we have $\Pi T \Pi = \Pi T$. This, together with the invertibility of (1.27), implies that $\text{row}(T_2^{k-i} R_2)_{i=1}^k$ is invertible. Therefore there exists a unique $Q_2 : X_2 \to Y$ such that $\theta_2 = (T_2, R_2, Q_2, 0; X_2, Y)$ is a monic node. This node, which has degree $k = \ell - m$, is called the right projection of θ associated with Π.

Let Π be a monic supporting projection for the monic node $\theta = (T, R, Q, 0; X, Y)$ and let θ_1 and θ_2 be the associated left and right projections. Then θ and $\theta_1 \theta_2$ are similar (see [3], Theorem 2.2). Conversely, if $\theta_1 = (T_1, R_1, Q_1, 0; X_1, Y)$ and $\theta_2 = (T_2, R_2, Q_2, 0; X_2, Y)$ are monic nodes such that θ and $\theta_1 \theta_2$ are similar, then there exists a monic supporting projection for θ such that the associated left and right projections of θ are similar to θ_1 and θ_2, respectively. To prove this we may assume that $\theta = \theta_1 \theta_2$. But then one can take Π to be the canonical projection of $X_1 \oplus X_2$ along X_1 onto X_2.

By formula (1.3) the factorization of a monic node implies a factorization of the corresponding transfer function. Since in this case the transfer functions are inverses of monic operator polynomials, we can employ the theory explained above to derive factorizations for monic operator polynomials. In fact, the following factorization theorem holds true (cf. [24], Theorem 8, [26], Theorem 13). Let $L(\lambda) = A_0 + \lambda A_1 + \ldots + \lambda^{\ell-1} A_{\ell-1} + \lambda^{\ell} I$ be a monic operator polynomial, and let $\theta = (T, R, Q, 0; X, Y)$ be a fixed monic node such that $W_\theta = L^{-1}$. Let Π be a monic supporting projection for θ of degree m, and let $\theta_1 = (T_1, R_1, Q_1, 0; X_1, Y)$ and $\theta_2 = (T_2, R_2, Q_2, 0; X_2, Y)$ be the associated left and right projections of θ. Put

$$L_1(\lambda) = \lambda^m I - \sum_{i=0}^{m-1} \lambda^i Q_1 T_1^m W_i,$$

$$L_2(\lambda) = \lambda^{\ell-m} I - \sum_{i=0}^{\ell-m-1} \lambda^i Q_2 T_2^{\ell-m} V_i,$$

where $\mathrm{row}(W_i)_{i=0}^{m-1} = [\mathrm{col}(Q_1 T_1^{i-1})_{i=1}^{m}]^{-1}$ and $\mathrm{row}(V_i)_{i=0}^{\ell-m-1} = [\mathrm{col}(Q_2 T_2^{i-1})_{i=1}^{\ell-m}]^{-1}$. Note that $W_{\theta_1} = L_1^{-1}$ and $W_{\theta_2} = L_2^{-1}$. As $\theta \simeq \theta_1\theta_2$, we may conclude from formula (1.3) that $L = L_2 L_1$. Conversely, given a factorization $L = L_2 L_1$ where L_1 and L_2 are monic operator polynomials, there exists a monic supporting projection Π of θ such that for the associated left and right projections θ_1 and θ_2 we have

$$L_1^{-1} = W_{\theta_1}, \quad L_2^{-1} = W_{\theta_2}.$$

In fact for Π we may take the projection $\Pi = I-P$, the projection P being defined by

$$P = [\mathrm{col}(QT^i)_{i=0}^{\ell-1}]^{-1}\mathrm{col}(Q_1 T_1^i)_{i=0}^{\ell-1}[\mathrm{col}(Q_1 T_1^i)_{i=0}^{m-1}]^{-1}\mathrm{col}(QT^i)_{i=0}^{m-1},$$

where m is the degree of L_1 and (Q_1, T_1, R_1) is a standard triple for L_1 (cf. [24], Section 5). By using an appropriate Möbius transformation, this factorization theorem for monic operator polynomials can also be deduced from Theorem 1.1; we shall come back to this at the end of Section 1.5.

In the previous paragraph the correspondence between the monic supporting projections Π of θ and the right divisors L_1 of L is not one-one. The reason may be explained as follows. Suppose Π is a monic supporting projection for θ of degree m, and let Π' be another projection of X such that $\mathrm{Ker}\,\Pi = \mathrm{Ker}\,\Pi'$. Then it is immediate from the definition that Π' is also a monic supporting projection for θ of degree m. Furthermore, the left projections of θ associated with Π and Π' coincide. So what really matters in the definition of the monic supporting projection Π is the existence of a T-invariant closed subspace X_1 of X such that the operator

$$\operatorname{col}(QT^{i-1})_{i=1}^{m}\Big|_{X_1} : X_1 \to Y^m$$

is invertible. Such a subspace X_1 is called a <u>supporting subspace</u> for θ (cf. [24], Section 5). The correspondence between the supporting subspaces of θ and the right divisors of L, $L^{-1} = W_\theta$, is one-one (cf. [26,3]; see also the discussion after Theorem 4.8).

For the companion type node (1.25) the supporting subspaces may be characterized in a simple way. Indeed, a closed subspace X_1 of Y^ℓ is a supporting subspace for the node (1.25) if and only if X_1 is invariant under the first companion operator $C_{1,L}$ and X_1 is an algebraic complement in Y^ℓ of the subspace of Y^ℓ consisting of all vectors for which the first m coordinates are zero. This is the contents of the first part of Theorem 1.6 in [26]. Note that condition (iii) in this theorem is superfluous.

<u>1.4.4 Polynomial nodes</u>. In the previous subsection we have seen that the inverses of monic operator polynomials can be seen as transfer functions of certain nodes. Now we shall deal with arbitrary polynomials. A node $\theta = (A,B,C,D;X,Y)$ is called a <u>polynomial node</u> if its main operator A is nilpotent. If, in addition, $D = I$, we say that θ is a <u>comonic polynomial node</u>. The transfer function of a (comonic) polynomial node is obviously a (comonic) polynomial in λ^{-1}.

Now conversely. Let P be an operator polynomial of degree ℓ whose coefficients are operators on Y. In order to show that $P(\lambda^{-1})$ is the transfer function of a polynomial node, it suffices to consider the comonic case where $P(0)$ is the identity operator on Y. Put $L(\lambda) = \lambda^\ell P(\lambda^{-1})$. Then L is a monic operator polynomial of degree ℓ.

Let $\Delta = (T,R,Q,0;X,Y)$ be a monic node such that the transfer function W_Δ is equal to L^{-1}. Then

$$\text{(1.28)} \qquad L(\lambda) = \lambda^\ell I - \sum_{i=0}^{\ell-1} \lambda^i Q T^\ell U_i,$$

where

$$\text{(1.29)} \qquad \operatorname{row}(U_{i-1})_{i=1}^{\ell} = [\operatorname{col}(QT^{i-1})_{i=1}^{\ell}]^{-1}.$$

Further, $U_{\ell-1} = R$ (see the previous section). So

$$U_0 Q + \dots + U_{\ell-2} Q T^{\ell-2} + RQT^{\ell-1} = I,$$

and hence

$$\text{(1.30)} \qquad T-RQT^\ell = \left[\operatorname{col}(QT^{i-1})_{i=1}^{\ell}\right]^{-1} \left[\delta_{i,j-1} I\right] \left[\operatorname{col}(QT^{i-1})_{i=1}^{\ell}\right].$$

It follows that $T-RQT^\ell$ is nilpotent of order ℓ. Also, using (1.29), one sees that $(T-RQT^\ell)U_j = U_{j-1}$ for $j=1,\dots,\ell-1$. But then

$$I - QT^\ell(\lambda - T + RQT\ )^{-1}R = I - \sum_{i=1}^{\ell} \lambda^{-i} QT^\ell U_{\ell-i}$$

$$= \lambda^{-\ell} L(\lambda) = P(\lambda^{-1}).$$

So $P(\lambda^{-1})$ is the transfer function of the comonic polynomial node

$$\text{(1.31)} \qquad \theta = (T-RQT^\ell,\ R,\ -QT^\ell; X,Y).$$

Summarizing we obtain: The class of transfer functions of (comonic) polynomial nodes coincides with that of the (comonic) polynomials in λ^{-1}. We observe that the node

$$\text{(1.32)} \qquad \theta = (T-T^\ell RQ,\ T^\ell R,\ -Q; X,Y)$$

is also a comonic polynomial node and its transfer function is also equal to $P(\lambda^{-1})$.

Consider the node (1.31). The associate node is given by

$\theta^{\times} = (T,R,-QT^{\ell};X,Y)$. On $\rho(T)\setminus\{0\}$ the transfer function of $\theta^{\times}$ coincides with $P(\lambda^{-1})^{-1}$. From this one easily infers that $P(\lambda^{-1}) = QT^{\ell-1}(I-\lambda T)^{-1}R$.

The product of two (comonic) polynomial nodes is again a (comonic) polynomial node. A node that is similar to a (comonic) polynomial node is also a (comonic) polynomial node. If $\theta = (A,B,C;X,Y)$ is a comonic polynomial node, then for any supporting projection Π of θ the nodes $pr_{\Pi}(\theta)$ and $pr_{I-\Pi}(\theta)$ are comonic polynomial nodes.

1.4.5 Final remarks. In the previous subsections we encountered several important subclasses of nodes. All these classes are closed under multiplication. Also they are closed under taking certain projections. In the case of Krein nodes we did not explicitly introduce the notion of a projection, but it is clear from our discussion how this could be done.

A striking feature of the Brodskii nodes and the Krein nodes is that the mapping $A \to A^{\times}$ which assigns to the main operator its associate operator coincides here with a natural "involution". In the case of Brodskii nodes this is the involution $A \to A^*$, while in the Krein case we have $A \to (A^*)^{-1}$. This suggests the following problem. Let p be an operator involution. Thus p is a rule that assigns to every operator A of a certain kind an operator $p(A)$ of the same kind such that $p(p(A)) = A$. It is easy to give examples of such involutions. Besides $p(A) = A^*$ and $p(A) = (A^*)^{-1}$ one can take, for instance, $p(A) = A$, $p(A) = A^{-1}$ and $p(A) = A^* + \frac{i}{4}(A+A^*)^2$. Now, given such an operator involution p, does there exist a class $@_p$ of nodes with invertible external operator such that the following properties hold:

(α) $@_p$ is closed under node multiplication;

(β) if $\theta = (A,B,C,D;X,Y)\in @_p$, then $A^{\times} = p(A)$.

As we have seen the answer is affirmative for the case when $p(A) = A^*$ (Brodskii nodes) or $p(A)=(A^*)^{-1}$ (Krein nodes). What about other possibilities for p?

Suppose p is an operator involution and $@_p$ is a class of nodes with invertible external operator satisfying (α) and (β). Let $\theta_i = (A_i,B_i,C_i,D_i;X_i,Y) \in @_p$ (i=1,2). Then also $\theta=\theta_1\theta_2 \in @_p$. Write $\theta = (A,B,C,D;X,Y)$. Then

$$p\left(\begin{bmatrix} A_1 & B_1C_2 \\ 0 & A_2 \end{bmatrix}\right) = p(A) = A^\times = A-BD^{-1}C =$$

$$= \begin{bmatrix} A_1^\times & 0 \\ B_2D_2^{-1}D_1^{-1}C_1 & A_2^\times \end{bmatrix} = \begin{bmatrix} p(A_1) & 0 \\ B_2D_2^{-1}D_1^{-1}C_1 & p(A_2) \end{bmatrix}.$$

This suggests that p should map operators of the form

$$\begin{bmatrix} A_1 & * \\ 0 & A_2 \end{bmatrix} \tag{1.33}$$

into operators of the form

$$\begin{bmatrix} p(A_1) & 0 \\ \# & p(A_2) \end{bmatrix}. \tag{1.34}$$

But then p(A) cannot be some analytic function of A in the sense of operational calculus. This makes the chances of finding interesting operator involutions in the general Banach space setting rather small. For the Hilbert space case one could be more optimistic. But, as the following theorem indicates, also there the possibilities seem to be rather restricted. The proof of the theorem is rather long and will be omitted.

THEOREM 1.7. *Suppose* $q = q(x,y)$ *is a polynomial with complex coefficients in two non-commuting variables* x *and* y. *For every Hilbert space operator, let* $p(A) = q(A,A^*)$. *Then* p *maps operators of the form* (1.33) *into operators of the form* (1.34) *if and only if* q *depends exclusively on* y *(and hence* $p(A)$ *is a polynomial in* A^**). In that case* p *is an involution if and only if* p *has the form*

$$p(A) = b+aA^*, \ |a| = 1 \ , \ b+a\bar{b} = 0.$$

As far as the necessity is concerned, it is sufficient to consider only operators on one finite dimensional Hilbert space of sufficiently high dimension N, where N depends on the degree of the polynomial q. In fact, if n is the degree of q, one can take $N = \frac{1}{2}(3^{n+1}-1)$.

In addition to Theorem 1.7 we note that in some cases the conditions (α) and (β) can be used to determine the class $@_p$ more explicitly. We shall illustrate this fact for the case that the underlying spaces are Hilbert spaces and $p(A) = A^*$. Let G be a fixed Hilbert space, and let $@_*$ be a class of nodes θ of the form $\theta = (A,B,C;H,G)$, where H is a Hilbert space too. Further suppose

(α) $@_*$ is closed under node multiplication;

$(\beta)'$ if $\theta = (A,B,C;H,G) \in @_*$, then $A^\times = A^*$.

THEOREM 1.8. *If for some* $\theta_0 = (A_0,B_0,C_0;H_0,G) \in @_*$ *the operator* B_0 *has a left inverse, then there exists a unique selfadjoint operator* $J : G \to G$ *such that*

$$C = 2iJB^*$$

for each $\theta = (A,B,C;H,G) \in @_*$.

PROOF. Since $A_0^\times = A_0^*$, we have $A_0 - A_0^* = B_0C_0$, and hence $C_0^*B_0^* = -B_0C_0$. Let B_0^+ be a left inverse of B_0, and define $J = -\frac{1}{2i} B_0^+C_0^*$. Then $J:G \to G$ and $C_0 = 2iJB_0^*$. Let us prove that J is selfadjoint. Take y_1,y_2 in G. As B_0 has a left inverse, the map B_0^* is surjective, and so there exist x_1,x_2 in H such that $B_0^*x_j = y_j$ $(j=1,2)$. But then

$$\langle Jy_1, y_2\rangle = \langle JB_0^* x_1, B_0^* x_2\rangle = \langle \frac{1}{2i} C_0 x_1, B_0^* x_2\rangle =$$

$$= \langle x_1, -\frac{1}{2i} C_0^* x_i\rangle = \langle x_1, \frac{1}{2i} B_0 C_0 x_2\rangle =$$

$$= \langle B_0^* x_1, JB_0^* x_2\rangle = \langle y_1, Jy_2\rangle .$$

So the map $J: Y \to Y$ is selfadjoint. From the surjectivity of the map B_0^* it also follows that J is uniquely determined by the formula $C_0 = 2iJB_0^*$.

Now, take an arbitrary node $\theta = (A,B,C;H,G)$ in the class $@_*$. Define $\tilde{\theta} = (\tilde{A},\tilde{B},\tilde{C};\tilde{H},G)$ to be the product $\theta\theta_0$. As $@_*$ is closed under node multiplication $\tilde{\theta} \in @_*$, and hence the associate main operator of $\tilde{\theta}$ is equal to $\tilde{A}^*$. Note that

$$\tilde{B} = \begin{pmatrix} B \\ B_0 \end{pmatrix}$$

has a left inverse, because this is true for B_0. In fact, if $B_0^+ B_0 = I$, then $[0 \ B_0^+]$ is a left inverse for $\tilde{B}$. So we may apply the result of the first paragraph to $\tilde{\theta}$. It follows that there exists a selfadjoint operator $\tilde{J}: G \to G$ such that $\tilde{C} = 2i\tilde{J}\tilde{B}^*$. But

$$\tilde{C} = [C \ C_0], \ \tilde{B}^* = [B^* \ B_0^*].$$

Hence $C = 2i\tilde{J}B^*$ and $C_0 = 2i\tilde{J}B_0^*$. The last formula implies $\tilde{J} = J$, and hence the proof is complete.

Observe that the formula $C = 2iJB^*$ is one of the defining properties for Brodskii J-nodes. However in the case of Brodskii nodes the operator J has to be not only selfadjoint but also unitary. On the other hand in many respects one can operate with the nodes of Theorem 1.8 in the same way as with Brodskii nodes.

1.5. Möbius transformations of nodes

From the definition of the transfer function of a node it is clear that such a function is always analytic at infinity. Therefore in general the theory developed in the previous sections can be applied to an arbitrary analytic operator function after a suitable transformation of the independent variable only. For this reason we study in this section the effect of a Möbius transformation on λ.

Throughout this section φ will be the Möbius transformation

(1.35) $$\varphi(\lambda) = \frac{p\lambda+q}{r\lambda+s}.$$

Here p,q,r and s are complex numbers and $ps-qr \neq 0$. We consider φ as a map from the Riemann sphere $\mathbb{C}_\infty$ onto itself. The inverse map φ^{-1} is given by

$$\varphi^{-1}(\lambda) = \frac{-s\lambda+q}{r\lambda-p}.$$

THEOREM 1.9. *Let* $W(\lambda) = D+C(\lambda-A)^{-1}B$ *be the transfer function of the node* $\theta = (A,B,C,D;X,Y)$, *and let* φ *be the Möbius transformation* (1.35). *Assume that* $T=p-rA$ *is invertible. Then* $W_\varphi(\lambda) = W(\varphi(\lambda))$ *is the transfer function of the node*

(1.36) $$\theta_\varphi = (-(q-sA)T^{-1},\ T^{-1}B,\ (ps-qr)CT^{-1}, D+rCT^{-1}B;\ X,Y).$$

PROOF. As $T = p-rA$ is invertible, the inverse map φ^{-1} is analytic on the spectrum of $\sigma(A)$. So $\varphi^{-1}(A)$ is well-defined. In fact, $\varphi^{-1}(A) = -(q-sA)T^{-1}$ is equal to the main operator of θ_φ. By the spectral mapping theorem

$$\rho(\varphi^{-1}(A)) = \{\lambda\in\mathbb{C} \mid \varphi(\lambda)\in\rho(A)\cup\{\infty\}\}.$$

It follows that the function W_φ as well as the transfer function of θ_φ are defined on the same open set, namely on the set $\rho(\varphi^{-1}(A))$.

To prove that the two functions coincide on $\rho(\varphi^{-1}(A))$, take $\lambda\in\rho(\varphi^{-1}(A))$. Assume first that $r\lambda+s \neq 0$. Then

$$
\begin{aligned}
W_\varphi(\lambda) &= D+C(\frac{\lambda p+q}{r\lambda+s} - A)^{-1}B \\
&= D+(r\lambda+s)C[\lambda(\rho-rA)+q-sA]^{-1}B \\
&= D+(r\lambda+s)C[\lambda-\varphi^{-1}(A)]^{-1}T^{-1}B \\
&= D+C\{r(\lambda-\varphi^{-1}(A))+r\varphi^{-1}(A)+s\}. \\
&\qquad\qquad \cdot[\lambda-\varphi^{-1}(A)]^{-1}T^{-1}B \\
&= D+rCT^{-1}B + (ps-qr)CT^{-1}[\lambda-\varphi^{-1}(A)]^{-1}T^{-1}B,
\end{aligned}
$$

where we use that $r\varphi^{-1}(A)+s = (ps-qr)(p-rA)^{-1}$.

Next, assume that $\lambda\in\rho(\varphi^{-1}(A))$ and $r\lambda+s = 0$. Then $\varphi(\lambda) = \infty$ and $W_\varphi(\lambda) = D$. On the other hand, it is not difficult to check that the value of the transfer function of θ_φ in $\lambda = -sr^{-1}$ is equal to D too. This completes the proof.

The node θ_φ introduced in formula (1.36) has several interesting properties; some of them will be discussed here below.

PROPOSITION 1.10. *Let* $\theta_1 = (A_1,B_1,C_1,D_1;X_1,Y)$ *and* $\theta_2 = (A_2,B_2,C_2,D_2;X_2,Y)$ *be nodes such that* $(\theta_1)_\varphi$ *and* $(\theta_2)_\varphi$ *exist. Then* $(\theta_1\theta_2)_\varphi$ *exists too and*

$$(1.37)\qquad (\theta_1\theta_2)_\varphi = (\theta_1)_\varphi(\theta_2)_\varphi.$$

PROOF. Recall that $\theta_1\theta_2 = (A,B,C,D;X_1\oplus X_2,Y)$, where

$$A = \begin{bmatrix} A_1 & B_1C_2 \\ 0 & A_2 \end{bmatrix}, \quad B = \begin{bmatrix} B_1D_2 \\ B_2 \end{bmatrix}, \quad C = [C_1 \;\; D_1C_2] \;, \quad D = D_1D_2.$$

The fact that $(\theta_1)_\varphi$ and $(\theta_2)_\varphi$ exist means nothing else than $p-rA_1$ and $p-rA_2$ are invertible. Since $\sigma(A)$ is a subset of $\sigma(A_1)\cup\sigma(A_2)$, it follows that $p-rA$ is invertible too. Thus $(\theta_1\theta_2)_\varphi$ is well-defined. Equality (1.37) follows now by a direct computation.

Let @ be a class of nodes such that for each $\theta\in$@ the node θ_φ is well-defined. Assume that @ is closed under multiplication. For instance, we could take for @ the class of Brodskii nodes for which θ_φ exists. Then we can form the class @$_\varphi$ = $\{\theta_\varphi | \theta\in$@$\}$, and by Proposition 1.10 the new class @$_\varphi$ is again closed under multiplication. In this way one can also establish certain relationships between different classes of nodes. For example (cf. [11]), let $\theta = (A,R,C,K;H,G)$ be a Krein J-node, and let Ψ be the Möbius transformation

$$\Psi(\lambda) = \alpha\left(\frac{\lambda+i}{\lambda-i}\right).$$

Here $|\alpha| = 1$, and we assume that $\alpha\in\rho(A)$. It follows that θ_Ψ is well-defined. Put $A_\Psi = -i(\alpha+A)(\alpha-A)^{-1}$, $B_\Psi = (\alpha-A)^{-1}R$, $C_\Psi = -2i\alpha C(\alpha-A)^{-1}$ and $D_\Psi = K+C(\alpha-A)^{-1}R$. Then $\theta_\Psi = (A_\Psi,B_\Psi,C_\Psi,D_\Psi;H,G)$. Using the properties of Krein J-nodes, one sees that

$$B_\Psi JB_\Psi^* = (\alpha-A)^{-1}(I-AA^*)(\bar{\alpha}-A^*)^{-1}. \tag{1.38}$$

It follows that

$$A_\Psi - A_\Psi^* = -2iB_\Psi JB_\Psi^*. \tag{1.39}$$

This last identity is one of the defining properties of a Brodskii (-J)-node. However, note that in general B_Ψ is not a Brodskii node, because its external operator D_Ψ may not be equal to the identity operator. As $A^{\times} = (A^*)^{-1}$ for Krein nodes, we have $\alpha \in \rho(A^*)$, and hence D_Ψ is invertible. We shall prove that the node

(1.40) $$\Delta = (A_\Psi, B_\Psi, D_\Psi^{-1}C_\Psi; H, G)$$

is a Brodskii(-J)-node. In view of (1.39) it suffices to prove that $D_\Psi^{-1}C_\Psi = -2iJB_\Psi^*$. In other words we have to show that $C_\Psi = -2iD_\Psi JB_\Psi^*$. To do this, observe (cf. (1.38)) that

$$B_\Psi JB_\Psi^* = A^*(\bar{\alpha}-A^*)^{-1} + \alpha(\alpha-A)^{-1}.$$

It follows that

(1.41) $$C_\Psi = -2i(-CA^*(\bar{\alpha}-A^*)^{-1} + CB_\Psi JB_\Psi^*).$$

From the definition of θ_Ψ it is clear that $D_\Psi = K+CB_\Psi$. So $-2iD_\Psi JB_\Psi^* = -2i(KJB_\Psi^*+CB_\Psi JB_\Psi^*)$. Employing the properties of Krein J-nodes, we have

$$\begin{aligned} KJR^* &= J(K^*)^{-1}(J-R^*R)JR^* \\ &= J(K^*)^{-1}R^* - J(K^*)^{-1}R^*(I-AA^*) \\ &= J(K^*)^{-1}R^*AA^* = -CA^*. \end{aligned}$$

Substituting this information in (1.41) yields $C_\Psi = -2iD_\Psi JB_\Psi^*$, and hence the node (1.40) is a Brodskii (-J)-node. The relationship between the nodes Δ and θ can also be expressed in terms of the corresponding characteristic operator functions W_Δ and W_θ. We have

$$W_\Delta(\lambda) = JW_\theta(\alpha)^*JW_\theta\left(\alpha\frac{\lambda+i}{\lambda-i}\right).$$

This is clear from the definition of Δ and the fact that $D_\Psi^{-1} = W_\theta(\alpha)^{-1} = JW_\theta(\alpha)^*J$.

PROPOSITION 1.11. Let $\theta = (A,B,C,D;X,Y)$ be a node such that θ_φ exists. Assume that the external operators of θ and

θ_φ <u>are invertible</u>. <u>Then</u> $(\theta^\times)_\varphi$ <u>and</u> $(\theta_\varphi)^\times$ <u>exist and</u>

$$(\theta^\times)_\varphi = (\theta_\varphi)^\times. \tag{1.42}$$

PROOF. Let W and W_φ be the transfer functions of θ and θ_φ, respectively. By assumption the operators $W(\infty) = D$ and $W_\varphi(\infty) = D+rC(p-rA)^{-1}B$ are invertible. If $r\neq 0$, then $W(pr^{-1}) = W_\varphi(\infty)$, and so $pr^{-1}\in\rho(A^\times)$, where $A^\times$ is the main operator of $\theta^\times$. Hence $p-rA^\times$ is invertible. This conclusion is also correct if $r = 0$, because then $p\neq 0$. It follows that $(\theta^\times)_\varphi$ exists. Also, as $D+rC(p-rA)^{-1}B$ is invertible, $(\theta_\varphi)^\times$ exists too. Finally, formula (1.42) is proved by direct computation, using

$$[D+rC(p-rA)^{-1}B]^{-1} = D^{-1}-rD^{-1}C(p-rA^\times)^{-1}BD^{-1}.$$

Let $\theta = (A,B,C,D;X,Y)$ be a node such that θ_φ exists. Assume that the external operators of θ and θ_φ are invertible. Let Π be a supporting projection for θ, i.e.,

$$A[\operatorname{Ker}\Pi]\subset \operatorname{Ker}\Pi\ ,\ A^\times[\operatorname{Im}\Pi]\subset \operatorname{Im}\Pi.$$

In general one may not conclude that Π is a supporting projection for θ_φ too. But if the state space of X is finite dimensional, then the conclusion is correct. So let us assume that $\dim X$ is finite. Let θ_1 and θ_2 be the factors of θ corresponding to Π and a factorization $D = D_1D_2$ of D with D_1 and D_2 invertible (i.e., θ_1 and θ_2 are given by formulas (1.5) and (1.6), respectively). As X is finite dimensional, the nodes $(\theta_1)_\varphi$ and $(\theta_2)_\varphi$ are well-defined, and we have (cf. Proposition 1.10)

$$\theta_\varphi = (\theta_1)_\varphi(\theta_2)_\varphi. \tag{1.43}$$

This factorization corresponds to Π (as a supporting projection for θ_φ) and a special factorization of $D+rC(p-rA)^{-1}B$ into invertible factors induced by $D = D_1D_2$. In the particular case that φ is a translation and the external operator of θ is the identity operator we may replace (1.43) by

$$\mathrm{pr}_{\Pi}(\theta_{\varphi}) = (\mathrm{pr}_{\Pi}(\theta))_{\varphi}\ ,\ \mathrm{pr}_{I-\Pi}(\theta_{\varphi}) = (\mathrm{pr}_{I-\Pi}(\theta))_{\varphi}.$$

Möbius transformations may be employed to derive from Theorem 1.1 factorization theorems for transfer functions that are irregular at infinity. To illustrate this we shall give a new proof of the division theorem for monic operator polynomials (cf. [26], Theorem 13) based on Theorem 1.1.

Suppose that L is a monic operator polynomial of degree ℓ, and let $\Delta = (T,R,Q,0;X,Y)$ be a monic node such that the transfer function of Δ is equal to L^{-1}. Let $X_1 \subset X$ be a supporting subspace, i.e., the space X_1 is a non-trivial (complemented) invariant subspace for T such that for some positive integer m (necessarily unique and less than ℓ)

$$\mathrm{col}(QT^{i-1})_{i=1}^{m}\Big|_{X_1} : X_1 \to Y^m$$

is invertible. Define $T_1 : X_1 \to X_1$ and $Q_1 : X_1 \to Y$ by $T_1x = Tx$ and $Q_1x = Qx$. Then $\mathrm{col}(Q_1T_1^{i-1})_{i=1}^{m}$ is invertible, say with inverse $\mathrm{row}(W_{i-1})_{i=1}^{m}$. Put

$$L_1(\lambda) = \lambda^m I - \sum_{i=0}^{m-1} \lambda^i Q_1T_1^m W_i .$$

We shall prove that L_1 is a right divisor of L.

Consider the Möbius transformation

$$\Psi(\lambda) = \frac{\alpha\lambda+1}{\lambda} .$$

Here α is a fixed complex number in the unbounded component of the resolvent set of T. As $T-\alpha$ is invertible, the node $\theta=\Delta_\varphi$ is well-defined. Put $A = -(\alpha-T)^{-1}$, $B = (\alpha-T)^{-1}R$, $C = -Q(\alpha-T)^{-1}$ and $D = Q(\alpha-T)^{-1}R$. Then $\theta = (A,B,C,D;X,Y)$ and the external operator D is equal to $L(\alpha)^{-1}$. Further, the associate main operator of θ is equal to

$$(1.44) \qquad A^\times = A-BD^{-1}C = -(\alpha-T)^{-1} + (\alpha-T)^{-1}RL(\alpha)Q(\alpha-T)^{-1}.$$

With the supporting subspace X_1 we associate the projection P defined by

$$Px = [\mathrm{col}(Q_1T_1^{i-1})_{i=1}^m]^{-1}[\mathrm{col}(QT^{i-1})_{i=1}^m]x.$$

We know that $\mathrm{Im}\, P = X_1$ is invariant under T. As α is in the unbounded component of T it follows that X_1 is also invariant under $A = -(\alpha-T)^{-1}$. Furthermore, we see that

$$(1.45) \qquad A\big|_{X_1} = -(\alpha-T_1)^{-1}.$$

Next we consider $X_2 = \mathrm{Ker}\, P$. From the theory of monic nodes we know that $X_2 = \mathrm{Im}\,[\mathrm{row}(T^{i-1}R)_{i=1}^{\ell-m}]$. We shall prove that X_2 is invariant under $A^\times$. In order to do this, recall that $QT^iR=0$ for $i=0,\dots,\ell-2$ and $QT^{\ell-1}R = I$. It follows that

$$(1.46) \qquad Q(\alpha-T)^{-1}T^sR = \alpha^sQ(\alpha-T)^{-1}R = \alpha^sL(\alpha)^{-1}, \quad s=0,\dots,\ell-1.$$

Using (1.44) we obtain $A^\times R = 0$ and for $1\leq s\leq \ell-1$

$$\begin{aligned} A^\times T^sR &= -(\alpha-T)^{-1}T^sR + (\alpha-T)^{-1}RL(\alpha)Q(\alpha-T)^{-1}T^sR \\ &= -(\alpha-T)^{-1}T^sR + \alpha^s(\alpha-T)^{-1}R \\ &= T^{s-1}R + \alpha T^{s-2}R + \dots + \alpha^{s-1}R. \end{aligned}$$

So we know the action of $A^{\times}$ on $T^{s}Ry$, $0\le s\le \ell-1$. It follows that X_2 is invariant under $A^{\times}$. Furthermore, we see that the restriction of $A^{\times}$ to X_2 is nilpotent of order $\ell-m$. Observe that by now we have proved that $\Pi = I-P$ is a supporting projection for θ.

As $\alpha-T_1$ is invertible, the same is true for the operator $L_1(\alpha)$. Put $D_1 = L_1(\alpha)^{-1}$ and $D_2 = L_1(\alpha)L(\alpha)^{-1}$. Then $D=D_1D_2$. Let

$$A = \begin{bmatrix} A_{11} & A_{12} \\ 0 & A_{22} \end{bmatrix}, \quad B = \begin{bmatrix} B_1 \\ B_2 \end{bmatrix}, \quad C = [C_1 C_2]$$

be the block matrix representations for A, B and C with respect to the decomposition $X = X_1 \oplus X_2$. Consider the nodes

$$\theta_1 = (A_{11}, B_1D_2^{-1}, C_1, D_1; X_1, Y),$$

$$\theta_2 = (A_{22}, B_2, D_1^{-1}C_2, D_2; X_2, Y),$$

and for $i = 1,2$ let W_i be the transfer function of θ_i. As $AX_1 \subset X_1$ and $A^{\times}X_2 \subset X_2$, we can apply Theorem 1.2 to show that $\theta = \theta_1\theta_2$, and hence

$$L(\Psi(\lambda))^{-1} = W_1(\lambda)W_2(\lambda). \tag{1.47}$$

First we shall prove that $L_1(\Psi(\lambda))^{-1} = W_1(\lambda)$. Put $\Delta_1 = (T_1, Q_1, R_1, 0; X_1, Y)$. Here T_1 and Q_1 are as before and $R_1 = W_{m-1}$. So Δ_1 is a monic node whose transfer function is equal to L_1^{-1}. Thus in order to prove that $L_1(\Psi(\lambda))^{-1}$ is equal to $W_1(\lambda)$, it suffices to show that $(\Delta_1)_{\Psi} = \theta_1$. Note that

$$(\Delta_1)_{\Psi} = (-(\alpha-T_1)^{-1}, (\alpha-T_1)R_1, -Q_1(\alpha-T_1)^{-1}, L_1(\alpha)^{-1}; X_1, Y).$$

We know already that $A_{11} = -(\alpha-T_1)^{-1}$ (cf. formula (1.45)). By definition $D_1=L_1(\alpha)^{-1}$. Further

$$C_1 = -Q(\alpha-T)\Big|_{X_1} = -Q_1(\alpha-T_1).$$

It remains to prove that $B_1D_2^{-1} = (\alpha-T_1)^{-1}R_1$. Take $y\in Y$. By applying (1.46) , first for T,Q,R and next for T_1,Q_1,R_1, we obtain

$$[\mathrm{col}(QT^{i-1})_{i=1}^m](\alpha-T)^{-1}RL(\alpha)L_1(\alpha)^{-1}y =$$

$$= [\mathrm{col}(\alpha^{i-1}L(\alpha)^{-1})_{i=1}^m]L(\alpha)L_1(\alpha)^{-1}y$$

$$= [\mathrm{col}(Q_1T_1^{i-1})_{i=1}^m](\alpha-T_1)^{-1}R_1y.$$

But then $B_1D_2^{-1}y = PBD_2^{-1}y = (\alpha-T_1)^{-1}R_1y$, and we have proved that $\theta_1 = (\Delta_1)_\Psi$.

As the restriction of $A^\times$ to X_2 is nilpotent of order ℓ-m, we know that $W_2(\lambda)^{-1}$ is a polynomial in λ^{-1} of degree at most ℓ-m. Put

$$L_2(\lambda) = W_2(\Psi^{-1}(\lambda))^{-1},$$

where Ψ^{-1} is the inverse map of the Möbius transformation Ψ. In other words, $\Psi^{-1}(\lambda) = (\lambda-\alpha)^{-1}$. It follows that $L_2(\lambda)$ is a polynomial in λ of degree at most ℓ-m. From (1.47) we see that $L(\lambda) = L_2(\lambda)L_1(\lambda)$, and hence L_1 is a right divisor of L.

Chapter II

REALIZATION AND LINEARIZATION

To apply the theory developed in the previous chapter to an operator function W it is important to have appropriate realizations of W. In the first two sections of the present chapter realizations are constructed for rational matrix and operator functions. In the first section the construction is carried out entirely in terms of the spectral data of W, while in the second section it is based on representations of the form $W(\lambda)=$ $=H(\lambda)L(\lambda)^{-1}$, where H and L are operator polynomials. In Section 2.3 realizations are constructed for arbitrary holomorphic operator functions. In Section 2.4 we compare realization with the method of linearization by extension [20], and it is shown that the main operator and the associate main operator $A^{\times}$ of the node $\theta = (A,B,C,D;X,Y)$ appear as linearizations of the transfer functions W_{θ}^{-1} and W_{θ}, respectively.

2.1 Realization for rational matrix functions

Let $W = W(\lambda)$ be a rational $n\times n$ matrix function. Throughout this section we assume that $\det W(\lambda) \not\equiv 0$. As usual the values of W will be identified with their canonical action on $\mathbb{C}^n$. Our aim is to construct a realization for W in terms of its spectral data. We begin with a review of the different notions that are relevant in this context.

Let $\lambda_0 \in \mathbb{C}$, and let

$$W(\lambda) = \sum_{j=-q}^{\infty}(\lambda-\lambda_0)^j A_j$$

be the Laurent expansion of W at λ_0. Here it is assumed that $q\geq 0$. We call λ_0 a <u>zero</u> (or <u>eigenvalue</u>) of W if in $\mathbb{C}^n$ there exist vectors $x_0,\dots,x_q$, $x_0 \neq 0$, such that

$$A_{-q}x_i + \dots + A_{-q+i}x_0 = 0 \quad (i=0,\dots,q).$$

In that case the vector x_0 is called an eigenvector (or rootvector) of W at the eigenvalue λ_0. Note that λ_0 is a zero of W if and only if λ_0 is a pole of $W^{-1} = W(\lambda)^{-1}$. The linear space of all eigenvectors of W at λ_0 together with the zero vector will be denoted by $\mathrm{Ker}(W;\lambda_0)$. The dimension of the space $\mathrm{Ker}(W;\lambda_0)$ is called the geometric multiplicity of λ_0 as a zero of W. If W is analytic at λ_0, then $\mathrm{Ker}(W;\lambda_0)$ is equal to $\mathrm{Ker}\, W(\lambda_0)$.

An ordered set $(x_0,\dots,x_{k-1})$ of vectors in $\mathbb{C}^n$ is called a Jordan chain for W at λ_0 if $x_0 \neq 0$ and there exist vectors $x_k,\dots, x_{q+k}$ in $\mathbb{C}^n$ such that

$$A_{-q}x_i + \dots + A_{-q+i}x_0 = 0 \quad (i=0,\dots,q+k).$$

The number k is called the length of the chain. Note that x_0 is an eigenvector of W at λ_0 if and only if x_0 is the first vector in a Jordan chain for W at λ_0. Given an eigenvector x_0 of W at λ_0, there are in general many Jordan chains for W at λ_0 which have x_0 as their first vector. However the lengths of these Jordan chains have a finite supremum, which we shall call the rank of the eigenvector x_0 (cf. [31]).

To organize the Jordan chains corresponding to the eigenvalue λ_0, we follow the procedure described in [31]. Choose an eigenvector x_{10} in $\mathrm{Ker}(W;\lambda_0)$ such that the rank r_1 of x_{10} is maximal, and let $(x_{10},\dots,x_{1r_1-1})$ be a corresponding Jordan chain. Now let N_1 be a direct complement in $\mathrm{Ker}(W;\lambda_0)$ of the linear space spanned by x_{10}. In N_1 we take an eigenvector x_{20} of maximal rank, r_2 say, and we choose a corresponding Jordan chain $(x_{20},\dots,x_{2r_2-1})$. Next let N_2 be a direct complement in N_1 of the space spanned by x_{20}, and repeat the procedure described above for N_2 instead of N_1. In this way we obtain a basis $x_{10},\dots,x_{p0}$ of $\mathrm{Ker}(W;\lambda_0)$ and corresponding Jordan chains

$$(x_{10},\dots,x_{1r_1-1}),\dots,(x_{p0},\dots,x_{pr_p-1}). \tag{2.1}$$

The system (2.1) we shall call a canonical system of Jordan chains for W at λ_0. The numbers $r_1,\dots,r_p$, which (see [31]) do not depend on the particular choices made above, are the so-called partial zero-multiplicities of W at λ_0. Their sum $r_1+\dots+r_p$ is called the zero-multiplicity of W at λ_0.

The information contained in the system (2.1) can be put into a pair of matrices. In order to do this, let Q_i be the $n\times r_i$ matrix whose j-th column is equal to the column vector $x_{i,j-1}$. In other words $Q_i = [x_{i0} \dots x_{ir_i-1}]$. Further, let J_i be the $r_i\times r_i$ Jordan block with λ_0 on the main diagonal. Finally, put

$$Q_0 = [Q_1Q_2 \dots Q_p] \ , \ J_0 = J_1\oplus J_2\oplus\dots\oplus J_p.$$

Note that J_0 is a Jordan matrix with one single eigenvalue, namely λ_0. The orders of its blocks are equal to the partial zero-multiplicities of W at λ_0. Hence the order of J_0 is precisely equal to the zero-multiplicity of λ_0 as an eigenvalue of W. Further

$$\dim \operatorname{Ker}(\lambda_0-J_0) = p = \dim \operatorname{Ker}(W;\lambda_0).$$

So the geometric multiplicity of λ_0 as a zero of W is equal to the geometric multiplicity of λ_0 as an eigenvalue of J_0. The pair (Q_0,J_0) is called a Jordan pair of W corresponding to the eigenvalue λ_0. The name Jordan pair will also be used for any pair of matrices $(\tilde{Q},\tilde{J})$, which is obtained from (Q_0,J_0) by some permutation of the blocks J_i in J_0 and the same permutation of the corresponding blocks in Q_0. From the construction of a canonical system of Jordan chains it follows that

$$\bigcap_{k=0}^{\infty} \operatorname{Ker} Q_0J_0^k = (0). \tag{2.2}$$

If λ_0 is a zero for W, then λ_0 is also a zero for the transposed matrix function $W^T=W(\lambda)^T$. The converse is also true. In fact one can show that the partial zero-multiplicities of λ_0 as an eigenvalue of W are the same as the partial zero-multiplicities of λ_0 as an eigenvalue of W^T (cf. [31]). Now let

$$(y_{10},\dots,y_{1r_1-1}),\dots,(y_{p0},\dots,y_{pr_p-1})$$

be a canonical system of Jordan chains for W^T at λ_0. For $1 \le i \le p$ let R_i be the $r_i \times n$ matrix whose ℓ-th row is formed by the entries of the vector $y_{i,r_i-\ell}$. In other words

$$R_i = [y_{ir_i-\ell} \cdots y_{i0}]^T.$$

As before, let J_i be the $r_i \times r_i$ Jordan block with λ_0 on the main diagonal, and put

$$\text{(2.3)} \qquad R_0 = \begin{bmatrix} R_1 \\ \cdot \\ \cdot \\ \cdot \\ R_p \end{bmatrix}, \quad J_0 = J_1 \oplus \cdots \oplus J_p.$$

The pair (J_0,R_0) is called a <u>dual Jordan pair</u> of W corresponding to the eigenvalue λ_0. This term will also be used for any pair of matrices $(\tilde{J},\tilde{R})$ which is obtained from (J_0,R_0) by some permutation of the blocks in (2.3). From the construction of a canonical system of Jordan chains, it follows that

$$\text{(2.4)} \qquad \bigcup_{k=0}^{\infty} \operatorname{Im}(R_0\ J_0R_0 \dots J_0^kR_0) = \mathbb{C}^{\rho_0},$$

where $\rho_0 = r_1+\dots+r_p$ is equal to the order of the matrix J_0. Observe that a Jordan pair and a dual Jordan pair have the same Jordan matrix J_0. So $(J_0,R_0,Q_0;\mathbb{C}^{\rho_0},\mathbb{C}^n)$ is a node.

Let (Q_0,J_0) be a Jordan pair and (J_0,R_0) a dual Jordan pair of W corresponding to the eigenvalue λ_0. Consider the function $Q_0(\lambda_0-J_0)^{-1}R_0$. As $\lambda_0 - J_0$ is nilpotent, we have

$$Q_0(\lambda_0-J_0)^{-1}R_0 = \sum_{j=1}^{s} (\lambda-\lambda_0)^{-j}Q_0(\lambda_0-J_0)^{j-1}R_0.$$

Here s is the order of nilpotency of λ_0-J_0. By Theorem 7.1 in [31] one can always choose Q_0, J_0, and R_0 in such a way that $Q_0(\lambda_0-J_0)^{-1}R_0$ is precisely equal to the principal part of the Laurent expansion of $W^{-1} = W(\lambda)^{-1}$ at λ_0. In that case we call the triple (Q_0,J_0,R_0) a <u>canonical Jordan triple</u> of W corresponding to the eigenvalue λ_0. The fact that a canonical Jordan triple always exists is trivial if $W(\lambda)$ has the Smith-McMillan canonical form and it can be proved in general by equivalence (see [31] for further details).

So far λ_0 has been a point in the finite complex plane. Now we consider the case that $\lambda_0 = \infty$. As W is a rational function, its behaviour in a neighbourhood of ∞ is given by the following expansion:

$$W(\lambda) = \sum_{j=-\infty}^{q} \lambda^j W_j .$$

Here q is an integer which we shall assume to be non-negative. We call $\lambda_0 = \infty$ a <u>zero</u> (or <u>eigenvalue</u>) of W if in $\mathbb{C}^n$ there exist vectors $x_0,\dots,x_q$, $x_0 \neq 0$, such that

$$W_q x_i + \dots + W_{q-i} x_0 = 0 \quad (i=0,\dots,q).$$

In that case the vector x_0 is called an <u>eigenvector</u> of W at the point ∞. Clearly, $\lambda_0 = \infty$ is a zero of W if and only if the point zero is an eigenvalue of the function $\widetilde{W}$ defined by

$$\widetilde{W}(\lambda) = W(\tfrac{1}{\lambda}). \tag{2.5}$$

This fact allows us (without any further explanation) to introduce for the point $\lambda_0 = \infty$ all notions defined above for a finite eigenvalue. For example, we define the <u>partial zero-multiplicities</u> of W at $\lambda_0 = \infty$ to be equal to the partial zero-multiplicities of $\widetilde{W}$ at the point 0. Similarly, a triple $(Q_\infty,J_\infty,R_\infty)$ is called a <u>canonical Jordan triple</u> of W corresponding to the point $\lambda_0 = \infty$ if $(Q_\infty,J_\infty,R_\infty)$ is a canonical Jordan triple of $\widetilde{W}$ corresponding to the point 0. Observe that in that case J_∞ is a nilpotent matrix.

THEOREM 2.1. <u>Let</u> $W(\lambda)$ <u>be a rational</u> $n\times n$ <u>matrix function. Let</u> $\lambda_1,\dots,\lambda_m$ <u>be the finite zeros of</u> W, <u>let</u> $\rho_1,\dots,\rho_m$ <u>be the corresponding zero-multiplicities, and for</u> $1\le i\le m$ <u>let</u> (Q_i,J_i,R_i)

be a canonical Jordan triple of W *corresponding to* λ_i. *Put* $\rho = \rho_1+\ldots+\rho_m$, *and set*

$$Q = \mathrm{row}(Q_i)_{i=1}^m , \quad J = J_1 \oplus\cdots\oplus J_m, \quad R = \mathrm{col}(R_i)_{i=1}^m.$$

Further, let $(Q_\infty, J_\infty, R_\infty)$ *be a canonical Jordan triple of* W *corresponding to* ∞. *Then*

$$W(\lambda)^{-1} = Q(\lambda-J)^{-1}R + D + \lambda Q_\infty(I-\lambda J_\infty)^{-1}R_\infty$$

for a suitable choice of D. *In particular, if* W^{-1} *is analytic at* ∞, *then* $D = W^{-1}(\infty)$ *and the node* $\theta = (J,R,Q,D;\mathbb{C}^\rho,\mathbb{C}^n)$ *is a realization of* W^{-1}.

PROOF. From the definition of Q, J and R it follows that $Q(\lambda-J)^{-1}R = \sum_{i=1}^m Q_i(\lambda-J_i)^{-1}R_i$. As (Q_i,J_i,R_i) is a canonical Jordan triple of W corresponding to λ_i, we know that for $1\le i\le m$ the function

$$W(\lambda)^{-1} - Q_i(\lambda-J_i)^{-1}R_i$$

has no pole at λ_i. It follows that $W(\lambda)^{-1} - Q(\lambda-J)^{-1}R$ is analytic on the whole of $\mathbb{C}$.

Similarly, $W(\frac{1}{\lambda})^{-1} - Q_\infty(\lambda-J_\infty)^{-1}R_\infty$ is analytic at 0. It follows that $W(\lambda)^{-1} - \lambda Q_\infty(I-\lambda J_\infty)^{-1}R_\infty$ is analytic at ∞, and hence the function

$$W(\lambda)^{-1} - Q(\lambda-J)^{-1}R - \lambda Q_\infty(I-\lambda J_\infty)^{-1}R_\infty \tag{2.6}$$

is analytic on the whole Riemann sphere $\mathbb{C}\cup\{\infty\}$. But this implies that the function (2.6) is equal to a constant $n\times n$ matrix D, say. This proves the theorem.

To obtain a realization for W we have to consider the pole-vectors of W. First take $\lambda_0 \in \mathbb{C}$. A non-zero vector x_0 in $\mathbb{C}^n$ is called pole-vector of W at λ_0 if there exist $\varphi_1,\ldots,\varphi_q$ in $\mathbb{C}^n$ such that

$$\begin{bmatrix} A_{-q} & A_{-q+1} & \cdots & A_{-1} \\ 0 & A_{-q} & \cdots & A_{-2} \\ \vdots & \vdots & \ddots & \vdots \\ 0 & 0 & \cdots & A_{-q} \end{bmatrix} \begin{bmatrix} \varphi_q \\ \varphi_{q-1} \\ \vdots \\ \varphi_1 \end{bmatrix} = \begin{bmatrix} x \\ 0 \\ \vdots \\ 0 \end{bmatrix}.$$

The linear space consisting of all pole-vectors of W at λ_0 together with the zero vector will be denoted by $\mathrm{Pol}(W;\lambda_0)$. Note that there exists a pole-vector of W at λ_0 if and only if W has a pole at λ_0. It is not difficult to prove (see [31]) that x_0 is a pole-vector of W at λ_0 if and only if x_0 is an eigenvalue of W^{-1} corresponding to λ_0. In other words $\mathrm{Pol}(W;\lambda_0) = \mathrm{Ker}(W^{-1};\lambda_0)$. The dimension of the space $\mathrm{Pol}(W;\lambda_0)$ is called the <u>geometric multiplicity</u> of λ_0 as a pole of W. By definition the <u>rank</u> of a pole-vector x_0 of W at λ_0 is the rank of x_0 as an eigenvector of W^{-1} at λ_0. Similarly, the <u>partial pole-multiplicities</u> of W at λ_0 are by definition equal to the partial zero-multiplicities of W^{-1} at λ_0. If $\eta_1,\dots,\eta_p$ are the partial pole-multiplicities of W at λ_0, then $\delta_0 = \eta_1+\dots+\eta_p$ is called the <u>pole-multiplicity</u> of W at λ_0. One can prove that this number is equal to the largest multiplicity λ_0 possesses as a pole of any minor of the matrix function W (cf. [52]).

To define the corresponding notions for $\lambda_0 = \infty$, formula (2.5) may be used. So, for example, a non-zero vector x_0 in $\mathbb{C}^n$ is called a <u>pole-vector</u> of W at ∞ if x_0 is a pole vector for $\tilde{W}$ at the point 0. Similarly, the partial pole-multiplicities of W at ∞ are by definition equal to the partial pole-multiplicities of $\tilde{W}$ at 0. In the same way one can define the other notions too.

Let λ_0 be a finite pole of W, and let (Q_0,J_0,R_0) be a canonical Jordan triple of W^{-1} corresponding to λ_0. Then

$Q_0(\lambda-J_0)^{-1}R_0$ is equal to the principal part of the Laurent expansion of W at λ_0. In other words,

$$A_{-j} = Q_0(\lambda_0-J_0)^{j-1}R_0 \ , \ j=1,\dots,q$$

and $Q_0(\lambda_0-J_0)^iR_0 = 0$ for $i\geq q$. It follows that

$$(2.7) \qquad \begin{bmatrix} A_{-q} & \cdot & \cdot & \cdot & \cdot & A_{-1} \\ 0 & \cdot & & & & \cdot \\ \cdot & 0 & \cdot & & & \cdot \\ \cdot & & 0 & \cdot & & \cdot \\ \cdot & & & 0 & \cdot & \cdot \\ 0 & \cdot & \cdot & \cdot & 0 & A_{-q} \end{bmatrix} = \Omega_1\Omega_2,$$

where $\Omega_1 = \mathrm{col}(Q_0(\lambda_0-J_0)^{i-1})_{i=1}^{s}$, $\Omega_2 = \mathrm{row}((\lambda_0-J_0)^{s-i})_{i=1}^{s}$ and $s\geq q$ is arbitrary. From (2.2) and (2.4) we see that for s sufficiently large Ω_1 is injective and Ω_2 is surjective. Therefore the rank of the matrix in the left hand side of (2.7) is equal to the order of J_0, which is equal to the pole-multiplicity of W at λ_0.

From Theorem 2.1 it is clear that we have the following realization theorem for W.

THEOREM 2.2. _Let_ $W(\lambda)$ _be a rational_ $n\times n$ _matrix function. Let_ $\lambda_1,\dots,\lambda_\ell$ _be the finite poles of_ W, _let_ $\delta_1,\dots,\delta_\ell$ _be the corresponding pole-multiplicities, and for_ $1\leq i\leq \ell$ _let_ (Q_i,J_i,R_i) _be a canonical Jordan triple of_ W^{-1} _corresponding to_ λ_i. _Put_ $\delta = \delta_1+\dots+\delta_m$, _and set_

$$Q = \mathrm{row}(Q_i)_{i=1}^{\ell},\ J = J_1\oplus\cdots\oplus J_\ell \ ,\ R = \mathrm{col}(R_i)_{i=1}^{\ell}.$$

Further, let $(Q_\infty,J_\infty,R_\infty)$ _be a canonical Jordan triple of_ W^{-1} _corresponding to_ ∞. _Then_

$$W(\lambda) = Q(\lambda-J)^{-1}R + D + \lambda Q_\infty(I-\lambda J_\infty)^{-1}R_\infty$$

for a suitable choice of D. *In particular, if* W *is analytic at* ∞, *then* $D = W(\infty)$ *and the node* $\theta = (J,R,Q,D;\mathbb{C}^{\delta},\mathbb{C}^{n})$ *is a realization of* W.

Because of formulas (2.2) and (2.4) the nodes θ in Theorems 2.1 and 2.2 have an additional minimality property, which will be discussed further in the next chapters.

2.2 Realization for rational operator functions

To construct a realization for a rational operator function the following theorem is often useful (cf. [1] Theorem 4.20).

THEOREM 2.3. *Let* $H(\lambda) = \sum_{j=0}^{\ell-1} \lambda^j H_j$ *and* $L(\lambda) = \lambda^{\ell} I + \sum_{j=0}^{\ell-1} \lambda^j A_j$ *be operator polynomials whose coefficients act on the complex Banach space* Y. *Put*

$$B = \begin{bmatrix} 0 \\ \cdot \\ \cdot \\ \cdot \\ 0 \\ I \end{bmatrix}, \quad A = \begin{bmatrix} 0 & I & \cdots & 0 \\ \vdots & & \ddots & \\ 0 & 0 & & I \\ -A_0 & -A_1 & \cdots & -A_{\ell-1} \end{bmatrix}, \quad C = [H_0 \ldots H_{\ell-1}].$$

Then $\theta = (A,B,C,0;Y^{\ell},Y)$ *is a node and*

$$W_{\theta}(\lambda) = H(\lambda)L(\lambda)^{-1}, \quad \lambda \in \rho(A).$$

PROOF. We know already (see Subsection 1.4.3) that

$$L(\lambda)^{-1} = Q(\lambda - A)^{-1}B, \quad \lambda \in \rho(A), \tag{2.8}$$

where $Q = [I\ 0 \ldots 0]$. Take $\lambda \in \rho(A)$, and define $C_1(\lambda), \ldots, C_{\ell}(\lambda)$ by

$$\operatorname{col}(C_j(\lambda))_{j=1}^{\ell} = (\lambda - A)^{-1}B.$$

From (2.8) we see that $C_1(\lambda) = L(\lambda)^{-1}$. As $(\lambda-A)[\mathrm{col}(C_j(\lambda))_{j=1}^{\ell}]$. B, the special form of A yields

$$C_i(\lambda) = \lambda^{i-1}C_1(\lambda), \quad 1\leq i\leq \ell.$$

It follows that $C(\lambda-A)^{-1}B = \sum_{j=0}^{\ell-1} H_j C_{j+1}(\lambda) = H(\lambda)L(\lambda)^{-1}$, and the proof is complete.

Let us employ the previous theorem to get a realization for a rational operator function W whose values act on the complex Banach space Y. Assume for the sake of simplicity that W is analytic at ∞, and put $D = W(\infty)$. As W is rational there exists a monic scalar polynomial $\ell(\lambda)$ such that $\ell(\lambda)W(\lambda)$ is analytic on the whole of $\mathbb{C}$. Put $H(\lambda) = \ell(\lambda)[W(\lambda)-D]$. Then $H(\lambda)$ is an operator polynomial whose coefficients act on Y. Clearly, $L(\lambda) = \ell(\lambda)I_Y$ is monic and $W(\lambda) = D + H(\lambda)L(\lambda)^{-1}$. Further, as $W(\infty) = D$, we have $\lim_{\lambda\to\infty} H(\lambda)L(\lambda)^{-1} = 0$, and hence the degree of $H(\lambda)$ is strictly less than the degree of $L(\lambda)$. So we can apply Theorem 2.3 to obtain a realization for $H(\lambda)L(\lambda)^{-1}$ and hence one for $W(\lambda)$ too.

2.3 Realization for arbitrary holomorphic operator functions

Let Γ be a Cauchy contour around zero, and let Y be a complex Banach space. With Γ and Y we associate the space $C(\Gamma,Y)$ of all Y-valued continuous functions on Γ endowed with the supremum norm. The canonical embedding of Y into $C(\Gamma,Y)$ will be denoted by τ, i.e., $\tau(y)(z) = y$ for each $y\in Y$ and $z\in\Gamma$. Further we define $\omega : C(\Gamma,Y) \to Y$ by setting

$$\omega f = \frac{1}{2\pi i}\int_{\Gamma} \frac{1}{z} f(z)dz.$$

THEOREM 2.4. <u>Let Ω be the interior domain of Γ, and let W be an operator function, holomorphic on Ω, continuous towards the boundary Γ, and with values in $L(Y)$. Define oper-</u>

ators V *and* M *on* $C(\Gamma,Y)$ *by*

$$(Vf)(z) = zf(z) \ , \ (Mf)(z) = W(z)f(z).$$

Then $W(\lambda) = I+\omega(V-VM)(\lambda-V)^{-1}\tau$ *for each* $\lambda\in\Omega$. *In other words, the node* $\theta = (V,\tau,\omega(V-VM);C(\Gamma,Y),Y)$ *is a realization for* W *on* Ω.

PROOF. First of all one shows that $\sigma(V) = \Gamma$ and

$$[(\lambda-V)^{-1}g](z) = \frac{1}{\lambda-z}\, g(z), \quad \lambda\notin\Gamma, z\in\Gamma.$$

It follows that for $\lambda\notin\Gamma$ we have

$$\omega(V-VM)(\lambda-V)^{-1}\tau y = \left(\frac{1}{2\pi i}\int_\Gamma \frac{I-W(z)}{\lambda-z}\,dz\right)y. \tag{2.9}$$

For $\lambda\in\Omega$ the right hand side of (2.9) is equal to $W(\lambda)y-y$, and the theorem is proved.

The associate main operator $V^\times$ of the node θ introduced in the previous theorem is given by $V^\times = V-\tau\omega(V-VM)$. It follows that

$$(V^\times f)(z) = zf(z) - \frac{1}{2\pi i}\int_\Gamma [I-W(\zeta)]f(\zeta)d\zeta. \tag{2.10}$$

So $V^\times$ is precisely equal to the linearization T of [20], Theorem 2.2. We shall come back to this connection in the next section.

Theorem 2.4 can be proved for any bounded open set Ω in $\mathbb{C}$, regardless of what the boundary conditions of W are. Of course, in that case the space $C(\Gamma,Y)$ must be replaced by an appropriate Banach space, which one has to define in terms of the behaviour of W near the boundary (cf., [44]; see also the next theorem).

If Ω is an unbounded open set containing zero, then one cannot expect that W admits a representation of the form $D+C(\lambda-A)^{-1}B$, because the behaviour of W near infinity may be irregular. However one can always write W as $D+\lambda C(I-\lambda A)^{-1}B$. This follows from the next theorem by changing λ into λ^{-1}.

THEOREM 2.5. Let Ω be an open neighbourhood of infinity in $\mathbb{C}\cup\{\infty\}$ not containing the point 0, and let $W:\Omega\to L(Y)$ be holomorphic. Define X to be the space of all Y-valued functions, holomorphic on Ω, such that

$$|||f||| = \sup_{z\in\Omega} \frac{\|f(z)\|}{\max(1, \|W(z)\|)} < \infty.$$

The space X endowed with the norm $|||\cdot|||$ is a Banach space. The canonical embedding of Y into X is denoted by τ. Further $\omega:X\to Y$ is defined by $\omega f = f(\infty)$. Let V and M be the operators on X given by

$$(Vf)(\lambda) = \lambda(f(\lambda)-f(\infty)),\quad (Mf)(\lambda) = W(\lambda)f(\infty).$$

Then $W(\lambda) = W(\infty) + \omega(\lambda-V)^{-1}VM\tau$ for $\lambda\in\Omega$. In other words, the node $(V,VM\tau,\omega,W(\infty);X,Y)$ is a realization for W on Ω.

PROOF. First one checks that the operators τ,ω,V and M are well-defined bounded linear operators. Next one proves that for each $\lambda\in\Omega\setminus\{\infty\}$ the operator $\lambda-V$ is invertible. Indeed, take $\lambda\in\Omega\setminus\{0\}$. For $g\in Y$, put

$$h(z) = \frac{\lambda g(z) - zg(\lambda)}{\lambda-z},\quad z\in\Omega.$$

Then $h\in Y$, and by direct computation one sees that

$$[(\lambda-V)h](z) = \lambda g(z),\quad z\in\Omega.$$

As $\lambda-V$ is injective, it follows that $\lambda\in\rho(V)$ and $(\lambda-V)^{-1}g=\frac{1}{\lambda}h$. Now take $g = VM\tau y$, i.e., $g(z) = z[W(z)y-W(\infty)y]$ for each $z\in\Omega$. Then

$$[(\lambda-V)^{-1}g](z) = \frac{z}{\lambda-z}[W(z)-W(\lambda)]y.$$

But then $\omega(\lambda-V)^{-1}VM\tau = W(\lambda) - W(\infty)$, and the theorem is proved.

In the previous theorem the condition that Ω does not contain the point 0 may be replaced by the requirement that $\mathbb{C}\setminus\Omega\neq\phi$. In the latter case one takes a point in $\mathbb{C}\setminus\Omega$, and with appropriate changes the theorem remains valid. If $\mathbb{C}\setminus\Omega = \phi$, i.e., if Ω is the full Riemann sphere $\mathbb{C}\cup\{\infty\}$, then the theorem does not go through, but on the other hand in that case the function W is constant.

Theorem 2.5 is related to the linearization result proved in [7]. For other versions of the above realization theorems we refer to [43].

2.4 Linearization

Let W be the transfer function of a node $\theta = (A,B,C,D;X,Y)$ with invertible external operator D. Then $W(\lambda)^{-1} = D^{-1} - D^{-1}C(\lambda-A^{\times})^{-1}BD^{-1}$ for λ in a neighbourhood of ∞. Here $A^{\times}=A-BD^{-1}C$ is the associate main operator. In this section we shall point out another connection between W and $A^{\times}$. In fact we shall prove that $A^{\times}$ appears as a linearization of W.

First we define the notion of linearization. Let Ω be an open set in $\mathbb{C}$, and let $W:\Omega \to L(Y)$ be holomorphic. An operator $T\in L(X)$ is called a <u>linearization</u> of W on Ω if there exist a Banach space Z and holomorphic operator functions E and F on Ω such that

(2.11) $$E(\lambda)(W(\lambda)\oplus I_Z) = (\lambda-T)F(\lambda), \quad \lambda\in\Omega,$$

while the maps $E(\lambda), F(\lambda) : Y\oplus Z \to X$ are bijective for each λ in Ω. The operator function $W(\cdot) \oplus I_Z$ is called the Z-<u>extension</u> of W. If two operator functions W_1 and W_2, holomorphic on Ω, are connected as in (2.11), i.e., if $E(\lambda)W_1(\lambda)=W_2(\lambda)F(\lambda)$ for $\lambda\in\Omega$, with E and F holomorphic on Ω and $E(\lambda)$ and $F(\lambda)$ invertible for each $\lambda\in\Omega$, then W_1 and W_2 are said to be <u>equivalent</u> on Ω.

THEOREM 2.6. *Let* $\theta = (A,B,C,D;X,Y)$ *be a node with an invertible external operator* D. *Assume that* B *has a left inverse* B^+, *and put* $Z = \operatorname{Ker} B^+$. *For* $y \in Y$, $z \in Z$ *and* $\lambda \in \rho(A)$ *define*

$$E(\lambda)(y,z) = BD^{-1}y + z + BD^{-1}C(\lambda - A)^{-1}z,$$

$$F(\lambda)(y,z) = (\lambda - A)^{-1}(By+z).$$

Then $E(\lambda), F(\lambda): Y \oplus Z \to X$ *are bijective,* E *and* F *are holomorphic on* $\rho(A)$ *and*

$$E(\lambda)[W_\theta(\lambda) \oplus I_Z] = (\lambda - A^\times)F(\lambda), \quad \lambda \in \rho(A). \tag{2.12}$$

In particular, $A^\times$ *is a linearization on* $\rho(A)$ *of the transfer function* W_θ.

PROOF. Note that $X = \operatorname{Im} B \oplus Z$. Put $P = BB^+$. Then P is the projection of X onto $\operatorname{Im} B$ along Z. Define $S: Y \oplus Z \to X$ by setting $S(y,z) = By+z$. The operator S is invertible. In fact, $S^{-1}x = (B^+x, (I-P)x)$.

Take $\lambda \in \rho(A)$. Put $V(\lambda) = I + BD^{-1}C(\lambda - A)^{-1}$. Note that $PV(\lambda)(I-P) = BD^{-1}C(\lambda - A)^{-1}(I-P)$. It follows that

$$\begin{aligned} E(\lambda)(y,z) &= BD^{-1}y + z + BD^{-1}C(\lambda - A)^{-1}z \\ &= BD^{-1}y + z + PV(\lambda)(I-P)z \\ &= [I + PV(\lambda)(I-P)](BD^{-1}y + z) \\ &= [I + PV(\lambda)(I-P)]S[D^{-1} \oplus I_Z](y,z). \end{aligned}$$

So $E(\lambda) = [I + PV(\lambda)(I-P)]S[D^{-1} \oplus I_Z]$, and hence $E(\lambda)$ is bijective. A straightforward computation shows that

$$E(\lambda)[W_\theta(\lambda) \oplus I_Z] = V(\lambda)S.$$

But $V(\lambda) = (\lambda-A^{\times})(\lambda-A)^{-1}$. As $F(\lambda) = (\lambda-A)^{-1}S$, we have (2.12). From $F(\lambda) = (\lambda-A)^{-1}S$ it is clear that $F(\lambda)$ is invertible. So the proof is complete.

By applying Theorem 2.6 to the associate node $\theta^{\times}$ we may conclude that under the conditions of Theorem 2.6 the operator A is a linearization on $\rho(A^{\times})$ of the transfer function $W_{\theta^{\times}}$. So, roughly speaking, the operator A appears as a linearization of W_{θ}^{-1} and $A^{\times}$ as a linearization of W_{θ}. For finite dimensional nodes this corresponds to the fact that the eigenvalues of A are related to the poles of W_{θ} and the eigenvalues of $A^{\times}$ are related to the zeros of W_{θ}. Note that Theorem 2.6 is applicable to the Livsic-Brodskiĭ characteristic operator function

$$W(\lambda) = I + 2iK^{*}(\lambda-A)^{-1}KJ,$$

provided K has a left inverse, and in that case the adjoint operator A^{*} is a linearization on $\rho(A)$ of W. A similar remark holds for Krein nodes.

If in Theorem 2.6 the assumption that B has a left inverse is replaced by the condition that C has a right inverse C^{+}, say, then the final conclusion of the theorem remains true. In fact, in that case one takes $Z = \operatorname{Ker} C$ and proves that

$$E(\lambda)[W_{\theta}(\lambda)\oplus I_{Z}] = (\lambda-A^{\times})F(\lambda), \quad \lambda\in\rho(A),$$

where $E(\lambda), F(\lambda)\colon Y\oplus Z \to X$ are given by

$$E(\lambda)(y,z) = (\lambda-A)C^{+}y + (\lambda-A)z,$$

$$F(\lambda)(y,z) = C^{+}DY - (I-C^{+}C)(\lambda-A)^{-1}By + z.$$

If B or C has a generalized inverse then one has to allow for extensions on both sides (see [43] for details). Always, irrespective of any invertibility condition on B or C, the functions $W_\theta(\lambda)\oplus I_X$ and $(\lambda-A^\times)\oplus I_Y$ are equivalent on $\rho(A)$. In fact, we have (cf. [20], Theorem 4.5):

$$E(\lambda)[I_Y\oplus(\lambda-A^\times)]F(\lambda) = W_\theta(\lambda)\oplus I_X \ , \ \lambda\in\rho(A), \tag{2.13}$$

where

$$E(\lambda) = \begin{pmatrix} W_\theta(\lambda) & C(\lambda-A)^{-1} \\ (\lambda-A)^{-1}B & (\lambda-A)^{-1} \end{pmatrix}, \ F(\lambda) = \begin{pmatrix} D^{-1}W_\theta(\lambda) & -D^{-1}C \\ -(\lambda-A)^{-1}B & I_X \end{pmatrix}.$$

This leads to the following corollary.

COROLLARY 2.7. *Let* $\theta = (A,B,C,D;X,Y)$ *be a node with an invertible external operator* D. *Then* $W_\theta(\lambda)$ *is invertible if and only if* $\lambda\in\rho(A)\cap\rho(A^\times)$.

PROOF. As invertibility properties do not change under extension and equivalence, the statement is clear from formula (2.13).

By applying the previous results to the operator function considered in Theorem 2.4 we obtain the following theorem (cf. [20], Theorems 2.2 and 2.3).

THEOREM 2.8. *Let* Γ *be a Cauchy contour around zero in* $\mathbb{C}$, *and let* W *be an operator function, holomorphic on the interior domain* Ω *of* Γ, *continuous towards the boundary* Γ *and with values in* $L(Y)$. *Let* T *on* $C(\Gamma,Y)$ *be defined by*

$$(Tf)(z) = zf(z) - \frac{1}{2\pi i}\int_\Gamma [I-W(\zeta)]f(\zeta)d\zeta.$$

Then T *is a linearization of* W *on* Ω *and*

$$\sigma(T) = \Gamma\cup\{\lambda\in\Omega \mid W(\lambda) \text{ not invertible}\}. \tag{2.14}$$

PROOF. By Theorem 2.4 we have $W(\lambda) = I+\omega(V-VM)(\lambda-V)^{-1}\tau$ for each $\lambda\in\Omega$. Note that τ has a left inverse, in fact $\omega\tau=I_Y$. As $\Omega\subset\rho(V)$, Theorem 2.6 shows that $W(\lambda)\oplus I_{\mathrm{Ker}\,\omega}$ is equivalent to $\lambda-V^\times$ on Ω, and we may conclude that $V^\times$ is a linearization of W on Ω. Here $V^\times$ is the associate main operator of the node $\theta = (V,\tau,\omega(V-VM);\ C(\Gamma,Y),Y)$. So $V^\times$ is given by formula (2.10), and hence $V^\times = T$.

To prove (2.14) consider the transfer function W_θ of the node $\theta = (V,\tau,\omega(V-VM);\ C(\Gamma,Y),Y)$. We know that $W_\theta(\lambda)=W(\lambda)$ for $\lambda\in\Omega$. For $\lambda\in\mathbb{C}\setminus\bar{\Omega}$ we have $W_\theta(\lambda) = I$. This is clear from (2.9). So $W_\theta(\lambda)$ is invertible for each λ in the exterior domain of Γ. As $\rho(V)=\mathbb{C}\setminus\Gamma$, we may apply Corollary 2.7 to show that $\sigma(V^\times)\cap\Omega = \{\lambda\in\Omega \mid W(\lambda) \text{ not invertible}\}$ and $\sigma(V^\times)\cap[\mathbb{C}\setminus\bar{\Omega}] = \phi$. So to prove (2.14) it remains to show that $\Gamma\subset\sigma(V^\times)$.

Take $\lambda_0\in\Gamma$, and assume that $\lambda_0\in\rho(V^\times)$. So $W_{\theta^\times}(\lambda)$ is defined in some open connected neighbourhood U of λ_0. Observe that on $[\mathbb{C}\setminus\bar{\Omega}]\cap U$ the function $W_{\theta^\times}$ is identically equal to I. By analyticity $W_{\theta^\times}(\lambda) = I$ for each $\lambda\in U$. But then, applying Corollary 2.7 to $\theta^\times$, one obtains $\lambda_0\in\rho(V)$. This contradicts $\Gamma = \sigma(V)$, and the proof is complete.

Theorem 2.6 is applicable only to nodes with an invertible external operator. To obtain a linearization of the transfer function of a node with a non-invertible external operator one can employ an appropriate Möbius transformation. In some cases a linearization can be given directly. For example, if $\theta = (T,R,Q,0;X,Y)$ is a monic node, then T is a linearization on $\mathbb{C}$ of $W_\theta(\lambda)^{-1}$. Recall (cf. Subsection 1.4.3) that in this case $W_\theta(\lambda)^{-1}$ is a monic operator polynomial. To describe the linearization in more detail, put $Z=Y^{\ell-1}$ where ℓ is the degree of θ, and let $E(\lambda),F(\lambda) : X\to Y\oplus Z$ be given by

$$E(\lambda)x = (Qx,\mathrm{col}(QT^i(T-\lambda)x)_{i=0}^{\ell-2}),$$

$$F(\lambda)x = (QT^{\ell-1}x + \sum_{j=1}^{\ell-1} L_j(\lambda)QT^{j-1}x, -\mathrm{col}(QT^i x)_{i=0}^{\ell-2}).$$

Here $L_j(\lambda) = \lambda^{\ell-j}I - \Sigma_{i=0}^{\ell-1-j}\lambda^i QT^{\ell}U_{i+j}$, where

$$[U_0 \dots U_{\ell-1}] = [\mathrm{col}(QT^{i-1})_{i=1}^{\ell}]^{-1}.$$

Then (cf. [3], Theorem 3.1) the operators $E(\lambda)$ and $F(\lambda)$ are invertible and

$$F(\lambda)(\lambda-T) = [W_\theta(\lambda)^{-1} \oplus I_Z]E(\lambda), \quad \lambda \in \mathbb{C}.$$

Chapter III

MINIMAL NODES

In this chapter the notion of a minimal node is considered. If two nodes are similar, then they have the same transfer function. The converse statement is not true. In fact nodes with rather different state spaces may have the same transfer function. For minimal nodes this phenomenon does not occur. In Section 3.1 minimal nodes are defined. In the finite dimensional case the connection between a minimal node θ and its transfer function W_θ is very close. For example in that case θ is determined up to similarity by W_θ. Also in that case the poles and zeros of W_θ determine completely the eigenvalue structure of the main operator and associate main operator of θ, respectively. This will be explained in Section 3.2. In Section 3.3 the notion of minimality is considered for Brodskii nodes, Krein nodes, monic nodes and polynomial nodes.

3.1 Minimality of nodes

Two similar nodes have the same transfer function. On the other hand, the transfer function will in general not determine the node up to similarity. For example, consider the nodes $\theta_1 = (A_1,B_1,0;X_1,Y)$ and $\theta_2 = (A_2,0,C_2;X_2,Y)$. The transfer functions of θ_1 and θ_2 are both identically equal to I, but if either B_1 or C_2 is non-zero, then θ_1 and θ_2 will never be similar. More generally, let $\theta_0 = (A_0,B_0,C_0;X_0,Y)$ be a node, and let X_1 and X_2 be arbitrary complex Banach spaces. Put $X = X_1 \oplus X_0 \oplus X_2$, and let $A:X \to X$, $B:Y \to X$ and $C:X \to Y$ be of the form

$$A = \begin{bmatrix} * & * & * \\ 0 & A_0 & * \\ 0 & 0 & * \end{bmatrix}, \quad B = \begin{bmatrix} * \\ B_0 \\ 0 \end{bmatrix}, \quad C = [0 \ C_0 \ *].$$

One easily verifies that the transfer function of the node $\theta = (A,B,C;X,Y)$ coincides on a neighbourhood of ∞ with the transfer function of θ_0. However, after a suitable choice of the spaces X_1 and X_2 or the unspecified operators $*$, the nodes θ and θ_0 will not be similar. Under certain minimality conditions, to be discussed below, more positive results can be obtained (cf. Section 3.2).

Let $\theta = (A,B,C,D;X,Y)$ be a node. Write

$$\mathrm{Ker}(C|A) = \bigcap_{j=0}^{\infty} \mathrm{Ker}\,CA^j \ , \ \mathrm{Im}(A|B) = \bigvee_{j=0}^{\infty} \mathrm{Im}\,A^jB.$$

Here $\bigvee_{j=0}^{\infty} N_j$ is defined to be the linear hull of $\bigcup_{j=0}^{\infty} N_j$. As in system theory we call θ _observable_ if $\mathrm{Ker}(C|A) = (0)$ and _controllable_ if $\mathrm{Im}(A|B)$ is dense in X. Further, we say that θ is _minimal_ if θ is both observable and controllable. By a _minimal realization_ of an operator function W we mean a minimal node that is a realization for W. Also, if W is given by

$$W(\lambda) = D + C(\lambda-A)^{-1}B, \tag{3.1}$$

we say that (3.1) is a minimal realization for W if the node determined by the operators A,B,C and D is minimal. In the same way one can define the notions of an _observable_ and a _controllable realization_.

Below we present some elementary facts concerning minimal nodes. With appropriate modifications the results are also valid for nodes that are observable or controllable only.

Suppose $\theta_1 = (A_1,B_1,C_1,D_1;X_1,Y)$ and $\theta_2 = (A_2,B_2,C_2,D_2;X_2,Y)$ are similar nodes. Then θ_1 is minimal if and only if θ_2 is minimal. If S_1 and S_2 are node similarities between θ_1 and θ_2, then

$$\mathrm{Im}(S_1-S_2) \subset \mathrm{Ker}(C_2|A_2).$$

So $S_1 = S_2$, provided that θ_1 and θ_2 are minimal. This proves the uniqueness of the node similarity between two minimal nodes.

If $\theta = (A,B,C,D;X,Y)$ is a node with invertible external operator D, then θ is minimal if and only if $\theta^\times$ is minimal. This is immediate from the fact that $\operatorname{Ker}(C|A) = \operatorname{Ker}(-D^{-1}C|A^\times)$ and $\operatorname{Im}(A|B) = \operatorname{Im}(A^\times|BD^{-1})$.

The product of two minimal nodes need not be minimal. To see this, multiply the minimal nodes $(0,1,1;\mathbb{C},\mathbb{C})$ and $(-1,1,-1;\mathbb{C},\mathbb{C})$. On the other hand, if the product of two nodes θ_1 and θ_2 is minimal, then so are θ_1 and θ_2. To prove this, write $\theta_1 = (A_1,B_1,C_1,D_1;X_1,Y)$ and $\theta_2 = (A_2,B_2,C_2,D_2;X\ ,Y)$. Then $\theta_1\theta_2 = (A,B,C,D;X_1 \oplus X_2,Y)$ with

$$A = \begin{bmatrix} A_1 & B_1C_2 \\ 0 & A_2 \end{bmatrix}, \quad B = \begin{bmatrix} B_1D_2 \\ B_2 \end{bmatrix}, \quad C = [C_1 \ \ D_1C_2], \quad D = D_1D_2.$$

Assume θ is minimal. Take x in $\operatorname{Ker}(C_1|A_1)$. Then clearly $(x,0)\in\operatorname{Ker}(C|A)$. But $\operatorname{Ker}(C|A) = (0)$, and so $x=0$. This proves that θ_1 is observable. Next take z in X. Then $(z,0)$ is in the closure of $\operatorname{Im}(A|B)$. So $(z,0)$ can be approximated arbitrarily close by sums of the form

$$\sum_{j=0}^{n-1} A^j By_j$$

with $y_0,\dots,y_{k-1}$ in Y. The first coordinate of such a sum is easily seen to belong to $\operatorname{Im}(A_1|B_1)$. Thus z is in the closure of $\operatorname{Im}(A_1|B_1)$ and we conclude that θ_1 is minimal. In the same way one can show that θ_2 is minimal too.

If Π is a supporting projection for a node θ, whose external operator is the identity, then

$$\theta = pr_{I-\Pi}(\theta)\cdot pr_{\Pi}(\theta).$$

Thus, if θ is minimal, then so are $pr_{I-\Pi}(\theta)$ and $pr_{\Pi}(\theta)$. An arbitrary projection of a minimal node need not be minimal, not even when the image of the projection is an invariant subspace for the main operator of the node. Indeed, if $\theta = (A,B,C;\mathbb{C}^3,\mathbb{C}^2)$

and Π are given by

$$A = \begin{pmatrix} 1 & 0 & 0 \\ 1 & 0 & 0 \\ 0 & 0 & 0 \end{pmatrix}, \quad B = \begin{pmatrix} 1 & 0 \\ 0 & 1 \\ 0 & 1 \end{pmatrix}, \quad C = \begin{pmatrix} 0 & 1 & 0 \\ 0 & 0 & 1 \end{pmatrix}, \quad \Pi = \begin{pmatrix} 0 & 0 & 0 \\ 0 & 1 & 0 \\ 0 & 0 & 1 \end{pmatrix},$$

then θ is minimal, but

$$\mathrm{pr}_\Pi(\theta) = \left(\begin{pmatrix} 0 & 0 \\ 0 & 0 \end{pmatrix}, \begin{pmatrix} 0 & 1 \\ 0 & 1 \end{pmatrix}, \begin{pmatrix} 1 & 0 \\ 0 & 1 \end{pmatrix}; \mathbb{C}^2, \mathbb{C}^2 \right)$$

is not. Note that $\mathrm{Im}\Pi$ is an invariant subspace for A.

3.2 Minimality for finite dimensional nodes

Let $\theta = (A,B,C,D;X,Y)$ be a finite dimensional node. Thus θ is a node and the spaces X and Y are finite dimensional. Let n be an integer larger than or equal to the degree of the minimal polynomial of A (for instance $n \geq \dim X$). Then

$$\mathrm{Ker}(C|A) = \bigcap_{j=0}^{n-1} \mathrm{Ker}CA^j, \quad \mathrm{Im}(A|B) = \bigvee_{j=0}^{n-1} \mathrm{Im}A^jB.$$

From this it is obvious that θ is minimal if and only if

$$\bigcap_{j=0}^{n-1} \mathrm{Ker}CA^j = (0), \quad \bigvee_{j=0}^{n-1} \mathrm{Im}A^jB = X.$$

An equivalent requirement is that the operators $\mathrm{col}(CA^j)_{j=0}^{n-1}$ and $\mathrm{row}(A^jB)_{j=0}^{n-1}$ are left and right invertible, respectively.

THEOREM 3.1. *Let $\theta_1 = (A_1,B_1,C_1,D_1;X_1,Y)$ and $\theta_2 = (A_2,B_2,C_2,D_2;X_2,Y)$ be finite dimensional minimal nodes whose transfer functions coincide (on some open set and hence on a neighbourhood of ∞). Then θ_1 and θ_2 are similar. Moreover, the (unique) node similarity S between θ_1 and θ_2 is given by*

$$S = [\mathrm{col}(C_2A_2^j)_{j=0}^{n-1}]^{+}\cdot[\mathrm{col}(C_1A_1^j)_{j=0}^{n-1}] =$$

$$= [\mathrm{row}(A_2^jB_2)_{j=0}^{n-1}]\cdot[\mathrm{row}(A_1^jB_1)_{j=0}^{n-1}]^{\dagger},$$

where n *is a positive integer larger than or equal to the degree of the minimal polynomial of* A_1, *the symbol* $+$ *indicates a left inverse and the symbol* $\dagger$ *indicates a right inverse.*

PROOF. For $k = 1,2,$ put

$$\Omega_k = \mathrm{col}(C_kA_k^j)_{j=0}^{n-1}, \quad \Delta_k = \mathrm{row}(A_k^jB_k)_{j=0}^{n-1},$$

where n is a positive integer larger than or equal to the maximum of the degrees of the minimal polynomials of A_1 and A_2. Since θ_k is minimal the operators Ω_k and Δ_k are left and right invertible, respectively. Let Ω_k^{+} be a left inverse of Ω_k and let $\Delta_k^{\dagger}$ be a right inverse of Δ_k.

Comparing the Laurent expansions of the transfer functions of θ_1 and θ_2 at ∞, we obtain

$$D_1 = D_2\ ,\ C_1A_1^jB_1 = C_2A_2^jB_i\ ,\ (j = 0,1,2,\ldots).$$

It follows that $\Omega_1\Delta_1 = \Omega_2\Delta_2$. But then

$$\Omega_2^{+}\Omega_1 = \Delta_2\Delta_1^{\dagger}.$$

We denote the operator appearing in this equality by S. Observe that $S:X_1 \to X_2$. A direct computation shows that S is invertible with inverse $\Omega_1^{+}\Omega_2 = \Delta_1\Delta_2^{\dagger}$ and that (1.1) is satisfied. Thus θ_1 and θ_2 are similar. Moreover we proved that S is of the form indicated in the theorem for n larger than or equal to the maximum of the degrees of the minimal polynomials of A_1 and A_2. But these polynomials are the same since A_1 and A_2 are similar. So the proof is complete.

THEOREM 3.2. <u>Let</u> $\theta = (A,B,C,D;X,Y)$ <u>be a finite dimensional node. Then there exist spaces</u> X_0, X_1 <u>and</u> X_2 <u>such that</u> $X = X_1 \oplus X_0 \oplus X_2$ <u>and with respect to this decomposition the operators</u> A, B <u>and</u> C <u>admit the representation</u>

$$(3.2) \qquad A = \begin{bmatrix} A_1 & * & * \\ 0 & A_0 & * \\ 0 & 0 & A_2 \end{bmatrix}, \quad B = \begin{bmatrix} * \\ B_0 \\ 0 \end{bmatrix}, \quad C = [0, C_0, *],$$

<u>where</u> $\theta_0 = (A_0,B_0,C_0,D;X_0,Y)$ <u>is a minimal node whose transfer function coincides with that of</u> θ (<u>on a neighbourhood of</u> ∞).

PROOF. Write $\theta = (A,B,C,D;X,Y)$ and let n be the degree of the minimal polynomial of A. Put $\Omega = \mathrm{col}(CA^j)_{j=0}^{n-1}$ and $\Delta = \mathrm{row}(A^jB)_{j=0}^{n-1}$. Then $\Omega : X \to Y^n$, $\Delta : Y^n \to X$ and

$$A[\mathrm{Ker}\,\Omega] \subset \mathrm{Ker}\,\Omega, \quad A[\mathrm{Im}\,\Delta] \subset \mathrm{Im}\,\Delta.$$

Put $X_1 = \mathrm{Ker}\,\Omega$, and let X_0 be a direct complement of $X_1 \cap \mathrm{Im}\,\Delta$ in $\mathrm{Im}\,\Delta$. Further, choose X_2 such that

$$X = X_1 \oplus X_0 \oplus X_2.$$

With respect to this decomposition the operators A,B and C can be written in the form (3.2). Put $\theta_0 = (A_0,B_0,C_0,D;X_0,Y)$. Then the transfer functions of θ_0 and θ coincide (on a neighbourhood of ∞). One verifies without difficulty that

$$\bigcap_{j=0}^{n-1} \mathrm{Ker}(C_0A_0^j) = (0), \quad \bigvee_{j=0}^{n-1} \mathrm{Im}(A_0^jB_0) = X_0.$$

Thus θ_0 is minimal, and the proof is complete.

The construction of the minimal node θ_0 can also be carried out by taking quotients instead of complements. This approach also works in the infinite dimensional case.

Let W be a rational function whose values are operators on a finite dimensional space Y. Of course W can be identified with a rational $n\times n$ matrix function, where n is the dimension of Y. Assume that W is analytic at ∞ and that $W(\infty) = D$ is invertible. Then we know from Theorem 2.2 that W admits a realization

$$W(\lambda) = D + Q(\lambda - J)^{-1}R,$$

where Q, J and R are constructed from the spectral data of W. By formulas (2.2) and (2.4) the node determined by the operators J, Q,R and D is minimal. In other words, the construction of Section 2.1 yields a minimal realization for W. From this construction it is also clear that a complex number λ_0 is an eigenvalue of J if and only if λ_0 is a pole of W. Moreover the partial multiplicities of λ_0 as an eigenvalue of J are the same as the partial pole multiplicities of W at λ_0. This, together with Theorem 2.1 gives the first part of the next theorem.

THEOREM 3.3. <u>Let W be the transfer function of the minimal finite dimensional node $\theta = (A,B,C,D;X,Y)$. Suppose D is invertible, and let $\lambda_0 \in \mathbb{C}$. Then λ_0 is an eigenvalue of A if and only if λ_0 is a pole of W and the partial multiplicities of λ_0 as an eigenvalue of A are the same as the partial pole multiplicities of W at λ_0. Also, λ_0 is an eigenvalue of $A^\times = A - BD^{-1}C$ if and only if λ_0 is a zero of W and the partial multiplicities of λ_0 as an eigenvalue of $A^\times$ are the same as the partial zero multiplicities of W at λ_0.</u>

PROOF. We only need to prove the second part of the theorem. Since θ is minimal, the node $\theta^\times$ is minimal too. The transfer function of $\theta^\times$ coincides with W^{-1}. Now apply the first part of the theorem to W^{-1} and $\theta^\times$.

The preceding theorem may be used to prove the following somewhat sharper version of Theorem 1.6 (cf. [15], [45]).

Theorem 3.4. _Let_ W _be an_ $n \times n$ _rational matrix function, analytic at infinity, such that_ $W(\infty)$ _is invertible. Assume that_ W _has poles of first order only. Then_ W _admits a factorization of the following form_

$$W(\lambda) = (I - \frac{1}{\lambda-\lambda_1}R_1) \dots (I - \frac{1}{\lambda-\lambda_\delta}R_\delta),$$

where $R_1,\dots,R_\delta$ _are_ $n \times n$ _matrices of rank one._

PROOF. Choose a minimal realization $\theta = (A,B,C,D;X,\mathbb{C}^n)$. Then θ is a finite dimensional node and $D=W(\infty)$ is invertible. As W has first order poles only, we see from Theorem 3.3 that A has simple eigenvalues only. So we can apply Theorem 1.6 to get the desired result.

The factorization of W constructed in the proof of Theorem 3.4 is a minimal factorization in the sense of Section 4.3 below. This implies that the points $\lambda_1,\dots,\lambda_\delta$ are precisely the poles of W counted according to pole-multiplicity (see Section 4.3) With minor modifications Theorem 3.4 can be extended to the case where $\det W(\lambda)$ does not vanish identically and W has a simple pole at ∞.

We conclude this section with a discussion of Möbius transformations of finite dimensional minimal nodes. We begin with a remark.

Let p,q,r and s be complex numbers. For $n=1,2,\dots$ and $t,j = 0,\dots,n-1$, we put

$$a_{bj}^{(n)} = \sum_{\substack{k=0,\dots,n-1-t\\ m=0,\dots,t\\ k+m=j}} (-1)^{k+t-m} \binom{n-1-t}{k}\binom{t}{m} p^{n-1-t-k} q^{t-m} r^k s^m.$$

In other words $a_{t0}^{(n)},\dots,a_{t,n-1}^{(n)}$ are the coefficients of the polynomial

$$(p-rx)^{n-1-t}(sx-q)^t.$$

The n×n matrix $\left(a_{tj}^{(n)}\right)_{t,j=0}^{n-1}$ will be denoted by $[p,q,r,s]_n$. For what follows it is important to note that

$$\det[p,q,r,s]_n = (ps-qr)^{\frac{1}{2}n(n-1)}.$$

The proof goes by an induction argument involving the following recurrence relations

$$a_{t0}^{(n+1)} = -qa_{t-1,0}^{(n)},$$

$$a_{tk}^{(n+1)} = sa_{t-1,k-1}^{(n)} - qa_{t-1,k}^{(n)}, \quad k=1,\dots,n-1,$$

$$a_{tn}^{(n+1)} = sa_{t-1,n-1}^{(n)}.$$

For the definition of a Möbius transformation θ_φ of a node θ, see Section 1.5.

THEOREM 3.5. _Let_ $\theta = (A,B,C,D;X,Y)$ _be a node, and let_

$$\varphi(\lambda) = \frac{p\lambda+q}{r\lambda+s}$$

be a Möbius transformation. Suppose $rA-p$ _is invertible. Then_ θ_φ _is minimal if and only if_ θ _is minimal._

PROOF. Write $\theta_\varphi = (A_1,B_1,C_1,D_1;X,Y)$. Then (see formula (1.36))

$$A_1 = -(q-sA)(p-rA)^{-1}, \quad C_1 = (ps-qr)C(p-rA)^{-1}.$$

A simple computation shows that for $n = 1,2,\dots$

$$\left[\operatorname{col}(C_1A_1^j)_{j=0}^{n-1}\right](p-rA)^n = (ps-qr)[p,q,r,s]_n \operatorname{col}(CA^j)_{j=0}^{n-1}.$$

Since φ is a Möbius transformation, we have $ps-qr \neq 0$.

So the matrix $[p,q,r,s]_n$ is invertible. By hypothesis $p-rA$ is invertible. It follows that $\mathrm{col}(C_1A_1^j)_{j=0}^{n-1}$ is left invertible if and only if $\mathrm{col}(CA^j)_{j=0}^{n-1}$ is left invertible. Thus θ_φ is observable if and only if θ is observable. In the same way one can show that θ_φ is controllable if and only if θ is controllable. This proves the theorem.

3.3 Minimality in special cases

In this section we discuss the notion of minimality for the classes of nodes considered in Section 1.4.

3.3.1 Brodskii nodes. Let $\theta = (A,KJ,2iK^*;H,G)$ be a Brodskii J-node. Following [8] we call θ simple if $\mathrm{Im}(A|K)$ is dense in H. Thus simplicity is synonymous to controllability. However, in view of the fact that $A-A^* = 2iKJK^*$, we have $\mathrm{Im}(A|K)=\mathrm{Im}(A^*|K)$, and hence $\mathrm{Ker}(K^*|A)$ is the orthogonal complement $\mathrm{Im}(A|K)^\perp$ of $\mathrm{Im}(A|K)$. Therefore, in this particular case, the notions of simplicity (controllability) and minimality coincide.

In [8] it is shown that given a Brodskii J-node $\theta = (A,KJ,2iK^*;H,G)$, there exists a simple Brodskii J-node θ_0 whose characteristic operator function (transfer function) coincides with that of θ on a neighbourhood of ∞. In fact, if Π is the orthogonal projection of H onto the closure of $\mathrm{Im}(A|K)$, then Π commutes with A and A^* and $\theta_0 = \mathrm{pr}_\Pi(\theta)$ has the desired properties. Observe that

$$\theta = \mathrm{pr}_{I-\Pi}(\theta) \cdot \theta_0 = \theta_0 \cdot \mathrm{pr}_{I-\Pi}(\theta).$$

The nodes $\theta_0 = \mathrm{pr}_\Pi(\theta)$ and $\mathrm{pr}_{I-\Pi}(\theta)$ are called the principal part and excess part of θ, respectively.

In [8] it is also shown that two simple Brodskii J-nodes whose characteristic operator functions coincide on a neighbourhood of ∞ are similar, the (unique) similarity transformation being a unitary operator. This fact plays an important role in [8]. For instance, it is used to prove the unicellularity of the

Volterra integral operator on $L_2(0,1)$.

3.3.2 Krein nodes. It can be shown that two minimal Krein J-nodes whose transfer function coincide on a neighbourhood of ∞ are similar, the (unique) similarity transformation being a unitary operator. In fact, this conclusion can be reached under the somewhat weaker assumption that the nodes are prime. Following [11], we call a Krein J-node $\Theta = (A,R,-J(K^*)^{-1}R^*A,K;H,G)$ prime if

$$\mathrm{Im}(A|R) + \mathrm{Im}(A^*|R)$$

is dense in H. In order to clarify this notion we make some general remarks.

Suppose $\Theta = (A,B,C,D;X,Y)$ is a node with an invertible main operator A. We say that Θ is biminimal if

$$\bigcap_{j=-\infty}^{\infty} \mathrm{Ker}CA^j = (0) , \quad \overline{\bigvee_{j=-\infty}^{\infty} \mathrm{Im}A^jB} = H.$$

Here the bar indicates taking the closure. Obviously, if Θ is minimal, then Θ is biminimal too. The converse is also true if, for example, A is an algebraic operator. The latter condition is automatically fulfilled when H is finite dimensional.

Now, returning to the subject of this subsection, assume that $\theta = (A,R,-J(K^*)^{-1}R^*A,K;H,G)$ is a Krein J-node. Using the relationship between A, A* and R appearing in Subsection 1.4.2, one can show that

$$\left(\bigvee_{j=-\infty}^{\infty} \mathrm{Im}\ A^jR\right)^{\perp} = \bigcap_{j=-\infty}^{\infty} \mathrm{Ker}\ R^*A^j$$

and

$$\bigvee_{j=-\infty}^{\infty} \mathrm{Im}\ A^jR = \mathrm{Im}(A|R) + \mathrm{Im}(A^*|R).$$

Hence θ is prime if and only if θ is biminimal. In particular, if θ is minimal, then certainly θ is prime.

Finally we mention that if θ is a Krein J-node, then there exists a prime Krein J-node θ_0 whose transfer function coincides with that of θ on a neighbourhood of ∞. The construction of θ_0 is suggested in [11], Sections 3 and 4.

<u>3.3.3 Monic nodes</u>. From the definition of a monic node it is clear that such a node is always minimal. So it is not surprising that the notion of minimality does not appear in [2,3]. Note however that a monic node θ is determined up to similarity by its transfer function (cf. [3] Theorem 1.2). Also, because of linearization, the spectral properties of the main operator of a monic node θ are determined completely by W_θ^{-1}.

<u>3.3.4 Polynomial nodes</u>. Let P be a comonic polynomial of degree ℓ whose coefficients are $n\times n$ matrices (i.e. operators acting on $\mathbb{C}^n$). Put $L(\lambda) = \lambda^\ell P(\lambda^{-1})$. Then L is a monic polynomial of degree ℓ. Let $\Delta = (T,R,Q,0;\mathbb{C}^{n\ell},\mathbb{C}^n)$ be a monic node whose transfer function coincides with L^{-1}. Then $\theta = (T,T^\ell R,Q;\mathbb{C}^{n\ell},\mathbb{C}^n)$ and its associate $\theta^\times = (T-T^\ell RQ,T^\ell R,-Q;\mathbb{C}^{n\ell},\mathbb{C}^n)$ are realizations for $P(\lambda^{-1})^{-1}$ and $P(\lambda^{-1})$, respectively (cf. Subsection 1.4.4). As $\mathrm{col}(QT^i)_{i=0}^{\ell-1}$ and $\mathrm{row}(T^iR)_{i=0}^{\ell-1}$ are both invertible, we have

$$\mathrm{Ker}(Q|T) = (0)\ , \ \mathrm{Im}(T^\ell R|T) = \mathrm{Im}\ T^\ell .$$

So θ is observable, but generally not controllable. The same is true for $\theta^\times$.

In order to obtain minimal realizations for $P(\lambda^{-1})^{-1}$ and $P(\lambda^{-1})$, we apply the method indicated in the proof of Theorem 3.2. Put $X_0 = \mathrm{Im}\ T^\ell$. Then X_0 is invariant under T. Let T_0 be the restriction of T to X_0 considered as an operator on X_0. For convenience we write B instead of $T^\ell R$. Note that B maps $\mathbb{C}^n$ into X_0. Let B_0 be the operator B viewed as an operator from $\mathbb{C}^n$ into X_0. Finally, let Q_0 be the restriction of Q to X_0. Then $\theta_0 = (T_0,B_0,Q_0;X_0,\mathbb{C}^n)$ and $\theta_0^\times = (T_0-B_0Q_0,B_0,-Q_0;X_0,\mathbb{C}^n)$ are minimal realizations for $P(\lambda^{-1})^{-1}$ and $P(\lambda^{-1})$, respectively.

In order to make the construction more explicit we make a special choice for T, R and Q. Let $\lambda_1,\ldots,\lambda_p$ be the different finite eigenvalues of P and for i = 1,...,p, let (Q_i,J_i) be a Jordan pair for λ_i as defined in Section 2.1. Put

$$Q_F = [Q_1 \ldots Q_p] \ , \ J_F = J_1 \oplus \ldots \oplus J_p .$$

Also, let (Q_∞, J_∞) be a Jordan pair corresponding to $\lambda_0 = 0$ for the monic matrix polynomial L with $L(\lambda) = \lambda^\ell P(\lambda^{-1})$. As P is comonic, all finite eigenvalues $\lambda_1,\ldots,\lambda_p$ are different from zero. Hence the Jordan matrix J_F is invertible. Put

$$Q = [Q_F \ Q_\infty] \ , \ J = J_F^{-1} \oplus J_\infty .$$

Then we know from Theorem 3.1 in [30] that (Q,J) is a standard pair for L in the sense of [22]. This means that $\mathrm{col}(QT^j)_{j=0}^{\ell-1}$ is invertible and if we define R by

$$\left[\mathrm{col}(QT^j)_{j=0}^{\ell-1}\right]^{-1} = [* \ \ldots \ * \ R],$$

then $(T,R,Q,0;\mathbb{C}^{n\ell},\mathbb{C}^n)$ is a monic node whose transfer function is L^{-1}.

Now, for this choice of T,R and Q, let us describe the operators J_0, B_0 and Q_0 as matrices. Recall that J_F and J_∞ are Jordan matrices. Let r be the order of J_F, and let $p_1 \geq p_2 \geq \ldots \geq p_\nu$ be the orders of the Jordan blocks in J_∞. Choose k such that $p_k > \ell \geq p_{k+1}$ and put

$$\alpha = \{j\}_{j=1}^{r} \cup \left(\bigcup_{i=0}^{k-1} \{r+p_0+\ldots+p_i+j\}_{j=1}^{p_{i+1}-\ell} \right),$$

$$\beta = \{j \mid j=1,\ldots,n\ell, j \notin \alpha\}.$$

Here $p_0 = 0$. Then X_0 is the subspace of $\mathbb{C}^{n\ell}$ spanned by the unit vectors e_j with $j \in \alpha$. Of course we identify X_0 with $\mathbb{C}^a$

where a is the number of elements in α. The matrix J_0 is now obtained from J by deleting all rows and columns with ordinal numbers in β. Similarly, Q_0 is the submatrix of Q which one gets by omitting all columns in Q with ordinal number in β. Finally B_0 is obtained from B by deleting all rows with ordinal number in β. Since $\operatorname{Im} B \subset X_0$, all these rows are zero.

To illustrate the above procedure, let us consider

$$P(\lambda) = \begin{pmatrix} 1 & \lambda^2 & \lambda \\ 0 & 1 & 0 \\ 0 & 0 & 1 \end{pmatrix}$$

Note that $P(\lambda)$ is invertible for each $\lambda \in \mathbb{C}$, and hence there is only spectrum at infinity. One computes that

$$Q = Q_\infty = \begin{pmatrix} 1 & 0 & 0 & 1 & 0 & 0 \\ 0 & 0 & -1 & 0 & 0 & -1 \\ 0 & 0 & 0 & 0 & 1 & 0 \end{pmatrix},$$

$$J = J_\infty = J_4 \oplus J_2,$$

where J_r is an $r \times r$ Jordan block with 0 on the main diagonal. It follows that

$$R = \begin{pmatrix} 0 & 1 & 0 \\ 1 & 0 & 0 \\ 0 & 0 & -1 \\ 0 & -1 & 0 \\ 0 & 0 & 0 \\ 0 & 0 & 1 \end{pmatrix}, \quad B = J^2 R = \begin{pmatrix} 0 & 0 & -1 \\ 0 & -1 & 0 \\ 0 & 0 & 0 \\ 0 & 0 & 0 \\ 0 & 0 & 0 \\ 0 & 0 & 0 \end{pmatrix}.$$

In this case we have $\alpha = \{-1,2\}$ and $\beta = \{3,4,5,6\}$. Hence, if

$$J_0 = \begin{pmatrix} 0 & 1 \\ 0 & 0 \end{pmatrix}, \quad Q_0 = \begin{pmatrix} 1 & 0 \\ 0 & 0 \\ 0 & 0 \end{pmatrix}, \quad B_0 = \begin{pmatrix} 0 & 0 & -1 \\ 0 & -1 & 0 \end{pmatrix},$$

then $\theta_0 = (J_0, B_0, Q_0; \mathbb{C}^2, \mathbb{C}^3)$ is a minimal realization for

$$P(\lambda^{-1})^{-1} = \begin{bmatrix} 1 & -\lambda^{-2} & -\lambda^{-1} \\ 0 & 1 & 0 \\ 0 & 0 & 0 \end{bmatrix}.$$

The associate node $\theta_0^\times = (J_0 - B_0Q_0, B_0, -Q_0; \mathbb{C}^2, \mathbb{C}^3)$ is a minimal realization for

$$P(\lambda^{-1}) = \begin{bmatrix} 1 & \lambda^{-2} & \lambda^{-1} \\ 0 & 1 & 0 \\ 0 & 0 & 1 \end{bmatrix}.$$

Observe that $J_0 - B_0Q_0 = J_0$.

Minimal realizations for $P(\lambda^{-1})^{-1}$ and $P(\lambda^{-1})$ can also be obtained by applying the method of Section 2.1. The alternative construction presented above however is somewhat more direct. Observe that it can also be used to produce a minimal realization for $P(\lambda^{-1})$ when P is an arbitrary, possibly non-comonic, $n \times n$ matrix polynomial. Indeed, one just constructs a minimal realization for $I - P(0) + P(\lambda^{-1})$ and adds $P(0) - I$ to the external operator.

Chapter IV

MINIMAL FACTORIZATIONS OF RATIONAL MATRIX FUNCTIONS

4.1 Local degree and local minimality

Let W be a rational $n\times n$ matrix function, and let $\lambda_0 \in \mathbb{C}$. In a deleted neighbourhood of λ_0 we have the following expansion

$$W(\lambda) = \sum_{j=-q}^{\infty} (\lambda-\lambda_0)^j W_j. \tag{4.1}$$

Here q is some positive integer. By the <u>local degree</u> of W at λ_0 we mean the number $\delta(W;\lambda_0) = \operatorname{rank} \Omega$, where

$$\Omega = \begin{bmatrix} W_{-q} & \cdot & \cdot & \cdot & \cdot & W_{-1} \\ 0 & \cdot & & & & \cdot \\ \cdot & & \cdot & & & \cdot \\ \cdot & & & \cdot & & \cdot \\ \cdot & & & & \cdot & \cdot \\ 0 & \cdot & \cdot & \cdot & 0 & W_{-q} \end{bmatrix}. \tag{4.2}$$

Of course this definition does not depend on the choice of q. We also introduce $\delta(W;\infty)$ by putting $\delta(W;\infty) = \delta(\tilde{W};0)$, where $\tilde{W}(\lambda) = W(\lambda^{-1})$. Observe that W is analytic at a point μ in the Riemann sphere $\mathbb{C}_\infty$ if and only if $\delta(W;\mu) = 0$. If $\det W(\lambda) \not\equiv 0$, then $\delta(W;\mu)$ is just the pole multiplicity of W at μ as defined in Section 2.1.

The local degree enjoys a sublogarithmic property. To see this, let W_1 and W_2 be rational $n\times n$ matrix functions, and write

$$W_k(\lambda) = \sum_{j=-p}^{\infty} W_j^{(k)} (\lambda-\lambda_0)^j \qquad (k = 1,2)$$

for some positive integer p. Put $W = W_1W_2$. Then W admits an expansion of the form (4.1) with $q = 2p$. Define, for $k = 1,2$,

$$\Omega_k = \begin{pmatrix} W_{-p}^{(k)} & \cdot & \cdot & \cdot & \cdot & W_{-1}^{(k)} \\ 0 & \cdot & & & & \cdot \\ \cdot & & \cdot & & & \cdot \\ \cdot & & & \cdot & & \cdot \\ \cdot & & & & \cdot & \\ 0 & \cdot & \cdot & \cdot & 0 & W_{-p}^{(k)} \end{pmatrix}.$$

The operator Ω given by (4.2) may then be written as

$$\Omega = \begin{pmatrix} \Omega_1 & * \\ 0 & \Omega_1 \end{pmatrix}\begin{pmatrix} \Omega_2 & * \\ 0 & \Omega_2 \end{pmatrix} = \begin{pmatrix} \Omega_1 \\ 0 \end{pmatrix}\begin{pmatrix} \Omega_2 & * \end{pmatrix} + \begin{pmatrix} * \\ \Omega_1 \end{pmatrix}\begin{pmatrix} 0 & \Omega_2 \end{pmatrix}.$$

It follows that $\operatorname{rank}\Omega \le \operatorname{rank}\Omega_1 + \operatorname{rank}\Omega_2$. In other words

$$\delta(W_1W_2;\lambda_0) \leqq \delta(W_1;\lambda_0) + \delta(W_1;\lambda_0). \tag{4.3}$$

Of course we also have $\delta(W_1W_2;\infty) \leqq \delta(W_1;\infty) + \delta(W_2;\infty)$.

The definitions and statements of the preceding two paragraphs also apply to rational functions whose values are operators on an arbitrary finite dimensional space Y. Indeed, if $\dim Y = n$, such functions can be identified with rational $n\times n$ matrix functions.

In this chapter we are mainly interested in factorizations W_1W_2 such that

$$\delta(W_1W_2;\lambda_0) = \delta(W_1;\lambda_0) + \delta(W_2;\lambda_0) \tag{4.4}$$

for each λ_0 in the Riemann sphere $\mathbb{C}_\infty$. Such factorizations are called <u>minimal</u>. We shall come back to this concept in Section 4.3. To understand the meaning of condition (4.4), we introduce the notion of local minimality of a node.

Let $\theta = (A,B,C,D;X,Y)$ be a finite dimensional node and $\lambda_0 \in \mathbb{C}$. We say that Θ is <u>minimal at the point</u> λ_0 if

$$(4.5) \qquad \bigcap_{j=0}^{\infty} \operatorname{Ker} CA^j P = \operatorname{Ker} P \ , \qquad \bigvee_{j=0}^{\infty} \operatorname{Im} PA^j B = \operatorname{Im} P.$$

Here P is the Riesz projection of A at λ_0. Note that Θ is minimal at each point in the resolvent set $\rho(A)$ of A. If the external operator D of Θ is the identity operator on Y, then Θ is minimal at λ_0 if and only if the projection $pr_P(\theta)$ of Θ is a minimal node.

The connection between local minimality and local degree is expressed by the following theorem.

THEOREM 4.1. *Let W be the transfer function of the finite dimensional node $\Theta = (A,B,C,D;X,Y)$, let $\lambda_0 \in \mathbb{C}$, and let P be the Riesz projection of A at λ_0. Then $\delta(W;\lambda_0) \le \operatorname{rank} P$, equality occurring if and only if Θ is minimal at λ_0.*

PROOF. Write W in the form (4.1). We may assume that q is larger than or equal to the degree of the minimal polynomial of A. In that case one has that Θ is minimal at λ_0 if and only if the rank of the operator

$$(4.6) \qquad \operatorname{col}(CA^{j-1})_{j=1}^{q} P \operatorname{row}(A^{q-i}B)_{j=1}^{q}$$

is equal to the rank of P. Recall now that

$$W_{-j} = CP(\lambda_0 - A)^j B, \quad j = 1,2,\dots \ .$$

Here $W_{-j} = 0$ for $j = q+1, q+2, \dots$. It follows that

$$(4.7) \qquad \operatorname{col}[C(\lambda_0 - A)^{j-1}]_{j=1}^{q} P \operatorname{row}[(\lambda_0 - A)^{q-j}B]_{j=1}^{q} = \Omega,$$

where Ω is as in (4.2). From this and the definition of $\delta(W;\lambda_0)$ we conclude $\delta(W;\lambda_0) \le \operatorname{rank} P$. Moreover, the operator appearing in the left hand side of (4.7) has the same rank as the operator (4.6). Hence Θ is minimal at λ_0 if and only if $\delta(W;\lambda_0) = \operatorname{rank} P$, and the proof is complete.

Suppose Θ_1 and Θ_2 are nodes with the same input/output space. Let $\lambda_0 \in \mathbb{C}$. If the product $\Theta_1\Theta_2$ is minimal at λ_0, then so are the factors Θ_1 and Θ_2. The converse of this is not true. In the next theorem we present a necessary and sufficient condition for $\Theta_1\Theta_2$ to be minimal at λ_0. Part of the condition involves a logarithmic property of the local degree (cf. formula (4.4)).

THEOREM 4.2. _For_ $j = 1,2$, _let_ W_j _be the transfer function of the node_ $\Theta_j = (A_j,B_j,C_j,D_j;X_j,Y)$, _and let_ $\lambda_0 \in \mathbb{C}$. _Then_ Θ_1 _and_ Θ_2 _are minimal at_ λ_0 _and_

$$\delta(W_1W_2;\lambda_0) = \delta(W_1;\lambda_0) + \delta(W_2;\lambda_0)$$

if and only if $\Theta_1\Theta_2$ _is minimal at_ λ_0.

PROOF. Recall that $\Theta_1\Theta_2 = (A,B,C,D;X_1 \oplus X_2,Y)$ where A,B,C and D are given by

$$A = \begin{pmatrix} A_1 & B_1C_2 \\ 0 & A_2 \end{pmatrix}, \quad B = \begin{pmatrix} B_1 \\ B_2 \end{pmatrix}, \quad C = [C_1 \;\; C_2], \; D = D_1D_2.$$

Let P, P_1 and P_2 be the Riesz projections of A, A_1 and A_2 at λ_0, respectively. Then, for a sufficiently small circle Γ around λ_0, we have

$$P = \begin{pmatrix} P_1 & \frac{1}{2\pi i}\int_\Gamma (\lambda-A_1)^{-1}B_1C_2(\lambda-A_2)^{-1}d\lambda \\ 0 & P_2 \end{pmatrix}.$$

The operator given by the integral is of the form $P_1Q_1+Q_2P_2$ with Q_1 and Q_2 acting from X_2 into X_1. To see this, write the Laurent expansions of $(\lambda-A_1)^{-1}$ and $(\lambda-A_2)^{-1}$ at λ_0 and compute the coefficient of $(\lambda-\lambda_0)^{-1}$ in the Laurent expansion of $(\lambda-A_1)^{-1}B_1C_2(\lambda-A_2)^{-1}$ at λ_0. It follows that

$$(4.8) \qquad P = \begin{bmatrix} I & Q_2 \\ 0 & I \end{bmatrix} \begin{bmatrix} P_1 & 0 \\ 0 & P_2 \end{bmatrix} \begin{bmatrix} I & Q_1 \\ 0 & I \end{bmatrix}.$$

But then

$$(4.9) \qquad \operatorname{rank} P = \operatorname{rank} P_1 + \operatorname{rank} P_2,$$

for the first and the last factor in the right hand side of (4.8) are invertible.

Suppose now that Θ_1 and Θ_2 are minimal at λ_0 and that (4.4) is satisfied. Then $\delta(W_1;\lambda_0) = \operatorname{rank} P_1$ and $\delta(W_2;\lambda_0) = \operatorname{rank} P_2$ by Theorem 4.1. Together with formulas (4.4) and (4.9) this gives $\operatorname{rank} P = \delta(W_1W_2;\lambda_0)$. Applying Theorem 4.1 we arrive at the conclusion that $\Theta_1\Theta_2$ is minimal at λ_0.

Conversely, assume that $\Theta_1\Theta_2$ is minimal at λ_0. Combining Theorem 4.1 and formulas (4.3) and (4.9), we get

$$\operatorname{rank} P = \delta(W_1W_2;\lambda_0) \leqq \delta(W_1;\lambda_0) + \delta(W_2;\lambda_0) \leqq$$

$$\leqq \operatorname{rank} P_1 + \operatorname{rank} P_2 = \operatorname{rank} P.$$

Since the first and last quantity in this expression are the same, all the inequalities are in fact equalities. In particular we have (4.4). Moreover, it is clear from Theorem 4.1 that $\delta(W_1;\lambda_0) = \operatorname{rank} P_1$ and $\delta(W_2;\lambda_0) = \operatorname{rank} P_2$. So, on account of the same theorem, Θ_1 and Θ_2 are minimal at λ_0.

If Θ is a minimal node, then clearly Θ is minimal at each point of $\mathbb{C}$. The converse of this is also true.

THEOREM 4.3. _Let_ $\Theta = (A,B,C,D;X,Y)$ _be a finite dimensional node and suppose that_ Θ _is minimal at each eigenvalue of_ A. _Then_ Θ _is a minimal node_.

PROOF. Let λ be an eigenvalue of A and P the corresponding Riesz projection. In view of (4.5), we have

$$P^{-1}[\mathrm{Ker}(C|A)] = \mathrm{Ker}\, P \ , \ P[\mathrm{Im}(A|B)] = \mathrm{Im}\, P.$$

Observe that $\mathrm{Ker}(C|A)$ and $\mathrm{Im}(A|B)$ are invariant subspaces for A. Since X is finite dimensional, it follows that they are invariant for P too. Hence $\mathrm{Ker}(C|A) \subset P^{-1}[\mathrm{Ker}(C|A)] = \mathrm{Ker}\, P$ and $\mathrm{Im}\, P = P[\mathrm{Im}(A|B)] \subset \mathrm{Im}(A|B)$. As the eigenvalue λ of A was taken arbitrarily, this proves the theorem.

Let $\Theta = (A,B,C,D;X,Y)$ be a finite dimensional node and $\lambda_0 \in \mathbb{C}$. Denote the Riesz projection of A at λ_0 by P. Then for n sufficiently large $\mathrm{Im}\, P = \mathrm{Ker}(\lambda_0 - A)^n$ and $\mathrm{Ker}\, P = \mathrm{Im}(\lambda_0 - A)^n$. Using this one easily verifies that Θ is minimal at the point λ_0 if and only if the operators

$$\begin{bmatrix} C \\ \lambda_0 - A \end{bmatrix} : X \to Y \oplus X \ , \ [\lambda_0 - A \ \ B] : X \oplus Y \to X$$

are injective and surjective, respectively. Applying now the preceding theorem we obtain the so-called Hautus test for minimality: The node Θ is minimal if and only if

$$\mathrm{rank} \begin{bmatrix} C \\ \lambda - A \end{bmatrix} = \mathrm{rank}[\lambda - A \ \ B] = \dim X$$

for each eigenvalue λ of A.

4.2 McMillan degree and minimality of nodes

Let W be a rational $n \times n$ matrix function. Recall that the local degree $\delta(W;\lambda)$ of W at λ vanishes if and only if W is analytic at λ. Therefore it makes sense to put

$$\delta(W) = \sum_{\lambda \in \mathbb{C}_\infty} \delta(W;\lambda).$$

This number is known in the literature as the <u>McMillan degree</u> of W. It plays an important role in network theory. Of course the definition applies to any rational operator function whose values act on a finite dimensional space.

A change of parameter involving a Möbius transformation does not affect the McMillan degree. Therefore we concentrate on the case when W is analytic at ∞. The next theorem is an immediate consequence of Theorems 4.1 and 4.3.

THEOREM 4.4. <u>Let</u> W <u>be the transfer function of the finite dimensional node</u> Θ. <u>If</u> X <u>is the state space of</u> Θ, <u>then</u> $\delta(W) \leq \dim X$, <u>equality occurring if and only if</u> Θ <u>is minimal</u>.

Let W be analytic at ∞. From Theorems 3.1 and 3.2 it is clear that the minimal realizations for W are just the realizations with smallest possible state space dimension. Theorem 4.4 adds to this that the smallest possible state space dimension is equal to the McMillan degree of W.

Suppose $W(\lambda)$ is invertible for some $\lambda \in \mathbb{C}_\infty$. Then W^{-1} is also a rational n×n matrix function. We claim that

$$\delta(W) = \delta(W^{-1}). \tag{4.10}$$

To see this, we may assume that W is analytic at ∞ and $W(\infty)$ is invertible. Otherwise we apply a suitable Möbius transformation. Let $\Theta = (A,B,C,D;X,\mathbb{C}^n)$ be a minimal node whose transfer function coincides with W. Since $D = W(\infty)$, we have that D is invertible. But then $\Theta^\times$ is well-defined and its transfer function is W^{-1}. The minimality of Θ implies that of $\Theta^\times$. Formula (4.10) is now an immediate consequence of Theorem 4.4.

As a second application of Theorem 4.4, we deduce another description of the McMillan degree for the case when W is analytic at ∞ (cf. [50]). Let

$$W(\lambda) = D + \frac{1}{\lambda}D_1 + \frac{1}{\lambda^2}D_2 + \dots$$

be the Laurent expansion of W at ∞, and put

$$T_m = (D_{i+j-1})_{i,j=1}^{m}.$$

Then, for m sufficiently large, we have $\delta(W) = \operatorname{rank} T_m$. To prove this, choose a minimal node $\Theta=(A,B,C,D;X,\mathbb{C}^n)$ whose transfer function coincides with W. Then

$$D_k = CA^{k-1}B , \quad k = 1,2,\dots .$$

Hence $T_m = [\operatorname{col}(CA^{j-1})_{j=1}^{m}].[\operatorname{row}(A^{j-1}B)_{j=1}^{m}]$. As Θ is minimal, we see that for m sufficiently large $\operatorname{rank} T_m = \dim X$. But $\dim X = \delta(W)$ by Theorem 4.4, and the proof is complete.

The next theorem is the global analogue of Theorem 4.2; it is one of the main tools for studying minimal factorizations (see next section).

THEOREM 4.5. *For* $j = 1,2,$ *let* W_j *be the transfer function of the finite dimensional node* Θ_j. *Then* $\delta(W_1W_2) \leq \delta(W_1)+\delta(W_2)$. *Furthermore,* $\Theta_1\Theta_2$ *is minimal if and only if* Θ_1 *and* Θ_2 *are minimal and* $\delta(W_1W_2) = \delta(W_1) + \delta(W_2)$.

4.3 Minimal factorization

Let W, W_1 and W_2 be rational $n\times n$ matrix functions, and assume that

$$W = W_1W_2. \tag{4.11}$$

Then we know from Section 4.1 that $\delta(W) \leq \delta(W_1) + \delta(W_2)$. The factorization (4.11) is called *minimal* if $\delta(W) = \delta(W_1) + \delta(W_2)$. An equivalent requirement is that this equality holds pointwise

$$\delta(W;\lambda) = \delta(W_1;\lambda) + \delta(W_2;\lambda), \quad \lambda\in\mathbb{C}_\infty. \tag{4.12}$$

Minimal factorizations are important in network theory (see [49] and the references given there).

Applying, if necessary, a suitable Möbius transformation, we may assume that W is analytic at ∞. But then, if (4.11) is a minimal factorization, the factors W_1 and W_2 are analytic at ∞ too. Indeed, from $0 = \delta(W;\infty) = \delta(W_1;\infty) + \delta(W_2;\infty)$ it follows that $\delta(W_1;\infty) = \delta(W_2;\infty) = 0$. In view of this we shall concentrate on the case when the rational matrix functions are analytic at ∞. In other words we assume that they appear as transfer functions of finite dimensional nodes.

For such functions there is an alternative way of defining the notion of a minimal factorization. The definition is suggested by Theorem 4.5 and reads as follows: The factorization (4.11) is minimal if, whenever Θ_1 and Θ_2 are minimal realizations for W_1 and W_2, respectively, then $\Theta_1\Theta_2$ is a minimal realization for W.

It is of interest to note that the alternative definition makes sense in a more general context. One just has to specify a suitable class of nodes together with the corresponding transfer functions. For the Livsic-Brodskii characteristic operator function this leads to the concept of a factorization into regular factors. For details, see [8], Section I.5. One could also consider Krein nodes and the corresponding transfer functions. However, for such nodes biminimality rather than minimality seems to be the natural property. As a final special case we mention the class of transfer functions of monic nodes with given fixed (possibly infinite dimensional) input/output space Y. This class coincides with that of the inverses of monic operator polynomials having coefficients in $L(Y)$. Recall that monic nodes are always minimal. So in this context every factorization is minimal. For the finite dimensional case this can also be seen directly from the behaviour of the McMillan degree. The argument may then be based on formula (4.10) and the observation that if L is a monic $n\times n$ matrix polynomial, then $\delta(L) = \delta(L;\infty) = n\ell$, where ℓ is the degree of L.

Now let us return to the study of minimal factorizations of rational $n\times n$ matrix functions. So suppose W, W_1 and W_2 are rational $n\times n$ matrix functions. In the remainder of this section we shall always suppose that $\det W(\lambda) \not\equiv 0$. This implies the existence of $a \in \mathbb{C}$ such that $W(a)$ is invertible. Put $\widetilde{W}(\lambda) = W(a)^{-1}W(\lambda^{-1}+a)$. Then $\widetilde{W}(\infty) = I_n$. There is a one-to-one correspondence between the (minimal) factorizations of W and those of $\widetilde{W}$. Therefore there is no loss of generality in assuming that $W(\infty) = I_n$.

Suppose $W(\infty) = I_n$. We are interested in the minimal factorizations of W. We claim that it suffices to consider only those factorizations (4.11) for which $W_1(\infty) = W_2(\infty) = I_n$. To make this claim more precise, assume that (4.11) is a minimal factorization of W. Then W_1 and W_2 are analytic at ∞ and $W_1(\infty)\cdot W_2(\infty) = I_n$. So $W_1(\infty)$ and $W_2(\infty)$ are each others inverse. By multiplying W_1 from the right with $W_2(\infty)$ and W_2 from the left by $W_1(\infty)$, we obtain a minimal factorization of W whose factors have the value I_n at ∞.

These considerations justify the fact that, <u>from now on, without further notice</u>, <u>we only deal with rational matrix functions that are analytic at</u> ∞ <u>with value the identity matrix</u>. In other words the rational matrix functions considered below appear as transfer functions of finite dimensional nodes whose external operator is the identity.

Intuitively, formula (4.12) means that in the product W_1W_2 pole-zero cancellations do not occur. The following theorem makes this statement more precise. Recall that A^T stands for the transpose of the matrix A. The meaning of the symbols $\mathrm{Ker}(W;\lambda)$ and $\mathrm{Pol}(W;\lambda)$ has been explained in Section 2.1.

THEOREM 4.6. *The factorization* $W = W_1W_2$ *is a minimal factorization if and only if for each* λ *in* $\mathbb{C}$

(i) $\mathrm{Ker}(W_1;\lambda)\cap\mathrm{Pol}(W_2;\lambda) = (0)$,

(ii) $\mathrm{Pol}(W_1^T;\lambda)\cap\mathrm{Ker}(W_2^T;\lambda) = (0)$.

To prove the theorem we need the following lemma.

LEMMA 4.7. *Let* W *be the transfer function of the minimal node* $\theta = (A,B,C;\mathbb{C}^\delta,\mathbb{C}^n)$. *Then* C *maps* $\mathrm{Ker}(A-\lambda)$ *in a one-one manner onto* $\mathrm{Pol}(W;\lambda)$.

PROOF. Using a similarity transformation we may assume without loss of generality that $A = J$, $B = R$ and $C = Q$, where J, R and Q are the operators constructed in Theorem 2.2. But for the minimal node $(J,R,Q;\mathbb{C}^{\delta},\mathbb{C}^n)$ the lemma is trivial.

Let W and θ be as in the preceding lemma, and apply this lemma to the associate node $\theta^{\times}$. Then one sees that C maps $\operatorname{Ker}(A^{\times}-\lambda)$ in a one-one manner onto $\operatorname{Ker}(W;\lambda_0)$.

PROOF OF THEOREM 4.6. Let $\theta_1 = (A_1,B_1,C_1;\mathbb{C}^{\delta_1},\mathbb{C}^n)$ and $\theta_2 = (A_2,B_2,C_2;\mathbb{C}^{\delta_2},\mathbb{C}^n)$ be minimal realizations for W_1 and W_2, respectively. Let $\theta = (A,B,C;\mathbb{C}^{\delta_1}\oplus\mathbb{C}^{\delta_2},\mathbb{C}^n)$ be the product $\theta_1\theta_2$. So

$$A = \begin{bmatrix} A_1 & B_1C_2 \\ 0 & A_2 \end{bmatrix}, \quad B = \begin{bmatrix} B_1 \\ B_2 \end{bmatrix}, \quad C = [C_1 C_2].$$

Take a fixed $m\geq 1$. By induction one proves that

$$A^m = \begin{bmatrix} A_1^m & T_m \\ 0 & A_2^m \end{bmatrix}, \quad T_m = \sum_{i+j=m-1} A_1^i B_1 C_2 A_2^j.$$

It follows that $CA^m = [C_1A_1^m \;\; Z_m]$, where

$$Z_m = C_2A_2^m + \sum_{j=0}^{m-1} C_1A_1^{m-1-j}B_1C_2A_2^j. \tag{4.13}$$

Again employing induction one shows that

$$C_1A_1^k = C_1(A_1^{\times})^k + \sum_{i=0}^{k-1} C_1(A_1^{\times})^{k-1-i}B_1C_1A_1^i, \quad k = 1,2,\ldots . \tag{4.14}$$

Using this in (4.13) one obtains

$$Z_m = C_2A_2^m + \sum_{j=0}^{m-1} C_1(A_1^{\times})^{m-1-j}B_1Z_j. \tag{4.15}$$

As $CA^m = [C_1A_1^m \; Z_m]$, we see from (4.14) and (4.15) that

$$\begin{pmatrix} I & 0 & 0 & & \\ -C_1B_1 & I & 0 & & \\ -C_1A_1^\times B_1 & -C_1B_1 & I & & \\ & & \ddots & \ddots & \\ -C_1(A_1^\times)^{m-1}B_1 & \cdots & & -C_1B_1 & I \end{pmatrix}\begin{pmatrix} C \\ CA \\ \vdots \\ CA^m \end{pmatrix} = \begin{pmatrix} C_1 & C_2 \\ C_1A_1^\times & C_2A_2 \\ \vdots & \vdots \\ C_1(A_1^\times)^m & C_2A_2^m \end{pmatrix}.$$

In particular,

$$(4.16) \qquad \bigcap_{j=0}^{m} \operatorname{Ker} CA^j = \bigcap_{j=0}^{m} \operatorname{Ker}[C_1(A_1^\times)^j \;\; C_2A_2^j].$$

Using (4.16) we shall prove that θ is observable if and only if $\operatorname{Ker}(W_1;\lambda)\cap\operatorname{Pol}(W_2;\lambda) = (0)$ for each $\lambda\in\mathbb{C}$. First, assume

$$(4.17) \qquad 0 \neq y_0\in\operatorname{Ker}(W_1;\lambda_0)\cap\operatorname{Pol}(W_2;\lambda_0).$$

Note that $\operatorname{Ker}(W_1;\lambda_0) = \operatorname{Pol}(W_1^{-1};\lambda_0)$. So applying Lemma 4.7 to $\theta_1^\times$ and θ_2, we see that there exist $x_1\in\operatorname{Ker}(A_1^\times-\lambda_0)$ and $x_2\in\operatorname{Ker}(A_2-\lambda_0)$ such that $C_1x_1 = C_2x_2 = y_0$. As $y_0 \neq 0$ we have $x_1,x_2 \neq 0$. Further,

$$C_1(A_1^\times)^j x_1 = \lambda_0^j y_0 = C_2A_2^j x_2, \; j\geq 0.$$

But then we can use (4.16) to show that

$$x_0 = \begin{pmatrix} x_1 \\ -x_2 \end{pmatrix}$$

is a non-zero element in $\operatorname{Ker}(C|A)$, and it follows that θ is not observable.

Next, assume that θ is not observable. Applying (4.16) we conclude that the space $K = \cap_{j=0}^{\infty} \mathrm{Ker}[C_1(A_1^\times)^j \; C_2A_2^j]$ is non-trivial. By [21], Lemma 2.2 (see also [22], Theorem 9.1) we have

$$K = \left\{ \begin{bmatrix} x_1 \\ -Sx_1 \end{bmatrix} \mid x_1 \in M \right\},$$

where M is a non-trivial $A_1^\times$-invariant subspace of $\mathbb{C}^{\delta_1}$ and $S : M \to \mathbb{C}^{\delta_2}$ is a linear map such that

$$C_1\big|_M = C_2S \; , \; S(A_1^\times\big|_M) = A_2S. \tag{4.18}$$

Since M is non-trivial, the operator $A_1^\times$ has an eigenvector, x_1 say, in M. Let λ_0 be the corresponding eigenvalue. Put $x_2 = Sx_1$ and $y_0 = C_1x_1$. Employing (4.18), we see that $A_2x_2 = \lambda_0x_2$ and $y_0 = C_2x_2$. But then, we can apply Lemma 4.7 to both $\theta_1^\times$ and θ_2 to show that

$$0 \neq y_0 \in \mathrm{Pol}(W_1^{-1};\lambda_0) \cap \mathrm{Pol}(W_2;\lambda_0).$$

As $\mathrm{Pol}(W_1^{-1};\lambda_0) = \mathrm{Ker}(W_1;\lambda_0)$, we obtain (4.17). So we have proved that θ is observable if and only if condition (i) is satisfied for each $\lambda \in \mathbb{C}$.

To finish the proof, observe that θ is controllable if and only if $\theta^T = (A^T, C^T, B^T; \mathbb{C}^\delta, \mathbb{C}^n)$ is observable. Since $W^T = W_2^TW_1^T$, we see from the first part of the proof that θ^T is observable if and only if

$$\mathrm{Ker}(W_2^T;\lambda) \cap \mathrm{Pol}(W_1^T;\lambda) = (0) \;, \quad \lambda \in \mathbb{C}.$$

In other words θ is controllable if and only if condition (ii) is satisfied for each $\lambda \in \mathbb{C}$. This completes the proof.

We now come to the main theorem of this section. It gives a complete description of minimal factorizations in terms of supporting projection (see Section 1.1) of minimal nodes.

THEOREM 4.8. *Let the node* Θ *with external operator the identity be a minimal realization of the rational matrix function* W.

(i) *If* Π *is a supporting projection for* Θ, W_1 *is the transfer function of* $pr_{I-\Pi}(\Theta)$ *and* W_2 *is the transfer function of* $pr_{\Pi}(\Theta)$, *then* $W = W_1W_2$ *is a minimal factorization of* W.

(ii) *If* $W = W_1W_2$ *is a minimal factorization of* W, *then there exists a unique supporting projection* Π *for the node* Θ *such that* W_1 *and* W_2 *are the transfer functions of* $pr_{I-\Pi}(\Theta)$ *and* $pr_{\Pi}(\Theta)$, *respectively*.

PROOF Let Π be a supporting projection for Θ. Then $\Theta = pr_{I-\Pi}(\Theta).pr_{\Pi}(\Theta)$. Since Θ is minimal, it follows that $pr_{I-\Pi}(\Theta)$ and $pr_{\Pi}(\Theta)$ are minimal. But then one can apply formula (1.3) and Theorem 4.5 to show that $W = W_1W_2$ is a minimal factorization. This proves (i).

Next assume that $W = W_1W_2$ is a minimal factorization. For $i = 1,2$, let Θ_i be a minimal realization of W_i with state space $\mathbb{C}^{\delta_i}$. Here $\delta_i = \delta(W_i)$ is the McMillan degree of W_i (see Theorem 4.4). By Theorem 4.5 the product $\Theta_1\Theta_2$ is minimal. Note that $\Theta_1\Theta_2$ is a realization for W. Hence $\Theta_1\Theta_2$ and Θ are similar, say with node similarity $S:\mathbb{C}^{\delta_1}\oplus\mathbb{C}^{\delta_2} \to \mathbb{C}^{\delta}$, where $\delta = \delta_1+\delta_2 = \delta(W)$. Let Π be the projection of $\mathbb{C}^{\delta}$ along $S[\mathbb{C}^{\delta_1}]$ onto $S[\mathbb{C}^{\delta_2}]$. Then Π is a supporting projection for Θ. Moreover $pr_{I-\Pi}(\Theta)$ is similar to Θ_1 and $pr_{\Pi}(\Theta)$ is similar to Θ_2. It remains to prove the unicity of Π.

Suppose P is another supporting projection of Θ such that $pr_{I-P}(\Theta)$ and $pr_P(\Theta)$ are realizations of W_1 and W_2, respectively. Then $pr_{I-P}(\Theta)$ and $pr_P(\Theta)$ are minimal again. Hence $pr_{I-\Pi}(\Theta)$ and $pr_{I-P}(\Theta)$ are similar, say with node similarity $U:\operatorname{Ker}\Pi \to \operatorname{Ker}P$, and $pr_{\Pi}(\Theta)$ and $pr_P(\Theta)$ are similar, say with node similarity $V:\operatorname{Im}\Pi \to \operatorname{Im}P$. Define T on $\mathbb{C}^{\delta}$ by

$$T = \begin{bmatrix} U & 0 \\ 0 & V \end{bmatrix} : \operatorname{Ker}\Pi \oplus \operatorname{Im}\Pi \to \operatorname{Ker}P \oplus \operatorname{Im}P.$$

Then T is a node similarity between Θ and itself. Since Θ is minimal it follows that T is the identity operatory on $\mathbb{C}^{\delta}$. But then $\Pi = P$, and the proof is complete.

Theorem 4.8 may be viewed as an analogue of Theorems 5.4 and 5.6 in [8] where the one-one correspondence between regular divisors of the Brodskii-Livsic characteristic operator function and the left divisors of a simple node is described. The one-one correspondence between the supporting subspaces of a monic node θ and the right divisors of $L = W_{\theta}^{-1}$ (cf. Subsection 1.4.3 and the references given there) is the variant of Theorem 4.8 for monic operator polynomials.

4.4 Canonical spectral factorization (2)

In this section we continue the discussion of canonical factorization begun in Section 1.2.

THEOREM 4.9. *Let* $\theta = (A,B,C;\mathbb{C}^{\delta},\mathbb{C}^{n})$ *be a minimal realization of the rational* $n\times n$ *matrix function* W. *Let* Γ *be a Cauchy contour such that* W *has no poles or zeros on* Γ. *Then* Γ *splits the spectra of* A *and* $A^{\times}$ *and* W *admits a right canonical factorization with respect to* Γ *if and only if*

$$\mathbb{C}^{\delta} = \operatorname{Im} P(A,\Gamma) \oplus \operatorname{Ker} P(A^{\times};\Gamma). \tag{4.19}$$

A similar statement holds true for left canonical factorization.

PROOF. If condition (4.19) is satisfied, then we know from Theorem 1.5 that W admits a right canonical factorization. So we have to prove the converse statement.

Suppose $W = W_{-}W_{+}$ is a right canonical factorization with respect to Γ. The functions W_{-} and W_{+} are rational $n\times n$ matrix functions, W_{-} has no poles and zeros in $\bar{F}_{-}$, and W_{+} has no poles and zeros in $\bar{F}_{+}$. Here F_{+} is the inner domain of Γ and F_{-} is the outer domain of Γ the point ∞ included. Without loss of generality we may assume that the values of W_{-} and W_{+}

at ∞ are equal to the unit matrix. Let $\Theta_1 = (A_1,B_1,C_1;\mathbb{C}^{\delta_1},\mathbb{C}^n)$ and $\Theta_2 = (A_2,B_2,C_2;\mathbb{C}^{\delta_2},\mathbb{C}^n)$ be minimal realizations for W_- and W_+, respectively. The conditions on the poles and zeros of W_- and W_+ imply that there are no pole-zero cancellations in the product $W = W_-W_+$. So we can apply Theorem 4.6 to show that the factorization $W = W_-W_+$ is a minimal factorization. But then $\Theta_1\Theta_2$ is a minimal realization for W, and hence $\Theta_1\Theta_2$ and Θ are similar.

The state space operator T of $\theta_1\theta_2$ and its associate $T^\times$ are given by

$$A = \begin{bmatrix} A_1 & B_1C_2 \\ 0 & A_2 \end{bmatrix}, \quad T^\times = \begin{bmatrix} A_1^\times & 0 \\ -B_2C_1 & A_2^\times \end{bmatrix}.$$

Here the matrix representations correspond to the decomposition $\mathbb{C}^\delta = \mathbb{C}^{\delta_1} \oplus \mathbb{C}^{\delta_2}$. Observe that $\sigma(A_1)$, being the set of poles of W_-, is contained in F_+. Similarly, $\sigma(A_2) \subset F_-$, $\sigma(A_1^\times) \subset F_+$ and $\sigma(A_2^\times) \subset F_-$. In particular, we see that

$$\sigma(A_1) \cap \sigma(A_2) = \sigma(A_1^\times) \cap \sigma(A_2^\times) = \phi.$$

But then $\sigma(T) = \sigma(A_1) \cup \sigma(A_2)$ and $\sigma(T^\times) = \sigma(A_1^\times) \cup \sigma(A_2^\times)$. It follows that Γ splits the spectra of T and $T^\times$, and we may apply Lemma 1.4 to show that

$$\mathbb{C}^{\delta_1} = \operatorname{Im} P(T;\Gamma), \quad \mathbb{C}^{\delta_2} = \operatorname{Ker} P(T^\times;\Gamma). \tag{4.20}$$

Now $\theta_1\theta_2 \simeq \theta$, say with node similarity $S: \mathbb{C}^{\delta_1} \oplus \mathbb{C}^{\delta_2} \to \mathbb{C}^\delta$. Thus $T = S^{-1}AS$ and $T^\times = S^{-1}A^\times S$. It follows that Γ splits the spectra of A and $A^\times$ and, by (4.20),

$$\operatorname{Im} P(A;\Gamma) = S[\mathbb{C}^{\delta_1}], \quad \operatorname{Ker} P(A^\times;\Gamma) = S[\mathbb{C}^{\delta_2}].$$

But $\mathbb{C}^\delta = S[\mathbb{C}^{\delta_1}] \oplus S[\mathbb{C}^{\delta_2}]$, and hence (4.19) holds.

4.5 Application to Wiener-Hopf integral equations

In this section the general division theory developed in the preceding sections is used to provide explicit formulas for solutions of finite systems of Wiener-Hopf integral equations. Such a system may be written as a single Wiener-Hopf equation:

$$\phi(t) - \int_0^\infty k(t-s)\phi(s)ds = f(t), \quad 0 \le t < \infty, \tag{4.21}$$

where ϕ and f are n-dimensional vector functions and $k \in L_1^{n\times n}(-\infty,\infty)$, i.e., the kernel k is an $n\times n$ matrix function whose entries are in $L_1(-\infty,\infty)$. We assume that the given vector function f has its component functions in $L_p(0,\infty)$, and we express this property by writing $f \in L_p^n(0,\infty)$. Throughout this section p will be fixed and $1 \le p < \infty$. The problem we shall consider is to find a solution ϕ for equation (4.21) that also belongs to the space $L_p^n(0,\infty)$.

The usual method (see [23]) to solve equation (4.21) is as follows. First assume that (4.21) has a solution ϕ in $L_p^n(0,\infty)$. Extend this solution to the whole real line by setting $\phi(t) = 0$ for $t < 0$. Then f extends to a $L_p^n(-\infty,\infty)$-function, also denoted by f, such that

$$\phi(t) - \int_{-\infty}^\infty k(t-s)\phi(s)ds = f(t)$$

for all $-\infty < t < \infty$. By applying the Fourier transformation and leaving the part of f that is given in the right hand side, one gets

$$[I_n - K(\lambda)]\Phi_+(\lambda) - F_-(\lambda) = F_+(\lambda), \quad \lambda \in \mathbb{R}, \tag{4.22}$$

where

$$K(\lambda) = \int_{-\infty}^\infty k(t)e^{it\lambda}dt \quad , \quad F_+(\lambda) = \int_0^\infty f(t)e^{it\lambda}dt, \tag{4.23}$$

$$(4.24)\qquad \Phi_+(\lambda) = \int_0^\infty \phi(t)e^{it\lambda}dt \quad , \quad F_-(\lambda) = \int_{-\infty}^0 f(t)e^{it\lambda}dt.$$

Note that the functions K and F_+ are given, but the functions Φ_+ and F_- have to be found. In fact in this way the problem to solve (4.21) is reduced to that of finding two functions Φ_+ and F_- such that (4.22) holds, while furthermore Φ_+ and F_- must be as in (4.24) with $\phi \in L_p^n(0,\infty)$ and $f \in L_p^n(-\infty,0)$.

To find Φ_+ and F_- of the desired form such that (4.22) holds, one factorizes the nxn matrix function $I_n - K(\lambda)$. This function is called the symbol of the integral equation (4.21). Assume that the symbol admits a factorization of the following form:

$$(4.25)\qquad I_n - K(\lambda) = (I_n + G_-(\lambda))(I_n + G_+(\lambda)),$$

where

$$G_+(\lambda) = \int_0^\infty g_1(t)e^{it\lambda}dt \quad , \quad G_-(\lambda) = \int_{-\infty}^0 g_2(t)e^{it\lambda}dt$$

with $g_1 \in L_1^{n\times n}(0,\infty)$, $g_2 \in L_1^{n\times n}(-\infty,0)$ and

$$\det(I_n + G_+(\lambda)) \quad , \quad \det(I_n + G_-(\lambda))$$

do not vanish in the closed upper and lower half plane, respectively. We shall refer to the factorization (4.25) as a right canonical factorization of $I_n - K(\lambda)$ with respect to the real line. Under the conditions stated above the functions $(I_n + G_+(\lambda))^{-1}$ and $(I_n + G_-(\lambda))^{-1}$ admit representations as Fourier transforms:

$$(4.26)\qquad (I_n + G_+(\lambda))^{-1} = I_n + \int_0^\infty \gamma_1(t)e^{it\lambda}dt,$$

$$(4.27)\qquad (I_n + G_-(\lambda))^{-1} = I_n + \int_{-\infty}^0 \gamma_2(t)e^{it\lambda}dt,$$

with $\gamma_1 \in L_1^{n\times n}(0,\infty)$ and $\gamma_2 \in L_1^{n\times n}(-\infty,0)$. Using the factorization (4.25) and omitting the variable λ, equation (4.22) can be rewritten as:

$$(4.28) \qquad [I_n + G_+]\Phi_+ - [I_n + G_-]^{-1}F_- = [I_n + G_-]^{-1}F_+.$$

Let P be the projection acting on the Fourier transforms of $L_p^n(-\infty,\infty)$-functions according to the following rule:

$$P(\int_{-\infty}^{\infty} h(t)e^{it\lambda}dt) = \int_0^{\infty} h(t)e^{it\lambda}dt.$$

By applying P to (4.28) one gets

$$[I_n + G_+]\Phi_+ = P[I_n + G_-]^{-1} F_+,$$

and hence

$$(4.29) \qquad \Phi_+ = [I_n + G_+]^{-1}P[I_n + G_-]^{-1}F_+,$$

which is the formula for the solution of equation (4.22). To obtain the solution ϕ of the original equation (4.21), i.e., to obtain the inverse Fourier transform of Φ_+, one can employ the formulas (4.26) and (4.27). In fact,

$$\phi(t) = f(t) + \int_0^{\infty} \gamma(t,s)f(s)ds,$$

where the kernel $\gamma(t,s)$ is given by

$$(4.30) \quad \gamma(t,s) = \gamma_1(t-s) + \gamma_2(t-s) + \int_0^{\min(t,s)} \gamma_1(t-r)\gamma_2(r-s)dr.$$

To conclude the description of this factorization method, let us mention (see [19,23]) that the equation (4.21) has a unique solution in $L_p^n(0,\infty)$ for each f in $L_p^n(0,\infty)$ if and only if its symbol admits a factorization as in (4.25).

To illustrate the factorization method described above, let us consider a special choice for f. Take (cf. [23])

$$(4.31) \qquad f(t) = e^{-itq}x_0,$$

where x_0 is a fixed vector in $\mathbb{C}^n$ and q is a complex number with $\operatorname{Im} q < 0$. Then

$$F_+(\lambda) = \int_0^\infty e^{it(\lambda-q)}x_0 dt = \frac{i}{\lambda-q} x_0, \quad \operatorname{Im}\lambda \geq 0.$$

Now observe that

$$\frac{i}{\lambda-q} \{(I_n + G_-(\lambda))^{-1} - (I_n + G_-(q))^{-1}\} x_0$$

is the Fourier transform of a $L_p^n(-\infty,0)$-function. So if one applies the projection P to this function one gets the zero function. It follows that in this case the formula for Φ_+ may be written as:

$$\Phi_+(\lambda) = \frac{i}{\lambda-q} (I_n + G_+(\lambda))^{-1}(I_n + G_-(q))^{-1}x_0.$$

Recall that the solution ϕ is the inverse Fourier transform of Φ_+. So we have

$$(4.32) \qquad \phi(t) = e^{-iqt} \{I_n + \int_0^t e^{isq}\gamma_1(s)ds\} (I_n + G_-(q))^{-1}x_0.$$

Our aim is to apply the division theory developed in the previous sections to get the factorization (4.25). Therefore, assume that the symbol $I_n - K(\lambda)$ is a rational $n\times n$ matrix function which is equal to I_n at ∞. As $K(\lambda)$ is the Fourier transform of an $L_1^{n\times n}(-\infty,\infty)$-function, the symbol $I_n - K(\lambda)$ is continuous on the real line. In particular $I_n - K(\lambda)$ has no poles on the real line. It follows that the conditions on $I_n - K(\lambda)$ are equivalent to the requirement that the kernel $k(t)$ is in the linear space spanned by all functions of the form

$$h(t) = \begin{cases} p(t)e^{i\alpha t} & \text{for } t > 0, \\ q(t)e^{i\beta t} & \text{for } t < 0, \end{cases}$$

where $p(t)$ and $q(t)$ are polynomials in t with coefficients in $\mathbb{C}^n$ and α and β are complex numbers with $\operatorname{Im}\alpha > 0$ and $\operatorname{Im}\beta < 0$. Since $I_n - K(\lambda)$ is rational and equal to I_n at ∞, one can construct (see Section 2.1) a minimal node $\theta = (A,B,C;\mathbb{C}^\delta,\mathbb{C}^n)$ such that

$$I_n - K(\lambda) = I_n + C(\lambda I_\delta - A)^{-1}B.$$

In the next theorem we express the solvability of equation (4.21) in terms of such a minimal realization and give explicit formulas for its solutions in the same terms.

THEOREM 4.10. *Let $I_n - K(\lambda) = I_n + C(\lambda I_\delta - A)^{-1}B$ be a minimal realization for the symbol of equation (4.21), and let $A^\times = A-BC$. In order that (4.21) has a unique solution ϕ in $L_p^n(0,\infty)$ for each f in $L_p^n(0,\infty)$ the following two conditions are necessary and sufficient:*

(1) $\det(I_n - K(\lambda)) \neq 0$ *for all* $\lambda\in\mathbb{R}$;

(2) $\mathbb{C}^\delta = M \oplus M^\times$, *where* $M(M^\times)$ *is the spectral subspace corresponding to the eigenvalues of* $A(A^\times)$ *in the upper (lower) half plane.*

Assume conditions (1) and (2) hold true, and let Π be the projection of $\mathbb{C}^\delta$ along M onto $M^\times$. Then $I_n - K(\lambda)$ admits a right canonical factorization with respect to the real line that has the form:

$$I_n - K(\lambda) = (I_n + G_-(\lambda))(I_n + G_+(\lambda)),$$

<u>where</u>

$$I_n + G_+(\lambda) = I_n + C\Pi(\lambda - A)^{-1}B,$$

$$I_n + G_-(\lambda) = I_n + C(\lambda - A)^{-1}(I - \Pi)B,$$

$$(I_n + G_+(\lambda))^{-1} = I_n - C(\lambda - A^\times)^{-1}\Pi B,$$

$$(I_n + G_-(\lambda))^{-1} = I_n - C(I - \Pi)(\lambda - A^\times)^{-1}B.$$

<u>Using this the formula for</u> Φ_+ <u>can be written as</u>:

$$\Phi_+(\lambda) = [I_n - C(\lambda - A^\times)^{-1}\Pi B]P[I_n - C(I - \Pi)(\lambda - A^\times)^{-1}B]F_+(\lambda),$$

<u>and the functions</u> γ_1 <u>and</u> γ_2 <u>in</u> (4.30) <u>are given by</u>

$$\gamma_1(t) = iCe^{-iA^\times t}\Pi B, \quad t \geq 0,$$

$$\gamma_2(t) = -iC(I - \Pi)e^{-iA^\times t}B, \quad t \leq 0.$$

PROOF. We have already mentioned (see [19,23]) that equation (4.21) has a unique solution in $L_p^n(0,\infty)$ for each f in $L_p^n(0,\infty)$ if and only if the symbol $I_n - K(\lambda)$ admits a canonical right factorization as in (4.25). So to prove the necessity and sufficiency of the conditions (1) and (2) it suffices to show that the conditions (1) and (2) together are equivalent to the statement that $I_n - K(\lambda)$ admits a right canonical factorization as in (4.25). But then we can apply Theorem 4.9 to prove the first part of the theorem.

Next assume that conditions (1) and (2) hold true. Then we can apply Theorem 1.5 to get the desired formulas for $I_n + G_+(\lambda)$, $I_n + G_-(\lambda)$ and their inverses. Using this in (4.29) gives the expression for Φ_+. Finally one obtains the formulas for γ_1 and γ_2 by noticing that

$$\int_0^\infty e^{-iA^\times t}\Pi e^{i\lambda t}dt = i(\lambda - A^\times)^{-1}\Pi, \quad \lambda \notin \sigma(A^\times), \quad \mathrm{Im}\,\lambda \geq 0,$$

$$\int_{-\infty}^0 (I - \Pi)e^{-iA^\times t}e^{i\lambda t}dt = -i(I - \Pi)(\lambda - A^\times)^{-1}, \; \lambda \notin \sigma(A^\times), \; \mathrm{Im}\,\lambda \leq 0.$$

Note that in the second part of the proof the minimality of the realization is not used.

Let us return to the special case that the known function is given by formula (4.31), and assume that the conditions (1) and (2) in the previous theorem hold true. Then the solution ϕ (cf. (4.32)) admits the following representation:

$$\phi(t) = e^{-iqt}\{I_n + i\int_0^t Ce^{i(q - A^\times)s}\Pi B\,ds\}\,. \tag{4.33}$$
$$.\;\{I_n + C(I - \Pi)(q - A^\times)^{-1}B\}\,x_0.$$

Finally, let us remark that with natural appropriate modifications Theorem 4.10 is also valid in the infinite dimensional case. Moreover in the infinite dimensional case we can sometimes allow for spectrum on the real line. In fact such a situation occurs in the theory of the energy transport equation which will be analysed in Chapter 6.

4.6 Application to block Toeplitz matrices

In the previous section the division theory was applied to finite systems of Wiener-Hopf integral equations. Here we shall deal with discrete Wiener-Hopf equations. So consider an equation of the type

$$(4.34)\qquad \sum_{k=0}^{\infty} a_{j-k}\xi_k = \eta_j, \quad j = 0,1,2,\ldots,$$

where the a_j are given complex nxn matrices,

$$\sum_{j=-\infty}^{\infty} \| a_j \| < \infty,$$

and $\eta = (\eta_j)_{j=0}^{\infty}$ is a given vector from $\ell_p^n = \ell_p(\mathbb{C}^n)$. The problem is to find $\xi = (\xi_k)_{k=0}^{\infty} \in \ell_p^n$ such that (4.34) is satisfied. We shall restrict ourselves to the case when $1 \le p \le 2$; the final results however are valid for $2 < p \le \infty$ as well.

Assume $\xi \in \ell_p^n$ is a solution of (4.34). Then one can write (4.34) in the form

$$(4.35)\qquad \sum_{k=-\infty}^{\infty} a_{j-k}\xi_k = \eta_j, \quad j = 0,\pm 1,\pm 2,\ldots,$$

where $\xi_k = 0$ for $k < 0$ and η_j is defined by (4.35) for $j < 0$. Multiplying both sides of (4.35) by λ^j with $|\lambda| = 1$ and summing over j, one gets

$$(4.36)\qquad a(\lambda)\xi_+(\lambda) - \eta_-(\lambda) = \eta_+(\lambda), \quad |\lambda| = 1,$$

where

$$(4.37)\qquad a(\lambda) = \sum_{j=-\infty}^{\infty} \lambda^j a_j, \quad \eta_+(\lambda) = \sum_{j=0}^{\infty} \lambda^j \eta_j,$$

$$(4.38)\qquad \xi_+(\lambda) = \sum_{j=0}^{\infty} \lambda^j \xi_j, \quad \eta_-(\lambda) = \sum_{j=-\infty}^{-1} \lambda^j \eta_j.$$

In this way the problem to solve (4.34) is reduced to that of finding two functions ξ_+ and η_- such that (4.36) holds, while moreover ξ_+ and η_- must be as in (4.38) with $(\xi_j)_{j=0}^{\infty}$ and $(\eta_{-j-1})_{j=0}^{\infty}$ from ℓ_p^n.

The usual way (cf. [19,23]) of solving (4.36) is again by factorizing the symbol $a(\lambda)$ of the given Wiener-Hopf equation. Assume that $a(\lambda)$ admits a right canonical factorization with respect to the unit circle, i.e., $a(\lambda)$ can be written as

$$a(\lambda) = h_-(\lambda)h_+(\lambda), \quad |\lambda| = 1,$$

(4.39)

$$h_+(\lambda) = \sum_{j=0}^{\infty} h_j^+\lambda^j, \quad h_-(\lambda) = \sum_{j=-\infty}^{0} h_j^-\lambda^j,$$

where $(h_j^+)_{j=0}^{\infty}$ and $(h_{-j}^-)_{j=0}^{\infty}$ belong to the space $\ell_1^{n\times n}$ of all absolutely convergent sequences of complex $n\times n$ matrices, $\det h_+(\lambda) \neq 0$ for $|\lambda| \leq 1$ and $\det h_-(\lambda) \neq 0$ for $|\lambda| \geq 1$ (including $\lambda = \infty$). Then h_+^{-1} and h_-^{-1} also admit a representation of the form

(4.40) $$h_+^{-1}(\lambda) = \sum_{j=0}^{\infty} \gamma_j^+\lambda^j, \quad h_-^{-1}(\lambda) = \sum_{j=-\infty}^{0} \gamma_j^-\lambda^j,$$

with $(\gamma_j^+)_{j=0}^{\infty}$ and $(\gamma_{-j}^-)_{j=0}^{\infty}$ from $\ell_1^{n\times n}$. Defining the projection P by

$$P\Big(\sum_{j=-\infty}^{\infty} b_j\lambda^j\Big) = \sum_{j=0}^{\infty} b_j\lambda^j,$$

one gets from (4.36) and (4.39)

(4.41) $$\xi_+ = h_+^{-1}P\, h_-^{-1}\eta_+.$$

Here, for convenience, the variable λ is omitted. The solution of the original equation (4.34) can now be written as

(4.42) $$\xi_k = \sum_{s=0}^{\infty} \gamma_{ks}\eta_s, \quad k = 0,1,\ldots,$$

where

$$(4.43) \qquad \gamma_{ks} = \sum_{r=0}^{\min(k,s)} \gamma^{+}_{k-r}\gamma^{-}_{r-s}.$$

The assumption that $a(\lambda)$ admits a right canonical factorization as in (4.39) is equivalent to the requirement that for each $\eta = (\eta_j)_{j=0}^{\infty}$ in ℓ_p^n the equation (4.34) has a unique solution $\xi = (\xi_k)_{k=0}^{\infty}$ in ℓ_p^n. For details we refer to [19,23].

By way of illustration, we consider the special case when

$$(4.44) \qquad \eta_j = q^j \eta_0, \quad j = 0,1,\dots .$$

Here η_0 is a fixed vector in $\mathbb{C}^n$ and q is a complex number with $|q| < 1$. Then clearly

$$\eta_+(\lambda) = \frac{1}{1-\lambda q}\,\eta_0, \quad |\lambda| \le 1,$$

and one checks without difficulty that formula (4.42) becomes

$$(4.45) \qquad \xi_k = q^k \sum_{s=0}^{k} q^{-s}\gamma_s^{+} h_-^{-1}(q^{-1})\eta_0, \quad k = 0,1,\dots .$$

This is the analogue of formula (4.32) in Section 4.5.

As before, we wish to apply our division theory. For that reason we assume that the symbol $a(\lambda)$ is a rational $n\times n$ matrix function whose value at ∞ is I_n. Note that $a(\lambda)$ has no poles on the unit circle. Therefore the conditions on $a(\lambda)$ are equivalent to the following assumptions:

(i) the sequence $(a_j - \delta_{j0}I_n)_{j=0}^{\infty}$ is a linear combination of sequences of the form

$$(\alpha^j j^r D)_{j=0}^{\infty},$$

where $|\alpha| < 1$, r is a non-negative integer and D is a complex $n\times n$ matrix;

(ii) the sequence $(a_{-j})_{j=1}^{\infty}$ is a linear combination of sequences of the form

$$(\beta^{-j} j^s E)_{j=1}^{\infty}, \qquad (\delta_{jm} F)_{j=1}^{\infty},$$

where $|\beta| > 1$, s and m are nonnegative integers and E and F are complex $n\times n$ matrices.

Since $a(\lambda)$ is rational and $a(\infty) = I_n$, one can construct (see Section 2.1) a node $\theta = (A,B,C;\mathbb{C}^{\delta},\mathbb{C}^{n})$ such that

$$a(\lambda) = I_n + C(\lambda I_{\delta} - A)^{-1}B \tag{4.46}$$

is a minimal realization for $a(\lambda)$. The next theorem is the analogue of Theorem 4.10.

THEOREM 4.11. *Let* (4.46) *be a minimal realization for the symbol* $a(\lambda)$ *of the equation* (4.34), *and let* $A^{\times} = A - BC$. *Then* (4.34) *has a unique solution* $\xi = (\xi_k)_{k=0}^{\infty}$ *in* ℓ_p^n *for each* $\eta = (\eta_j)_{j=0}^{\infty}$ *in* ℓ_p^n *if and only if the following two conditions are satisfied*:

(1) $\det a(\lambda) \neq 0$ *for all* λ *with* $|\lambda| = 1$,

(2) $\mathbb{C}^{\delta} = M \oplus M^{\times}$, *where* $M(M^{\times})$ *is the spectral subspace corresponding to the eigenvalues of* $A(A^{\times})$ *inside (outside) the unit circle*.

Assume conditions (1) *and* (2) *are satisfied, and let* Π *be the projection of* $\mathbb{C}^{\delta}$ *along* M *onto* $M^{\times}$. *Then* $a(\lambda)$ *admits a right canonical factorization with respect to the unit circle that has the form*

$$a(\lambda) = h_{-}(\lambda)h_{+}(\lambda), \quad |\lambda| = 1,$$

where

$$h_{+}(\lambda) = I_n + C\Pi(\lambda - A)^{-1}B,$$

$$h_-(\lambda) = I_n + C(\lambda - A)^{-1}(I - \Pi)B,$$

$$h_+^{-1}(\lambda) = I_n - C(\lambda - A^\times)^{-1}\Pi B,$$

$$h_-^{-1}(\lambda) = I_n - C(I - \Pi)(\lambda - A^\times)^{-1}B.$$

Using this, formula (4.41) for ξ_+ can be written as

$$\xi_+(\lambda) = [I_n - C(\lambda I_\delta - A^\times)^{-1}\Pi B]P[I_n - C(I - \Pi)(\lambda I_\delta - A^\times)^{-1}B]\eta_+(\lambda),$$

and the sequences $(\gamma_j^+)_{j=0}^\infty$ and $(\gamma_{-j}^-)_{j=0}^\infty$ in (4.43) are given by

$$\gamma_0^+ = I_n - C(A^\times)^{-1}\Pi B,$$

$$\gamma_j^+ = -C(A^\times)^{-(j+1)}\Pi B, \quad j = 1,2,\dots ,$$

$$\gamma_0^- = I_n,$$

$$\gamma_j^- = -C(I_\delta - \Pi)(A^\times)^{-(j+1)}B, \quad j = -1,-2,\dots .$$

With respect to the formulas for γ_j^+, we note that $\operatorname{Im}\Pi$ is $A^\times$-invariant and the restriction of $A^\times$ to $\operatorname{Im}\Pi$ is invertible. The proof of Theorem 4.11 is similar to that of Theorem 4.10.

Now let us again consider the special case where $(\eta_j)_{j=0}^\infty$ is of the form (4.44). Combining formula (4.45), with those appearing in Theorem 4.11, one gets

$$\xi_k = q^k[I_n - \sum_{s=0}^{k} q^{-s}C(A^\times)^{-(s+1)}\Pi B].$$

$$\cdot\ [I_n - C(I_\delta - \Pi)(q^{-1} - A^\times)^{-1}B]\eta_0,$$

$k = 0,1,\dots$. This is the analogue of formula (4.33).

The main step in the factorization method for solving the equation (4.34) is to construct a right canonical factorization of the symbol $a(\lambda)$ with respect to the unit circle. In Theorem 4.11 we obtained explicit formulas for the case when $a(\lambda)$ is rational and has the value I_n at ∞. The latter condition is not essential. Indeed, by a suitable Möbius transformation one can transform the symbol $a(\lambda)$ into a function which is invertible at infinity (see Section 1.5). Next one makes the Wiener-Hopf factorization of the transformed symbol relative to the image of the unit circle under the Möbius transformation. Here one can use the same formulas as in Theorem 4.11. Finally, using the inverse Möbius transformation, one can obtain explicit formulas for the factorization with respect to the unit circle, and hence also for the solution of equation (4.34).

4.7 Application to singular integral equations

In this section we apply Theorem 4.9 to the theory of singular integral equations. For a detailed account of this theory we refer to I. Gohberg: The factorization problem in normed rings, functions of isometric and symmetric operators, and singular integral equations, Russian Math. Surveys 19 (1964), nr. 1, 63-114 and I. Gohberg, N. Krupnik: Einführung in die Theorie der eindimensionalen singulären Integral operatoren, Birkhäuser Verlag, 1979. Here we only give a brief description.

Consider the singular integral equation

$$(4.47)\qquad a(t)\phi(t) + b(t)\frac{1}{\pi i}\int_\Gamma \frac{\phi(\tau)}{t-\tau}\,d\tau = f(t), \quad t\in\Gamma.$$

Here Γ consists of a finite number of disjoint smooth simple Jordan curves, a and b are given continuous $n\times n$ matrix functions defined on Γ, and f is a given function from $L_p^n(\Gamma)$, p fixed, $1 < p < \infty$. As usual in the theory of singular integral equations, it is assumed that the inner domain F_+ of Γ is connected and contains 0, while the outer domain F_- of Γ contains ∞. The problem is to find $\phi \in L_p^n(\Gamma)$ such that (4.47) is satisfied.

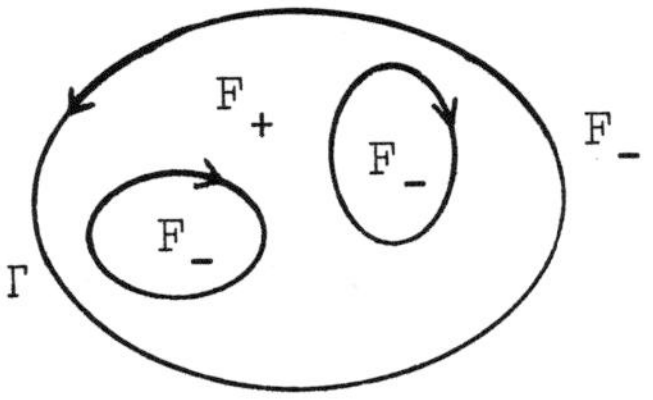

For ϕ a rational function without poles on Γ, we put

$$(S\phi)(t) = \frac{1}{\pi i} \int_\Gamma \frac{\phi(\tau)}{t-\tau}\, d\tau, \quad t \in \Gamma,$$

where the integral is taken in the sense of the Cauchy principal value. The operator S defined in this way can be extended by continuity to a bounded linear operator, again denoted by S, on all of $L_p^n(\Gamma)$. Equation (4.47) can now be written as

$$aI\phi + bS\phi = f. \tag{4.48}$$

In other words, the study of the equation (4.47) reduces to that of the operator $aI + bS$. Here a and b are viewed as multiplication operators. Equation (4.47) has a unique solution $\phi \in L_p^n(\Gamma)$ for each choice of $f \in L_p^n$ if and only if the operator $aI + bS$ is invertible. In the remainder of this section we shall discuss a necessary and sufficient condition for this to happen and we shall give formulas for $(aI + bS)^{-1}$.

The operator S enjoys the property that $S^2 = I$. Hence $P_\Gamma = \frac{1}{2}(I + S)$ and $Q_\Gamma = \frac{1}{2}(I - S)$ are complementary projections. The image of P_Γ consists of all functions in $L_p^n(\Gamma)$ that admit an analytic continuation into F_+. Similarly, the image of Q_Γ is the set of all functions in $L_p^n(\Gamma)$ that admit an analytic continuation into F_- vanishing at ∞. Putting $c = a + b$ and $d = a - b$, one can rewrite the equation (4.48) in the form

$$cP_\Gamma\phi + dQ_\Gamma\phi = f.$$

The following is known: The operator $aI + bS = cP_\Gamma + d\phi_\Gamma$ is invertible if and only if $c(\lambda)$ and $d(\lambda)$ are invertible for all $\lambda \in \Gamma$ and $w(\lambda) = d^{-1}(\lambda)c(\lambda)$ admits a right canonical factorization with respect to Γ.

Suppose these conditions are satisfied and

$$w(\lambda) = w_-(\lambda)w_+(\lambda), \quad \lambda \in \Gamma,$$

is such a factorization. Then clearly

$$aI + bS = dw_-(w_+P_\Gamma + w_-^{-1}Q_\Gamma),$$

and the inverse of $aI + bS$ is given by

$$\begin{aligned}(aI + bS)^{-1} &= (w_+^{-1}P_\Gamma + w_-Q_\Gamma)w_-^{-1}d^{-1} \\ &= w_+^{-1}P_\Gamma\, w_-^{-1}d^{-1} + w_-Q_\Gamma w_-^{-1}d^{-1}.\end{aligned}$$

Replacing P_Γ and Q_Γ by $\frac{1}{2}(I + S)$ and $\frac{1}{2}(I - S)$, respectively, one gets

$$\begin{aligned}(aI + bS)^{-1} &= \tfrac{1}{2}(c^{-1} + d^{-1})I + \tfrac{1}{2}(w_+^{-1} - w_-)S\, w_-^{-1}d^{-1} \\ &= \tfrac{1}{2}[(a + b)^{-1} + (a - b)^{-1}]I + \tfrac{1}{2}(w_+^{-1} - w_-)S\, w_-^{-1}(a - b)^{-1} \\ &= (a + b)^{-1}a(a - b)^{-1}I + \tfrac{1}{2}(w_+^{-1} - w_-)S\, w_-^{-1}(a - b)^{-1}.\end{aligned}$$

The next theorem deals with the case when $w(\lambda)$ is rational and has the value I_n at ∞.

THEOREM 4.12. (1) *The operator* $aI + bS$ *is invertible if and only if* $\det[a(\lambda) + b(\lambda)]$ *and* $\det[a(\lambda) - b(\lambda)]$ *do not vanish on* Γ *and* $w(\lambda) = [a(\lambda) - b(\lambda)]^{-1}[a(\lambda) + b(\lambda)]$ *admits a right canonical factorization with respect to* Γ.

(2) *Suppose* $\det[a(\lambda)+b(\lambda)]$ *and* $\det[a(\lambda)-b(\lambda)]$ *do not vanish on* Γ, *and* $w(\lambda) = [a(\lambda)-b(\lambda)]^{-1}\cdot[a(\lambda)+b(\lambda)]$ *is a rational function whose value at* ∞ *is* I_n. *Let*

$$w(\lambda) = I_n + C(\lambda I_\delta - A)^{-1}B$$

be a minimal realization for $w(\lambda)$, *and let* $A^\times = A - BC$. *Then* $aI + bS$ *is invertible if and only if* $\mathbb{C}^\delta = M \oplus M^\times$, *where* $M(M^\times)$ *is the spectral subspace corresponding to the eigenvalues of* $A(A^\times)$ *inside (outside)* Γ. *In that case the functions* w_+, w_+^{-1}, w_- *and* w_-^{-1} *appearing in the expressions for* $(aI + bS)^{-1}$ *can be specified as follows*:

$$w_+(\lambda) = I_n + C\Pi(\lambda - A)^{-1}B,$$

$$w_-(\lambda) = I_n + C(\lambda - A)^{-1}(I - \Pi)B,$$

$$w_+^{-}(\lambda) = I_n - C(\lambda - A^\times)^{-1}\Pi B,$$

$$w_-^{-1}(\lambda) = I_n - C(I - \Pi)(\lambda - A^\times)^{-1}B.$$

Here Π *is the projection of* $\mathbb{C}^\delta$ *along* M *onto* $M^\times$.

By way of illustration, we consider the important special case when

$$f(t) = \frac{1}{t-\alpha}[a(t) - b(t)]\eta,$$

where α is a complex number outside Γ and $\eta \in \mathbb{C}^n$. Put

$$g(t) = \frac{1}{t-\alpha}\eta.$$

Then one can write $f = dg$, where as before $d = a - b$. Hence $w_-^{-1}d^{-1}f = w_-^{-1}g$. Observe now that the function

$$\frac{1}{t-\alpha}\,[w_-^{-1}(t) - w_-^{-1}(\alpha)]\,\eta$$

is analytic outside Γ and vanishes at ∞. So if we apply P_Γ to it we get zero. It follows that

$$(P_\Gamma w_-^{-1} g)(t) = \frac{1}{t-\alpha}\, w_-^{-1}(\alpha)\,\eta.$$

But then

$$(Q_\Gamma w_-^{-1} g)(t) = \frac{1}{t-\alpha}\,[w_-^{-1}(t) - w_-^{-1}(\alpha)]\,\eta,$$

and hence

$$[(aI + bS)^{-1} f](t) = \frac{1}{t-\alpha}\, w_+^{-1}(t)\, w_-^{-1}(\alpha)\eta + \\ + \frac{1}{t-\alpha}\,[I_n - w_-(t) w_-^{-1}(\alpha)]\,\eta.$$

In the situation of Theorem 4.12 (2), the right hand side of this equality becomes

$$\frac{1}{t-\alpha}\,\eta - \frac{1}{t-\alpha}\, C[(t - A^\times)^{-1}\Pi + (t - A)^{-1}(I - \Pi)]B\ . \\ .\ [I_n - C(I - \Pi)(\alpha - A^\times)^{-1}B]\,\eta.$$

The case when $w(\lambda)$ is rational, but does not have the value I_n at ∞, can be treated by applying a suitable Möbius transformation. The argument is similar to that presented at the end of Section 4.6.

Chapter V

DIVISIBILITY AND RICCATI EQUATION

5.1 Angular subspaces and angular operators

Throughout this section X is a complex Banach space and Π is a projection of X onto X_2 along X_1. Matrix representations of operators acting on X will always be taken with respect to the decomposition $X = X_1 \oplus X_2$.

A closed subspace N of X is called _angular_ (with respect to Π) if $X = \operatorname{Ker} \Pi \oplus N$. If R is a bounded linear operator from X_2 into X_1, then the space

$$N_R = \{Rx+x \mid x \in X_2\}$$

is angular with respect to Π. The next proposition shows that any angular subspace is of this form.

PROPOSITION 5.1. _Let_ N _be a closed subspace of_ X. _Then_ N _is angular with respect to_ Π _if and only if_ $N = N_R$ _for some bounded linear operator_ R _from_ X_2 _into_ X_1.

PROOF. If $N = N_R$, then one checks easily that N is angular. To prove the converse, assume that N is angular with respect to Π, and let Q be the projection of X onto N along X_1. Put $Rx = (Q-\Pi)x$ for $x \in X_2$. Then $N = N_R$.

The operator R appearing in the preceding proposition is uniquely determined. It is called the _angular operator_ for N. The notion has been introduced by M.G. Krein in [40]. In this section we shall describe a few different ways to express the angular operator.

PROPOSITION 5.2. _Let_ N _be a closed subspace of_ X. _Then_ N _is angular with respect to_ Π _if and only if the restriction_ $\Pi|_N : N \to X_2$ _is bijective, and in that case the angular operator_

R *for* N *is given by*

$$(5.1) \qquad Rx = (I-\Pi)(\Pi|_N)^{-1}x \ , \ x\in X_2.$$

PROOF. Suppose that N is angular with angular operator R. The bijectivity of $\Pi|_N$ is clear from the fact that $\Pi(Rx+x)=x$ for all $x\in X_2$.

Next, assume that $\Pi|_N$ is bijective and define R by (5.1). We shall prove that $N = N_R$. First, take $x\in X_2$. Then $Rx+x = (\Pi|_N)^{-1}x\in N$, and hence $N_R\subset N$. Conversely, if $u\in N$, then $v = \Pi u\in X_2$ and $Rv+v = u$. It follows that $N\subset N_R$, and the proof is complete.

PROPOSITION 5.3. *Let*

$$S = \begin{bmatrix} S_{11} & S_{12} \\ S_{21} & S_{22} \end{bmatrix}$$

be an invertible bounded linear operator on X. *Then* SX_2 *is angular with respect to* Π *if and only if* S_{22} *is bijective, and in that case* $R = S_{12}S_{22}^{-1}$ *is its angular operator.*

PROOF. Put $N = SX_2$, and let S_0 be the restriction of S to X_2 considered as an operator from X_2 into N. Then S_0 is bijective. Also, let $\Pi|_N$ be the restriction of Π to N considered as an operator into X_2. Since $(\Pi|_N)\circ S_0 = S_{22}$, we see that $\Pi|_N$ is bijective if and only if this is the case for S_{22}. Apply now the previous proposition and use that $(I-\Pi)S_0u = S_{12}u$ for each $u\in X_2$.

PROPOSITION 5.4. *Let* P *be a projection of* X. *Then* Ker P *is angular with respect to* Π *if and only if the restriction*

$P|_{\operatorname{Ker}\Pi} : \operatorname{Ker}\Pi \to \operatorname{Im} P$ _is bijective, and in that case the angular operator_ R _for_ Ker P _is given by_

$$(5.2) \qquad Rx = -(P|_{\operatorname{Ker}\Pi})^{-1}Px \ , \ x \in X_2.$$

PROOF. Observe that Ker P is angular with respect to Π if and only if Ker Π is angular with respect to P. So the first part of the theorem follows by applying Proposition 5.2 to Ker Π and P.

Next, assume that $P|_{\operatorname{Ker}\Pi}$ is bijective. To determine the angular operator R for Ker P, note that

$$0 = P(Rx+x) = (P|_{\operatorname{Ker}\Pi})Rx + Px$$

for each $x \in X_2$. From this, formula (5.2) is clear.

To factorize a node $\theta = (A,B,C,D;X,Y)$ with invertible external operator D, one has to look for two closed subspaces N_1 and N_2 of X such that N_1 is invariant under A and N_2 is invariant under $A^{\times}$. Such a pair of subspaces yields a factorization of θ if $X = N_1 \oplus N_2$ (cf. Theorem 1.1). For this reason we include the following lemma:

LEMMA 5.5. _Let_ N_1 _and_ N_2 _be closed subspaces of_ X _such that_

$$(5.3) \qquad X = X_1 \oplus N_2 = N_1 \oplus X_2.$$

In other words N_2 _is angular with respect to_ Π _and_ N_1 _is angular with respect to_ $I-\Pi$. _Let_ $R_{12}: X_2 \to X_1$ _and_ $R_{21}: X_1 \to X_2$ _be the corresponding angular operators. Then the following statements are equivalent._

(i) $X = N_1 \oplus N_2$;

(ii) $I - R_{21} R_{12}$ _is invertible_;

(iii) $I - R_{12}R_{21}$ <u>is invertible</u>;

(iv) $F = \begin{bmatrix} I & R_{12} \\ R_{21} & I \end{bmatrix}$ <u>is invertible</u>.

PROOF. The equivalence of (ii), (iii) and (iv) is an immediate consequence of Remark 1.2. Observe that F maps $X_1(X_2)$ in a one-one manner onto $N_1(N_2)$. As $X = X_1 \oplus X_2$, it is clear that $X = N_1 \oplus N_2$ if and only if F is invertible. So (i) and (iv) are equivalent, and the proof is complete.

Let N_1 and N_2 be as in Lemma 5.5, and assume that the operator F introduced in Lemma 5.5 is invertible. Then $X = N_1 \oplus N_2$, and so we have a projection Q from X onto N_2 along N_1. It is not difficult to show that

$$F^{-1} = (I-\Pi)(I-Q) + \Pi Q.$$

Conversely, assume that N_1 and N_2 are closed subspaces of X such that $X = N_1 \oplus N_2$, and let Q be the projection of X onto N_2 along N_1. Then the invertibility of the map $(I-\Pi)(I-Q) + \Pi Q$ implies that (5.3) holds. A case of this type we shall meet in Section 6.4

5.2 Angular operator and the division theorem

In this section we use the concepts introduced in the previous section to bring the division theorem for nodes in a somewhat different form. The main point is that throughout we work with a fixed decomposition $X = X_1 \oplus X_2$ of the state space X of the node that has to be factorized and the factors are described with respect to this decomposition. In the finite dimensional case this corresponds to working with a fixed coordinate system.

THEOREM 5.6. <u>Let</u> $\theta = (A,B,C,D;X,Y)$ <u>be a node with an</u>

invertible external operator D, *let* Π *be a projection of* X *onto* X_2 *along* X_1, *and let* N *be an angular subspace of* X *with respect to* Π. *Assume that*

$$A X_1 \subset X_1 \ , \ A^{\times} N \subset N \tag{5.4}$$

and $D = D_1 D_2$ *with* D_1 *and* D_2 *invertible operators on* Y. *Let*

$$A = \begin{pmatrix} A_{11} & A_{12} \\ A_{21} & A_{22} \end{pmatrix}, \quad B = \begin{pmatrix} B_1 \\ B_2 \end{pmatrix}, \quad C = [C_1 \quad C_2]$$

be the matrix representations of A, B *and* C *with respect to the decomposition* $X = X_1 \oplus X_2$, *let* R *be the angular operator for* N *with respect to* Π, *and put*

$$\theta_1 = (A_{11}, (B_1 - RB_2)D_2^{-1}, C_1, D_1; X_1, Y),$$

$$\theta_2 = (A_{22}, B_2, D_1^{-1}(C_1 R + C_2), D_2, X_2, Y).$$

Then $\theta \simeq \theta_1\theta_2$. *More precisely*

$$\theta_1\theta_2 = (E^{-1}AE,\ E^{-1}B,\ CE,\ D; X, Y),$$

where E *is the invertible operator*

$$E = \begin{pmatrix} I & R \\ 0 & I \end{pmatrix}.$$

PROOF. For conveninece, put $\hat{A} = E^{-1}AE$, $\hat{B} = E^{-1}B$, $\hat{C} = CE$ and $\hat{\theta} = (\hat{A}, \hat{B}, \hat{C}, D; X, Y)$. Observe that $\hat{A}^{\times} = E^{-1}A^{\times}E$. Now E maps X_1 onto X_1 and X_2 onto N. Thus (5.4) implies that

$$\hat{A}\, X_1 \subset X_1, \quad \hat{A}^{\times} X_2 \subset X_2.$$

Apply now Theorem 1.1 to show that $\hat{\theta} = \hat{\theta}_1\hat{\theta}_2$, where

$$\hat{\theta}_1 = (\hat{A}_{11}, \hat{B}_1 D_2^{-1}, \hat{C}_1, D_1; X_1, Y),$$

$$\hat{\theta}_2 = (\hat{A}_{22}, \hat{B}_2, D_1^{-1}\hat{C}_2, D_2; X_2, Y).$$

But $\hat{\theta}_1 = \theta_1$ and $\hat{\theta}_2 = \theta_2$, and the proof is complete.

Suppose that the angular subspace N in Theorem 5.6 is the image of X_2 under the invertible operator S on X. Then we know from Proposition 5.3 that S_{22} is invertible and the angular operator R for N is given by $R = S_{12}S_{22}^{-1}$. So then the formulas for θ_1 and θ_2 become

$$\theta_1 = (A_{11}, (B_1 - S_{12}S_{22}^{-1}B_2)D_2^{-1}, C_1, D_1; X_1, Y),$$

$$\theta_2 = (A_{22}, B_2, D_1^{-1}(C_1S_{12}S_{22}^{-1} + C_2)D_2; X_2, Y).$$

For the particular case when $D = D_1 = D_2 = I$, we get

$$\theta_1 = (A_{11}, B_1 - S_{12}S_{22}^{-1}B_2, C_1; X_1, Y), \tag{5.5}$$

$$\theta_2 = (A_{22}, B_2, C_1S_{12}S_{22}^{-1} + C_2; X_2, Y). \tag{5.6}$$

We shall use this to prove the following node analogue of Theorem 4 in Sahnovic paper [45] (see also [38]).

COROLLARY 5.7. *Let* $\theta = (A,B,C;X,Y)$ *and* $\tilde{\theta} = (\tilde{A},\tilde{B},\tilde{C};X,Y)$ *be nodes such that*

$$AS - S\tilde{A} = B\tilde{C}, \quad S\tilde{B} = B, \quad CS = \tilde{C} \tag{5.7}$$

for some operator $S: X \to X$. *Let* Π *be a projection of* X *onto* X_2 *along* X_1, *and assume*

$$AX_1 \subset X_1, \quad \tilde{A}X_2 \subset X_2.$$

If the operators $S:X \to X$ and $S_{22} = \Pi S \Pi : X_2 \to X_2$ are invertible, then $\theta \simeq \theta_1\theta_2$, where θ_1 and θ_2 are given by (5.5) and (5.6), respectively.

PROOF. Formula (5.7) and the invertibility of S imply that the associate node $\theta^\times$ and $\tilde{\theta}$ are similar, the similarity being given by S. As

$$S^{-1}(A^\times)S = S^{-1}AS - S^{-1}BCS = \tilde{A},$$

the space $N = SX_2$ is invariant under $A^\times$. The fact that S_{22} is invertible implies that N is angular with respect to Π. But then the remarks made in the paragraph preceding this corollary yield the desired factorization.

The next theorem is the symmetric version of Theorem 5.6.

THEOREM 5.8. Let $\theta = (A,B,C,D;X,Y)$ be a node with an invertible external operator, let Π be a projection of X onto X_2 along X_1. Further, let N_1 and N_2 be closed subspaces of X such that

$$X = X_1 \oplus N_2 = N_1 \oplus X_2,$$

and let $R_{12}:X_2 \to X_1$ and $R_{21}:X_1 \to X_2$ be the corresponding angular operators. Assume that

$$X = N_1 \oplus N_2 \ , \ AN_1 \subset N_1 \ , \ A^\times N_2 \subset N_2, \tag{5.8}$$

and $D = D_1D_2$ with D_1 and D_2 invertible operators on Y. Let

$$A = \begin{pmatrix} A_{11} & A_{12} \\ A_{21} & A_{22} \end{pmatrix}, \quad B = \begin{pmatrix} B_1 \\ B_2 \end{pmatrix}, \quad C = [C_1 \ \ C_2]$$

be the matrix representations of A, B and C with respect to the decomposition $X = X_1 \oplus X_2$. For $i = 1,2$, put

$$\theta_i = (A_i, B_i, C_i, D_i, X_i, Y),$$

with

$$A_1 = R(A_{11}+A_{12}R_{21}-R_{12}A_{21}-R_{12}A_{22}R_{21}),$$

$$B_1 = R(B_1-R_{12}B_2)D_2^{-1},$$

$$C_1 = C_1 + C_2R_{21},$$

$$A_2 = R_{21}R(-A_{11}R_{12}-A_{12}+R_{12}A_{21}R_{12}+R_{12}A_{22}) + A_{21}R_{12}+A_{22},$$

$$B_2 = -R_{21}RB_1+R_{21}RR_{12}B_2+B_2,$$

$$C_2 = D_1^{-1}(C_1R_{12}+C_2),$$

where $R = (I-R_{12}R_{21})^{-1}$. *Then* $\theta \simeq \theta_1\theta_2$. *More precisely*

$$\theta_1\theta_2 = (F^{-1}AF, F^{-1}B, CF, D; X, Y),$$

where F *is the operator*

$$F = \begin{pmatrix} I & R_{12} \\ R_{21} & I \end{pmatrix}.$$

PROOF. From Lemma 5.5 and the fact that $X = N_1 \oplus N_2$ it follows that F is invertible. Also $I-R_{12}R_{21}$ is invertible, and so $R = (I-R_{12}R_{21})^{-1}$ is well-defined. From Remark 1.2 we see that

$$F^{-1} = \begin{pmatrix} R & -RR_{12} \\ -R_{21}R & R_{21}RR_{12}+I \end{pmatrix}. \tag{5.9}$$

Put $\hat{A} = F^{-1}AF$, $\hat{B} = F^{-1}B$, $\hat{C} = CF$ and $\hat{\theta} = (\hat{A},\hat{B},\hat{C},D;X,Y)$. Observe that $\hat{A}^{\times} = F^{-1}A^{\times}F$. Now F maps X_1 onto N_1 and X_2 onto N_2. Thus (5.8) implies that

$$\hat{A}X_1 \subset X_1 \ , \ \hat{A}^{\times}X_2 \subset X_2 .$$

Apply Theorem 1.1 to show that $\hat{\theta} = \hat{\theta}_1\hat{\theta}_2$, where

$$\hat{\theta}_1 = (\hat{A}_{11},\hat{B}_1 D_2^{-1},\hat{C}_1,D_1;X_1,Y),$$

$$\hat{\theta}_2 = (\hat{A}_{22},\hat{B}_2,D_1^{-1}\hat{C}_2,D_2;X_2,Y).$$

Using (5.9), a simple computation shows that $\hat{\theta}_1 = \theta_1$ and $\hat{\theta}_2 = \theta_2$, and the proof is complete.

5.3 The Riccati equation

As in the previous sections X is a complex Banach space and Π is a projection of X onto X_2 along X_1. In view of Theorem 5.6 the following question is of interest. Given an angular subspace N of X and an operator T on X, when is N invariant under T. The next proposition shows that the answer involves an operator Riccati equation.

PROPOSITION 5.9. Let N be an angular subspace of X with respect to Π, and let

$$T = \begin{pmatrix} T_{11} & T_{12} \\ T_{21} & T_{21} \end{pmatrix} : X_1 \oplus X_2 \to X_1 \oplus X_2$$

be an operator on X. Then N is invariant under T if and only if the angular operator R for N satisfies the Riccati equation

$$RT_{21}R + RT_{22} - T_{11}R - T_{12} = 0. \qquad (5.10)$$

PROOF. The operator

$$E = \begin{pmatrix} I & R \\ 0 & I \end{pmatrix} : X_1 \oplus X_2 \to X_1 \oplus X_2$$

is invertible and maps X_2 onto N. So

$$(5.11) \qquad E^{-1}TE = \begin{pmatrix} T_{11} - RT_{21} & -RT_{21}R - RT_{22} + T_{11}R + T_{12} \\ T_{21} & T_{22} + T_{21}R \end{pmatrix}$$

leaves X_2 invariant if and only if T leaves N invariant. But $E^{-1}TE$ leaves X_2 invariant if and only if (5.10) is satisfied, and the proof is complete.

In view of formula (1.3) and Theorem 5.6, the problem of finding factorizations for transfer functions or nodes is related to that of solving a certain Riccati operator equation. As a matter of fact, in the situation of Theorem 5.6, the condition that $A^{\times}N \subset N$ is equivalent to the requirement that

$$RA_{21}^{\times}R + RA_{22}^{\times} - A_{11}^{\times}R - A_{12}^{\times} = 0.$$

Using the fact that $A^{\times} = A - BD^{-1}C$ and $A_{21} = 0$, this equation may be written as

$$RB_2D^{-1}C_1R + R(B_2D^{-1}C_2 - A_{22}) + (A_{11} - B_1D^{-1}C_1)R +$$

$$+ A_{12} - B_1D^{-1}C_2 = 0.$$

In Chapter 7 the space N in Theorem 5.6 will often be a spectral subspace for $A^{\times}$. For this reason we include the following proposition

PROPOSITION 5.10. *Let* N *be an angular subspace of* X *with respect to* Π, *and let*

$$T = \begin{bmatrix} T_{11} & T_{12} \\ T_{21} & T_{22} \end{bmatrix} : X_1 \oplus X_2 \to X_1 \oplus X_2$$

be an operator on X. *Then* N *is a spectral subspace for* T *if and only if the angular operator* R *for* N *satisfies the Riccati equation* (5.10) *and*

$$\sigma(T_{11} - RT_{21}) \cap \sigma(T_{22} + T_{21}R) = \phi .$$

In fact, if $N = \operatorname{Im} P(T;\Gamma)$, *where* Γ *is a Cauchy contour that splits the spectrum of* T, *then* $\sigma(T_{22}+T_{21}R)$ *is inside* Γ *and* $\sigma(T_{11}-RT_{21})$ *is outside* Γ.

PROOF. Define E as in the proof of Proposition 5.9. It is clear that N is a spectral subspace for T if and only if X_2 is a spectral subspace for $E^{-1}TE$. But then we can apply Lemma 1.4 to get the desired result.

Chapter VI

APPLICATION TO TRANSPORT EQUATION

In this chapter the division theory developed in the previous chapters is applied to solve the transport equation. It is known that the transport equation may be transformed into a Wiener-Hopf integral equation with an operator valued kernel (see [17]). An equation of the latter type can be solved explicitly if a certain spectral factorization of its symbol is available (cf. Section 4.5). In our case the symbol may be represented as a transfer function, and to make the spectral factorization the general division theorem of the first chapter may be applied. A new difficulty is that in this case the curve cuts through the spectra of the main operator and the associate main operator. Nevertheless, due to the special structure of the operators involved, the factorization can be made and explicit formulas are obtained. Since our main purpose is to show how our method works we restrict ourselves to the case of a degenerate kernel.

According to the division theorem to make the factorization it is necessary to find the appropriate pair of invariant subspaces. In this case the choice of the subspaces is evident, but to prove that their direct sum is the whole space requires some effort. In fact, the matching of the subspaces was recently proved in [33,34,35] in connection with another method to solve the transport equation. In [33,34,42] one can also find analytic descriptions for the subspaces concerned.

For a general text about the transport equation see K.M. Case and P.F. Zweifel, Linear Transport Theory. Reading, Mass., Addison-Wesley, 1967.

6.1 The transport equation

For the plane symmetric case the mathematical equation describing the transport of energy through a medium is an integral-differential equation of the following form:

$$(6.1)\qquad \mu\frac{\partial\psi(x,\mu)}{\partial x} + \psi(x,\mu) = \int_{-1}^{1} k(\mu,\mu')\psi(x,\mu')d\mu', \quad 0\leq x<\infty .$$

The kernel $k(\mu,\mu')$ is a given real-valued and symmetric L_1-function on $-1\leq\mu,\mu'\leq 1$. Throughout this chapter (cf. [34,35,42]) we assume that

$$(6.2)\qquad k(\mu,\mu') = \sum_{j=0}^{n} a_j p_j(\mu)p_j(\mu'),$$

where $p_j(\mu)$ is the j-th normalized Legendre polynomial and

$$(6.3)\qquad -\infty < a_j < 1 \quad , \quad j = 0,1,\ldots,n.$$

The problem is to solve (6.1) under the boundary conditions:

$$(6.4)\qquad \begin{cases} \lim\limits_{x\to\infty} \psi(x,\mu)\exp(\frac{x}{\mu}) = 0 \ , & -1\leq\mu<0, \\ \psi(0,\mu) = f_+(\mu) \ , & 0\leq\mu\leq-1. \end{cases}$$

Here f_+ is a given function.

By writing $\psi(x)(\mu) = \psi(x,\mu)$, we may consider the unknown function ψ as a vector function on $[0,\infty)$ with values in $H = L^2[-1,1]$. In this way equation (6.1) can be written as an operator differential equation:

$$(6.5)\qquad T\frac{d\psi}{dx}(x) + \psi(x) = B_0\psi(x) \ , \quad 0\leq x<\infty,$$

where the derivative is taken with respect to the norm in H. In (6.5) the operators T and B_0 are defined by

$$(6.6)\qquad (Tf)(\mu) = \mu f(\mu) \ , \quad B_0 f = \sum_{j=0}^{n} a_j (f,p_j)p_j .$$

Because of (6.3), the operator $I-B_0$ is strictly positive, and hence (6.5) is equivalent to

$$[I-B_0]^{-1}T\,\frac{d\psi}{dx} = -\psi .$$

In [33,35,42] this equation is solved by diagonalizing the operator $[I-B_0]^{-1}T$.

Equation (6.1) with boundary conditions (6.4) can also be written as a Wiener-Hopf integral equation with an operator valued kernel (cf. [17]). In order to do this, let us introduce some notation. By $P_+(P_-)$ we denote the orthogonal projection of $H = L^2[-1,1]$ onto the subspace $H_+(H_-)$ consisting of all functions that are zero almost everywhere on [-1,0] ([0,1]). Further, h(x) will be the operator-valued function defined by

$$(h(x)f)(\mu) = \begin{cases} \frac{1}{\mu}\exp(-\frac{x}{\mu})(P_+B_0f)(\mu) & \text{for } x > 0, \\ -\frac{1}{\mu}\exp(-\frac{x}{\mu})(P_-B_0f)(\mu) & \text{for } x < 0, \end{cases}$$

and F(x) is the vector-valued function given by

$$F(x)(\mu) = \begin{cases} f_+(\mu)\exp(-\frac{x}{\mu}) & \text{for } 0<\mu\leq+1, \\ 0 & \text{for } -1\leq\mu\leq 0. \end{cases}$$

Then equation (6.1) with the boundary condition (6.3) can be written as

$$\psi(x) - \int_0^\infty h(x-y)\psi(y)dy = F(x) \ , \ 0\leqslant x<\infty. \tag{6.7}$$

To see this one multiplies equation (6.1) by $\frac{1}{\mu}\exp(\frac{x}{\mu})$ and integrates over (0,x) if $\mu > 0$ or over (x,∞) whenever $\mu<0$. Using the boundary conditions one gets in this way the integral equation (6.7). In [17] the asymptotics of solutions of equation (6.7) are found and used to describe the asymptotics of solutions of the transport equation.

6.2 Wiener-Hopf equations with operator-valued L_1-kernels

It is well-known that the Wiener-Hopf integral equation:

(6.8) $$\psi(x) - \int_0^\infty k(x-y)\psi(y)dy = F(x)\ ,\ 0\leq x<\infty,$$

may be solved by constructing certain factorizations of its symbol (cf. Section 4.5 and [18,28]. In this section we shall describe this method for the case that $k(\cdot)$ is an L_1-kernel whose values are compact operators on a separable Hilbert space H. So we assume that $k(t)$ is a compact operator for each $-\infty<t<\infty$, that $(k(\cdot)f,g)$ is measurable on the real line for each f and g in H and that

$$\int_{-\infty}^{\infty} \|k(t)\|dt < \infty.$$

Note that the kernel $h(\cdot)$ considered in the previous section falls into this category.

By definition the symbol of equation (6.8) is the function $I-K(\lambda)$, where $K(\lambda)$ is the Fourier transform of the kernel $k(\cdot)$, i.e.,

$$K(\lambda) = \int_{-\infty}^{\infty} k(x)e^{i\lambda x}dx\ ,\ -\infty\leq\lambda\leq+\infty\ .$$

We say that the symbol admits a (right) Wiener-Hopf factorization with respect to the real line if

(6.9) $$I-K(\lambda) = \tilde{G}_-(\lambda)\{P_0+\sum_{\nu=1}^{n}\left(\frac{\lambda-i}{\lambda+i}\right)^{\kappa_\nu}P_\nu\}\tilde{G}_+(\lambda),$$

for $-\infty\leq\lambda\leq\infty$. Here, by definition, $P_1,\ldots,P_n$ are mutually disjoint projections of H of rank one and $P_0+P_1+\ldots+P_n$ is the identity on H. The operator functions $\tilde{G}_-$ and $\tilde{G}_+$ are holomorphic inside (infinity included) and continuous up to the boundary in the half-planes $\operatorname{Im}\lambda\leq 0$ and $\operatorname{Im}\lambda\geq 0$, respectively. Further $\tilde{G}_-(\lambda)$ is an invertible operator on H for $\operatorname{Im}\lambda\leq 0$ and the same is true for $\tilde{G}_+(\lambda)$ for $\operatorname{Im}\lambda\geq 0$. The numbers $\kappa_1,\ldots,\kappa_n$ are integers which are called the (right) partial indices. If all partial indices are zero the factorization (6.9) is called canonical. According to [18], because of the fact that $k(\cdot)$ is an L_1-kernel whose values are compact operators on H, the factorization (6.9) can always be made, while moreover $\tilde{G}_+(\lambda)^{-1}$ and $\tilde{G}_-(\lambda)^{-1}$ can be written as

$$(6.10)\quad \tilde{G}_+(\lambda)^{-1} = I+\int_0^\infty \gamma_1(t)e^{i\lambda t} , \quad \tilde{G}_-(\lambda)^{-1} = I+\int_{-\infty}^0 \gamma_2(t)e^{i\lambda t}dt.$$

Here, γ_1 and γ_2 are L_1-functions on $(0,\infty)$ and $(-\infty,0)$, respectively, whose values are compact operators on H.

Let $L^2(\mathbb{R}_+,H)$ denote the space of all L^2-integrable functions on $[0,\infty)$ with values in H. The identities (6.10) are important, because they allow for explicit formulas for the solutions of (6.8) in the case when all partial indices are zero. Indeed, by [18] equation (6.8) has a unique solution ψ in $L^2(\mathbb{R}_+,H)$ for each $F\in L^2(\mathbb{R}_+,H)$ if and only if in (6.9) all partial indices are zero, and in that case (cf. Section 4.5)

$$\psi(x) = F(x) + \int_0^\infty \gamma(x,t)F(t)dt,$$

where

$$\gamma(x,t) = \gamma_1(x-t) + \gamma_2(t-x) + \int_0^{\min(x,t)} \gamma_1(x-s)\gamma_2(s-t)ds.$$

As we observed already, in (6.7) the kernel $h(\cdot)$ is an L_1-function on the real line whose values are compact (in fact finite rank) operators on $L^2[-1,1]$. In the next section we shall prove that the corresponding symbol admits a Wiener-Hopf factorization with zero partial indices, and we shall describe the factors explicitly.

6.3 Construction of the Wiener-Hopf factorization

We now return to equation (6.7). Note that its symbol is given by $I-H(\lambda)$, where

$$H(\lambda) = \int_{-\infty}^{\infty} e^{i\lambda t} h(t) B_0 dt = (I - i\lambda T)^{-1} B_0.$$

Here T and B_0 are as in formula (6.6). The operator function $H(\lambda)$ is analytic on the strip $|\mathrm{Im}\ \lambda| < 1$. In this section we show that $I-H(\lambda)$ admits a canonical Wiener-Hopf factorization with respect to the real line. In fact we shall prove that

$$I-H(\lambda) = G_-(\lambda)G_+(\lambda), \quad -\infty \leq \lambda \leq \infty,$$

where

$$G_-(\lambda) = I-(I-i\lambda T)^{-1}(I-P)B_0(I-PB_0)^{-1},$$

$$G_+(\lambda) = I-(I-Q^*B_0)^{-1}[(I+i\bar{\lambda}T)^{-1}(I-Q)]^*B_0,$$

$$G_-(\lambda)^{-1} = I+(I-Q^*B_0)^{-1}[(I+i\bar{\lambda}T^\times)^{-1}Q]^*B_0,$$

$$G_+(\lambda)^{-1} = I+(I-i\lambda T^\times)^{-1}PB_0(I-PB_0)^{-1}.$$

The operator $T^\times = (I-B_0)^{-1}T$ while P and Q are projections whose definition will be given below.

In order to make this factorization we replace λ by $(i\bar{\lambda})^{-1}$ and consider the operator function

$$W(\lambda) = [I-B_0]^{-1}[I-H((i\bar{\lambda})^{-1})]^*. \tag{6.11}$$

Recall that $I-B_0$ is a strictly positive operator because of the condition (6.3). So $[I-B_0]^{-1}$ exists and is a positive operator on $H = L^2[-1,1]$. As T and B_0 are both selfadjoint we have

$$\begin{aligned} W(\lambda) &= (I-B_0)^{-1}[I-B_0(I-\tfrac{1}{\lambda}T)^{-1}] \\ &= (I-B_0)^{-1}[I-\lambda B_0(\lambda-T)^{-1}] \\ &= I-B_0(I-B_0)^{-1}T(\lambda-T)^{-1}. \end{aligned}$$

So $W(\lambda)$ appears as the transfer function of the node

$$\theta = (T, I, -B_0(I-B_0)^{-1}T; H, H) .$$

In this case the associate main operator $T^\times = (I-B_0)^{-1}T$.

Our problem is that we have to make a right canonical Wiener-Hopf factorization of $W = W_\theta$ with respect to the imaginary axis. In terms of the division theory developed in Chapter I this means that we have to find subspaces M and $M^\times$ invariant under T and $T^\times$, respectively, such that $\sigma(T|_M)$ lies in the half-plane $\mathrm{Re}\,\lambda \geq 0$ and $\sigma(T^\times|_{M^\times})$ lies in the half-plane $\mathrm{Re}\,\lambda \leq 0$. Since T is self-adjoint the choice of the space M is clear, in fact we must take $M = H_+$. As we shall see below the operator $T^\times$ is (with respect to an equivalent inner product) self-adjoint too. So for $M^\times$ we have to take the spectral subspace of $T^\times$ corresponding to the part of the spectrum on $(-\infty, 0]$. The first difficulty is to prove the matching of the subspaces M and $M^\times$, i.e., to show that $H = M \oplus M^\times$. When this has been established a second difficulty appears, because in this case the imaginary axis does not split the spectra of T and $T^\times$. So we cannot apply Theorem 1.5, but we have to prove that the factors obtained by applying the first division theorem (i.e., Theorem 1.1) have the desired boundary behaviour. The purpose of this section is to show that this procedure works indeed. Here we use some calculations carried out by C. van der Mee.

We begin with some further information about $T^\times$. As $I-B_0$ is strictly positive, $[f,g] = ([I-B_0]f, g)$ defines an equivalent inner product on H. The space H endowed with this inner product we shall denote by H_0. If $A^\sim$ denotes the adjoint of an operator on the space H_0, then

$$A^\sim = [I-B_0]^{-1}A^*(I-B_0). \tag{6.12}$$

In particular, we see that the operator $T^\times$ is self-adjoint with respect to the inner product $[\cdot,\cdot]$. Let $F(t)$ be the corresponding spectral resolution. Put $H_m = \operatorname{Im} F(0)$ and $H_p = \operatorname{Ker} F(0)$. Then H_m and H_p are both invariant under $T^\times$ and

$$(6.13)\qquad \sigma(T^\times|_{H_m}) \subset (-\infty,0],\ \sigma(T^\times|_{H_p}) \subset [0,\infty).$$

The operator T is self-adjoint with the original inner product on H and T leaves invariant the spaces H_- and H_+. Further

$$(6.14)\qquad \sigma(T|_{H_-}) = [-1,0]\ ,\ \sigma(T|_{H_+}) = [0,1].$$

The matching of the subspaces M and $M^\times$ referred to above now means that we have to show that $H = H_+ \oplus H_m$. In [34] (cf. [35], Section 2) for a purpose different from the one here it has been proved that

$$(6.15)\qquad H = H_- \oplus H_p\ ,\quad H = H_+ \oplus H_m.$$

A proof of (6.15), somewhat different from the one given in [34], will be presented in the next section. Let $P(Q)$ be the projection of H along $H_-(H_+)$ onto $H_p(H_m)$. Since H_- and H_+ are invariant under T and H_m and H_p are invariant under $T^\times$, both P and Q are supporting projections for the node θ. Put

$$\Delta_1 = \mathrm{pr}_{I-P}(\theta)\ ,\ \Delta_2 = \mathrm{pr}_P(\theta),$$

$$\theta_1 = \mathrm{pr}_{I-Q}(\theta)\ ,\ \theta_2 = \mathrm{pr}_Q(\theta).$$

Then for λ outside $\sigma(T) = [-1,1]$ we have

$$(6.16)\qquad W(\lambda) = W_{\theta_1}(\lambda)W_{\theta_2}(\lambda)\ ,\quad W(\lambda) = W_{\Delta_1}(\lambda)W_{\Delta_2}(\lambda).$$

Both factorizations in (6.16) are canonical Wiener-Hopf factorizations of $W(\lambda)$ with respect to the imaginary axis. We shall prove this for the first factorization.

First let us write the nodes θ_1 and θ_2:

$$\theta_1 = (T|_{H_+}, I-Q, -B_0(I-B_0)^{-1}T|_{H_+}; H_+, H),$$

$$\theta_2 = (PT|_{H_m}, Q, -B_0(I-B_0)^{-1}T|_{H_m}; H_m, H).$$

As $\theta_1^\times = \mathrm{pr}_{I-Q}(\theta^\times)$ and $\theta_2^\times = \mathrm{pr}_Q(\theta^\times)$, we also have

$$\theta_1^\times = ((I-Q)T^\times|_{H_+}, I-Q, B_0(I-B_0)^{-1}T|_{H_+}; H_+, H),$$

$$\theta_2^\times = (T^\times|_{H_m}; Q, B_0(I-B_0)^{-1}T|_{H_m}; H_m, H).$$

The transfer functions of θ_1, $\theta_1^\times$, θ_2 and $\theta_2^\times$ are given by:

$$W_{\theta_1}(\lambda) = I-B_0(I-B_0)^{-1}T(\lambda I-T)^{-1}(I-Q),$$

$$W_{\theta_2}(\lambda) = I-B_0(I-B_0)^{-1}TQ(\lambda I-T)^{-1},$$

$$W_{\theta_1^\times}(\lambda) = I+B_0(I-B_0)^{-1}T(I-Q)(\lambda I-T^\times)^{-1},$$

$$W_{\theta_2^\times}(\lambda) = I+B_0(I-B_0)^{-1}T(\lambda I-T^\times)^{-1}Q.$$

As the main operator of θ_1 is equal to $T|_{H_+}$, we know from (6.14) that W_{θ_1} is analytic outside $[0,1]$. In particular, W_{θ_1} is analytic on the left half-plane $\mathrm{Re}\,\lambda < 0$. As $H = H_m \oplus H_+ = H_m \oplus H_p$, we may apply Lemma 1.4 to show that $(I-Q)T^\times|_{H_+}$ is similar to $T^\times|_{H_p}$. By (6.13) this implies that the spectrum of the main operator of $\theta_1^\times$ is on the half-line $[0,\infty)$. But then we may conclude that $W_{\theta_1}(\lambda)$ is invertible for $\mathrm{Re}\,\lambda < 0$. In a similar way one can prove that W_{θ_2} is analytic on the right half-plane $\mathrm{Re}\,\lambda > 0$ and on $\mathrm{Re}\,\lambda > 0$ the values of W_{θ_2} are invertible. So we have almost proved that the first factorization in (6.16) is a (right) canonical Wiener-Hopf factorization. To make the proof complete we have to investigate the behaviour of the functions on the imaginary axis. For this we need the following simple lemma about self-adjoint operators.

LEMMA 6.1. *Let* S *be a bounded self-adjoint operator. Then*

$$\|S(i\alpha-S)^{-1}\| \le 1 \ , \ 0\neq\alpha\in\mathbb{R}, \tag{6.17}$$

and for each $f \perp \operatorname{Ker} S$ *we have*

(i) $\lim\limits_{\alpha\to 0,\alpha\in\mathbb{R}} S(i\alpha-S)^{-1}f = -f,$

(ii) $\lim\limits_{\lambda\to 0,\mathrm{Re}\lambda\le 0} S(\lambda-S)^{-1}f = -f,$ *whenever* $S \ge 0$.

PROOF. Let $E(t)$ be the spectral resolution of the identity for S. Take f in the Hilbert space. Then

$$\|S(i\alpha-S)^{-1}f\|^2 \le \int \frac{t^2}{\alpha^2+t^2}\, d\|E(t)f\|^2$$

$$\le \int d\|E(t)f\|^2 = \|f\|^2.$$

This proves (6.17). Next, observe that

$$\|f+S(i\alpha-S)^{-1}f\|^2 \le \int \frac{\alpha^2}{\alpha^2+t^2}\, d\|E(t)f\|^2.$$

So by Lebesgue's dominated convergence theorem we get

$$\lim_{\substack{\alpha\to 0\\ \alpha\in\mathbb{R}}} \|f+S(i\alpha-S)^{-1}f\|^2 \le \|E(0+)f\|^2 - \|E(0-)f\|^2$$

$$= \|(E(0+) - E(0-))f\|^2,$$

which is zero if $f \perp \operatorname{Ker} S$. Hence (i) is proved. Finally, part (ii) is proved in exactly the same way as part (i).

As Ker T = (0), we see from Lemma 6.1 (i) that

$$T(i\alpha-T)^{-1}f \to -f \quad (\alpha\to 0,\ \alpha\in\mathbb{R})$$

for each $f\in H$. But if a sequence of operators converges in the strong operator topology, then the convergence is uniform on compact subsets of the underlying space. So, as B_0 has finite rank, we may conclude that $T(i\alpha-T)^{-1}B_0 \to -B_0$ in the operator norm if $\alpha \to 0$, $\alpha\in\mathbb{R}$. By taking adjoints we obtain that $B_0T(i\alpha-T)^{-1} \to -B_0$ in the operator norm if $\alpha \to 0$, $\alpha\in\mathbb{R}$. But then we see that in the operator norm

$$W(i\alpha) \longrightarrow [I-B_0]^{-1} \quad (\alpha\to 0,\ \alpha\in\mathbb{R}).$$

So we may view W as a continuous function on the imaginary axis all whose values are invertible operators on H. It is this operator function on $\operatorname{Re}\lambda = 0$ we want to factorize.

At each non-zero point of the imaginary axis the functions W_{θ_1}, W_{θ_2}, $W_{\theta_1^\times}$, $W_{\theta_2^\times}$ are analytic and their values are invertible operators acting on H. So we are interested in the behaviour of these functions near zero. The following equalities hold:

(6.18) $$\lim_{\lambda\to 0,\operatorname{Re}\lambda\le 0} W_{\theta_1}(\lambda) = [I-B_0]^{-1}(I-B_0Q),$$

(6.19) $$\lim_{\lambda\to 0,\operatorname{Re}\lambda\ge 0} W_{\theta_2}(\lambda) = [I-B_0]^{-1}(I-B_0P^*),$$

(6.20) $$\lim_{\lambda\to 0,\mathrm{Re}\,\lambda\le 0} W_{\theta_1^\times}(\lambda) = [I-B_0]^{-1}(I-B_0P^*)(I-B_0),$$

(6.21) $$\lim_{\lambda\to 0,\mathrm{Re}\,\lambda\le 0} W_{\theta_2^\times}(\lambda) = I-B_0Q.$$

To prove these equalities we need the following intertwining lemma (due to Hangelbroek [34]; cf. [42], formula (5.4)).

LEMMA 6.2. <u>We have</u> $(I-Q^*)T = TP$.

PROOF. We shall prove that

(6.22) $$(I-Q^*)T(I-P) = Q^*TP = 0.$$

Indeed $((I-Q^*)T(I-P)f,g) = (T(I-P)f,(I-Q)g)$. Now $(I-P)f\in H_-$ and $(I-Q)g\in H_+$. As H_- is T-invariant we also have $T(I-P)f\in H_-$. But $H_- \perp H_+$. So $((I-Q^*)T(I-P)f, g) = 0$ for all f and g in H. It follows that $(I-Q^*)T(I-P) = 0$. Next, we consider

$$(Q^*TPf,g) = (TPf,Qg) = [T^\times Pf,Qg].$$

As $Pf \in H_p$ and H_p is invariant under $T^\times$, we have $T^\times Pf\in H_p$. Further $Qg\in H_m$. But $H_m \perp H_p$ in H endowed with the inner product $[\cdot,\cdot]$. It follows that $(Q^*TPf,g) = 0$ for all f and g. Hence $Q^*TP = 0$.

Using (6.22) we obtain

$$\begin{aligned}(I-Q^*)T &= (I-Q^*)T(I-P) + (I-Q^*)TP\\ &= (I-Q^*)TP = TP-Q^*TP = TP.\end{aligned}$$

This completes the proof of the lemma.

Note that W_{θ_1} can be written as

$$W_{\theta_1}(\lambda) = I-B_0(I-B_0)^{-1}\Big|_{H_+}(T\Big|_{H_+})[\lambda-(T\Big|_{H_+})]^{-1}(I-Q).$$

The operator $T\big|_{H_+}$ is a nonnegative self-adjoint operator with a trivial kernel. So we can apply Lemma 6.1 (ii) to show that for each $f\in H$

$$(T\Big|_{H_+})[\lambda-(T\Big|_{H_+})]^{-1}f \longrightarrow -f \quad (\lambda\to 0,\ \mathrm{Re}\ \lambda \le 0).$$

As $B_0(I-B_0)^{-1}$ is of finite rank, it follows that

$$B_0(I-B_0)^{-1}\Big|_{H_+}(T\Big|_{H_+})[\lambda-(T\Big|_{H_+})]^{-1} \longrightarrow -B_0(I-B_0)^{-1}$$

in the operator norm if $\lambda \to 0$, $\mathrm{Re}\ \lambda \le 0$. Now

$$I+B_0(I-B_0)^{-1}(I-Q) = [I-B_0]^{-1}(I-B_0Q),$$

and hence (6.18) has been proved.

Using the intertwining lemma, we have

$$W_{\theta_2}(\lambda) = I-B_0(I-B_0)^{-1}[(\bar{\lambda}-T)^{-1}T(I-P)]^*.$$

As $\mathrm{Im}\ (I-P) = H_-$ and $T\big|_{H_-}$ is a nonpositive self-adjoint operator with zero kernel, we may apply Lemma 6.1 (ii) to show that in the operator norm

$$(\bar{\lambda}-T)^{-1}T(I-P)(I-B_0)^{-1}B_0 \longrightarrow -(I-P)(I-B_0)^{-1}B_0.$$

By passing to the adjoints, one sees that (6.19) holds true.

To prove (6.20) and (6.21) we first note that $W_{\theta_1^\times}$ and $W_{\theta_2^\times}$ may be written as

(6.23) $$W_{\theta_1^\times}(\lambda) = I+B_0[(\bar{\lambda}-T^\times)^{-1}T^\times P]^\sim,$$

(6.24) $$W_{\theta_2^\times}(\lambda) = I+B_0T^\times(\lambda-T^\times)^{-1}Q.$$

Here the symbol $\sim$ denotes the adjoint operation in the space $H_0 = (H,[\cdot,\cdot])$. By the intertwining lemma, $T(I-Q) = P^*T$. So, using (6.12), we have

$$\begin{aligned}(I-B_0)^{-1}T(I-Q) &= (I-B_0)^{-1}P^*T\\ &= P^\sim(I-B_0)^{-1}T = P^\sim T^\times.\end{aligned}$$

As $T^\times$ is self-adjoint on H_0, we see that $W_{\theta_1^\times}$ may be written as in (6.23). As $T^\times = [I-B_0]^{-1}T$ the formula (6.24) is clear.

Now observe that $\operatorname{Im} P = H_p$ is invariant under $T^\times$, and $T^\times|_{H_p}$ is a nonnegative self-adjoint operator with respect to $[\cdot,\cdot]$. Also $T^\times|_{H_p}$ is injective, because $T^\times = [I-B_0]^{-1}T$ is injective. So we can repeat the arguments used in the proof of (6.19) to show that in the operator norm

$$B_0\, P^\sim T^\times(\lambda-T^\times)^{-1} \longrightarrow -B_0P^\sim$$

if $\lambda \to 0$, $\operatorname{Re}\lambda \le 0$. From this (6.20) is easily deduced. Finally, using (6.24), one can prove (6.21) in the same way as (6.18) has been proved.

From the formulas (6.18) - (6.21) it follows that W_{θ_1} and $W_{\theta_1^\times}$ may be viewed as continuous functions on $\operatorname{Re}\lambda \le 0$. From

$$W_{\theta_1}(\lambda)W_{\theta_1^\times}(\lambda) = W_{\theta_1^\times}(\lambda)W_{\theta_1}(\lambda) = I\ ,\ \operatorname{Re}\lambda < 0,$$

we see that on $\text{Re}\,\lambda \leq 0$ the values of W_{θ_1} and $W_{\theta_1^\times}$ are invertible operators. Similarly, W_{θ_2} and $W_{\theta_2^\times}$ are continuous functions on $\text{Re}\,\lambda \geq 0$ whose values are invertible. So indeed the factorization

$$W(\lambda) = W_{\theta_1}(\lambda)W_{\theta_2}(\lambda)\ ,\ \text{Re}\,\lambda = 0,$$

is a canonical Wiener-Hopf factorization of W with respect to the imaginary axis.

Note that (6.19) and (6.21) may be used to show that $I-B_0Q$ and $I-B_0P^*$ are invertible and

$$(I-B_0Q)^{-1} = [I-B_0]^{-1}(I-B_0P^*).$$

By passing to the adjoints we see that $I-Q^*B_0$ and $I-PB_0$ are invertible and

$$(I-Q^*B_0)^{-1} = (I-PB_0)(I-B_0)^{-1}. \tag{6.25}$$

Let us return to the symbol $I-H(\lambda) = W(i/\bar{\lambda})^*(I-B_0)$. Put

$$G_-(\lambda) = W_{\theta_2}(i/\bar{\lambda})^*(I-Q^*B_0),$$

$$G_+(\lambda) = (I-Q^*B_0)^{-1}W_{\theta_1}(i/\bar{\lambda})^*(I-B_0).$$

From what we have proved so far it is clear that

$$I-H(\lambda) = G_-(\lambda)G_+(\lambda)\ ,\ \text{Im}\,\lambda = 0$$

is a right canonical Wiener-Hopf factorization with respect to the real line. It remains to prove that G_+, G_-, G_+^{-1} and G_-^{-1} can be written in the form mentioned in the first paragraph of this section. For G_+ and G_- this follows by direct computation using the intertwining lemma, the representations for W_{θ_1}

and W_{θ_2} and formula (6.25). To get the formulas for G_+^{-1} and G_-^{-1} we first note (using (6.12) and (6.25)) that

$$G_-(\lambda)^{-1} = (I-PB_0)W_{\theta_2^\times}(i/\bar{\lambda})^{\sim}(I-B_0)^{-1},$$

$$G_+(\lambda)^{-1} = W_{\theta_1^\times}(i/\bar{\lambda})^{\sim}(I-PB_0)^{-1}.$$

Next we use the representations (6.23) and (6.24) to get the desired formulas.

6.4 The matching of the subspaces

In the Wiener-Hopf factorization, carried out in the previous section, we used heavily that

$$H = H_- \oplus H_p \ , \ H = H_+ \oplus H_m \tag{6.26}$$

(cf. formula (6.15)). In this section we shall prove that indeed the space H may be decomposed in these two ways.

Recall that $P_-(P_+)$ is the orthogonal projection of H onto $H_-(H_+)$. Define $P_m = F(0)$ and $P_p = I-F(0)$, where $F(t)$ is the spectral resolution of the identity for the operator $T^\times = [I-B_0]^{-1}T$ with respect to the inner product $[f,g] = ((I-B_0)f,g)$. By definition

$$H_- = \mathrm{Im}\ P_-,\ H_+ = \mathrm{Im}\ P_+,\ H_m = \mathrm{Im}\ P_m,\ H_p = \mathrm{Im}\ P_p.$$

As $H = H_- \oplus H_+$, we can apply Proposition 5.2 to show that $H=H_-\oplus H_p$ if and only if

$$P_+P_p\big|_{H_p} : H_p \longrightarrow H_+$$

is bijective. Similarly, $H = H_- \oplus H_p$ if and only if

$$P_-P_m\big|_{H_m} : H_m \longrightarrow H_-$$

is bijective. Since $H = H_m \oplus H_p$ and $H = H_- \oplus H_+$, we see that (6.26) holds true if and only if the operator $V = P_-P_m + P_+P_p$ is bijective (cf. [34], [35] Theorem 1).

It is not difficult to prove that V is injective. Indeed, take $f \in H$ and assume $Vf = 0$. Put $f_m = P_m f$ and $f_p = P_p f$. Then $P_-f_m + P_+f_p = 0$, and hence $P_-f_m = 0$ and $P_+f_p = 0$. Note that

$$0 \geq [T^{\times} f_m, f_m] = (Tf_m, f_m) = (TP_+f_m, f_m) \geq 0.$$

It follows that $P_+f_m \in \operatorname{Ker} T$. But T is injective. So $P_+f_m = 0$. As $P_-f_m = 0$ too, we have $f_m = 0$. In the same way one proves that $f_p = 0$. Hence $f = 0$, and we conclude that V is injective.

Next, to prove that V is surjective, one shows that $I-V$ is compact (cf. [34], [35]). Because, if $I-V$ is compact, then $V = I-(I-V)$ is surjective if and only if V is injective. In [34] and [35] it is proved that $I-V$ is Hilbert-Schmidt. We shall show (see the next lemma) that $I-V$ is trace class. The method of proof we use is different from the one employed in [34] and [35] and is due to C. van der Mee.

LEMMA 6.3 The operator $I-V$ is trace class.

PROOF. As $I-V = (P_+-P_-)(P_m-P_-)$ and P_+-P_- is invertible, it suffices to prove that $P_m - P_-$ is trace class. Now $P_m = F(0)$, where $F(t)$ is the spectral resolution of the identity for $T^{\times}$ with respect to the inner product $[\cdot,\cdot]$. Similarly, $P_- = E(0)$, where $E(t)$ is the spectral resolution of the identity for T. As T and $T^{\times}$ are injective, in both cases the spectral resolutions are continuous at zero. So using a standard formula for the spectral resolution (see [37], Exercise VI.5.7) we may write for each $f\in H$

$$(P_m-P_-)f = \lim_{\varepsilon\downarrow 0} \frac{1}{2\pi i} \int_{\Gamma_\varepsilon} [(T^\times-\lambda)^{-1} - (T-\lambda)^{-1}]f d\lambda. \tag{6.27}$$

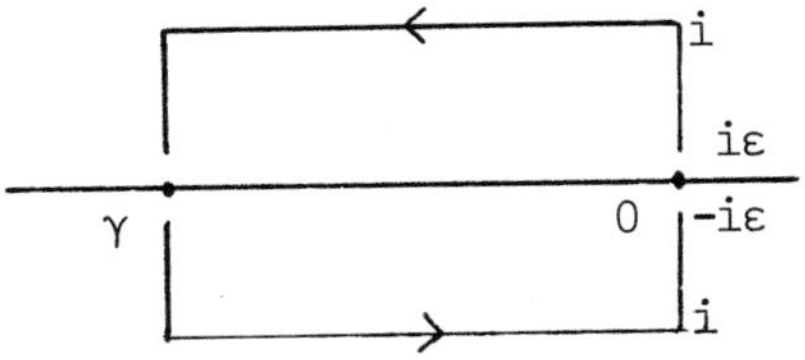

Here Γ_ε is an oriented curve as in the picture on the right hand side. The number γ is chosen such that the spectra of T and $T^\times$ both are in the open half-line (γ,∞). Now let us consider the intergrand in (6.27). We have

$$\begin{aligned}(T^\times-\lambda)^{-1} - (T-\lambda)^{-1} &= (\lambda-T)^{-1}[I-(\lambda-T)(\lambda-T^\times)^{-1}]\\ &= (\lambda-T)^{-1}(T-T^\times)(\lambda-T^\times)^{-1}\\ &= -(\lambda-T)^{-1}B_0T^\times(\lambda-T^\times)^{-1}.\end{aligned}$$

Let Δ be the closed contour obtained from Γ_ε be letting ε go to zero. As $T^\times$ is self-adjoint in H endowed with the inner product $[\cdot,\cdot]$, we know from Lemma 6.1 (i) and the choice of γ that $T^\times(\lambda-T^\times)^{-1}$ is bounded in norm on $\Delta\setminus\{0\}$. Next, let us investigate $(\lambda-T)^{-1}B_0$. First we shall prove that for the trace class norm we have

$$\|(i\alpha-T)^{-1}B_0\|_{tr} \leq q|\alpha|^{-\frac{1}{2}}, \quad 0\neq\alpha\in\mathbb{R}. \tag{6.28}$$

Here q is some positive constant. Indeed, from the definition of T it follows that

$$\|(i\alpha-T)^{-1}B_0\|_{tr} \leq \sum_{j=0}^{n} |a_j| \, \|p_j\| \, \|(i\alpha-T)^{-1}p_j\| .$$

For each j the function p_j is a polynomial in t. So to find an upper bound for $\|(i\alpha-T)^{-1}p_j\|$, $0\neq\alpha\in\mathbb{R}$, we have to estimate

$$\left(\int_{-1}^{1} \frac{t^{2k}}{\alpha^2+t^2}\, dt\right)^{1/2} . \tag{6.29}$$

As $t^{2k+2} \leqslant t^{2k}$ for $|t| \leqslant 1$, it suffices to find an upper bound for (6.29) for the case $k = 0$. But

$$\left(\int_{-1}^{1} \frac{dt}{\alpha^2+t^2}\right)^{1/2} = \left(\frac{2}{|\alpha|} \arctan \frac{1}{|\alpha|}\right)^{1/2}, \quad 0 \neq \alpha \in \mathbb{R}.$$

This proves (6.28). Note that in the trace class norm $(\lambda - T)^{-1}B_0$ is continuous on $\Delta \setminus \{0\}$. It follows that

$$\lim_{\varepsilon \downarrow 0} \int_{\Gamma_\varepsilon} [(T^\times - \lambda)^{-1} - (T-\lambda)^{-1}]d\lambda$$

exists in trace class norm. But then we can use (6.27) to show that $P_m - P_-$ is trace class.

6.5 Formulas for solutions

Let $I-H(\lambda)$ be the symbol of equation (6.7). In Section 3 we have constructed a right Wiener-Hopf factorization for $I-H(\lambda)$ with respect to the real line with zero partial indices:

$$\text{(6.30)} \qquad I-H(\lambda) = G_-(\lambda)G_+(\lambda), \quad -\infty \leqslant \lambda \leqslant \infty.$$

This implies that any other right Wiener-Hopf factorization for $I-H(\lambda)$ with respect to the real line has no non-zero partial indices too. To see this, assume

$$I-H(\lambda) = \tilde{G}_-(\lambda)\left\{P_0 + \sum_{\nu=1}^{n} \left(\frac{\lambda - i}{\lambda + i}\right)^{\kappa_\nu} P_\nu\right\}\tilde{G}_+(\lambda)$$

is a right Wiener-Hopf factorization with respect be the real line. Then

$$\tilde{G}_-(\lambda)^{-1}G_-(\lambda) = \left\{P_0 + \sum_{\nu=1}^{n} \left(\frac{\lambda - i}{\lambda + i}\right)^{\kappa_\nu} P_\nu\right\}\tilde{G}_+(\lambda)G_+(\lambda)^{-1}$$

for $-\infty \leqslant \lambda \leqslant \infty$. Take ν such that $\kappa_\nu > 0$. Then

$$(6.31)\qquad P_\nu \tilde{G}_-(\lambda)^{-1}G_-(\lambda) = \left(\frac{\lambda-i}{\lambda+i}\right)^{\kappa_\nu} P_\nu \tilde{G}_+(\lambda)G_+(\lambda)^{-1}.$$

In (6.31) the left hand side term is analytic in the lower half-plane (infinity included) and continuous up to the real line. For the right hand side term the same is true with respect to the upper half-plane. So by Liouville's theorem both terms are constant. But the term on the right hand side has a zero. It follows that $P_\nu \tilde{G}_-(\lambda)^{-1}G_-(\lambda)$ is zero. But this contradicts the invertibility of $\tilde{G}_-(\lambda)$ and $G_-(\lambda)$. So there are no positive partial indices. In the same way one proves that there are no negative partial indices.

The previous arguments also show that

$$(6.32)\qquad \tilde{G}_+(\lambda) = SG_+(\lambda)\ ,\ \tilde{G}_-(\lambda) = G_-(\lambda)S^{-1},$$

where S is a fixed invertible operator. From Section 3 we know that $G_+(\alpha) \to I$ if $|\alpha| \to \infty$ $(\alpha\in\mathbb{R})$. So S is uniquely determined by the behaviour of $\tilde{G}_+$ at infinity. According to the general theory developed in [18] (cf. Section 2) we may assume that

$$\tilde{G}_+(\lambda)^{-1} = I + \int_0^\infty \gamma_1(t)e^{i\lambda t}dt,\ \tilde{G}_-(\lambda)^{-1} = I+\int_{-\infty}^0 \gamma_2(t)e^{i\lambda t}dt,$$

where γ_1 and γ_2 are L_1-functions whose values are compact operators on H. But then it follows that the operator S appearing in (6.32) is the identity operator. So we have

$$(6.33)\qquad G_+(\lambda)^{-1} = I + \int_0^\infty \gamma_1(t)e^{i\lambda t}dt,\ G_-(\lambda)^{-1} = I + \int_{-\infty}^0 \gamma_2(t)e^{i\lambda t}dt$$

for an appropriate choice of operator-valued L_1-functions γ_1 and γ_2. But in Section 3 we have obtained explicit formulas for $G_+(\lambda)^{-1}$ and $G_-(\lambda)^{-1}$. This allows us to derive formulas for γ_1

and γ_2 too. In fact

$$\gamma_1(t) = -A_1^{-1}\exp(tA_1^{-1})PB_0(I - PB_0)^{-1}, \quad t > 0,$$

$$\gamma_2(t) = -(I - Q^*B_0)^{-1}Q^*(I - B_0)A_2^{-1}\exp(-tA_2^{-1}) \,.$$

$$\cdot\, P_m(I - B_0)^{-1}B_0, \quad t < 0,$$

where $A_1 = -T^\times|_{H_p}$ and $A_2 = T^\times|_{H_m}$. Note that both A_1 and A_2 are nonpositive self-adjoint operators, and hence for $i = 1,2$ the term $A_i^{-1}\exp(tA_i^{-1})$ is a well-defined bounded linear operator. Given the expressions for γ_1 and γ_2 equation (6.7) can be solved explicitly, as has been explained at the end of Section 2.

Using the formulas for G_+^{-1} and G_-^{-1} one can also give an explicit formula for the Fourier transform Ψ_+ of the solution ψ of equation (6.7). Since the Fourier transform of the known function F is equal to

$$F_+(\lambda) = T(I - i\lambda T)^{-1}f_+, \quad \mathrm{Im}\,\lambda \geq 0,$$

we have (cf. formula (4.29))

$$\Psi_+(\lambda) = [I - (I - i\lambda T^\times)^{-1}PB_0(I - PB_0)^{-1}] \,.$$

$$\cdot\, \mathcal{P}[I + (I - Q^*B_0)^{-1}\{(I + i\bar{\lambda}T^\times)^{-1}Q\}^*B_0]T(I - i\lambda T)^{-1}f_+,$$

where $\mathcal{P}$ is the projection defined by

$$\mathcal{P}\left(\int_{-\infty}^{\infty} f(t)e^{it\lambda}dt\right) = \int_0^{\infty} f(t)e^{it\lambda}dt.$$

The method explained in this chapter can also be applied to more general equations; presently research in this direction is being carried out by C. van der Mee for non-degenerate kernels $k(\mu,\mu')$ and the multigroup case.

CHAPTER VII

STABILITY OF SPECTRAL DIVISORS

In numerical computations of minimal factors of a given transfer function questions concerning the conditioning of the factors turn up naturally. According to the division theory developed in the previous chapters, all minimal factorizations may be obtained in an explicit way in terms of supporting projections of minimal nodes. This fact allows one to reduce questions concerning the conditioning of minimal factorizations to questions concerning the stability of divisors of a node. In the present chapter we study the matter of stability for spectral divisors mainly. In this case the investigation can be carried out for finite as well as for infinite dimensional state spaces. The invariant subspace method employed in this chapter will also be used to prove that "spectral" solutions of an operator Riccati equation are stable. The case of minimal non-spectral factorizations will be considered in the next chapter. For the connections with the practical computational aspects, we refer to [5], where among other things rough estimates are given for the number of computations involved in the construction of a minimal factorization of a transfer function.

7.1 Examples and first results for finite dimensional case

The property of having non-trivial minimal factorizations is ill-conditioned. For example it may happen that a transfer function admits non-trivial minimal factorizations while after a small perturbation the perturbed function has no such factorizations. On the other hand it may also happen that the perturbed function admits non-trivial minimal factorizations while the original function does not have this property. To see this we consider the following examples. Let

$$W_\varepsilon(\lambda) = \begin{bmatrix} 1+\frac{1}{\lambda} & \varepsilon\frac{1}{\lambda^2} \\ 0 & 1+\frac{1}{\lambda} \end{bmatrix}. \tag{7.1}$$

For each ε this is the transfer function of the minimal node $\theta_\varepsilon = (A_\varepsilon, I, I; \mathbb{C}^2, \mathbb{C}^2)$, where I is the identity on $\mathbb{C}^2$ and $A_\varepsilon(x_1,x_2)^T = (\varepsilon x_2, 0)^T$. To find a non-trivial minimal factorization of the function (7.1), we have to find non-trivial divisors of the node θ_ε (cf. Theorem 4.8), i.e., we must look for non-trivial subspaces M and $M^\times$ of $\mathbb{C}^2$, invariant under A_ε and $A_\varepsilon - I$, respectively, such that

$$M \oplus M^\times = \mathbb{C}^2.$$

Note that A_ε and $A_\varepsilon - I$ have the same invariant subspaces, and for $\varepsilon \neq 0$ there is only one such space of dimension one, namely the first coordinate space. It follows that for $\varepsilon \neq 0$ the function (7.1) has no non-trivial minimal factorizations. For $\varepsilon = 0$ we have

$$W_0(\lambda) = \begin{bmatrix} 1+\frac{1}{\lambda} & 0 \\ 0 & 1 \end{bmatrix} \cdot \begin{bmatrix} 1 & 0 \\ 0 & 1+\frac{1}{\lambda} \end{bmatrix}$$

and this factorization is minimal, because the McMillan degree of $W_0(\lambda)$ is equal to 2 and the McMillan degree of each of the factors is one.

Next we consider the function

$$W_\varepsilon(\lambda) = \begin{bmatrix} 1 & (\lambda^2-\varepsilon^2)^{-1} \\ 0 & 1 \end{bmatrix}.$$

Put

$$A_\varepsilon = \begin{bmatrix} \varepsilon & 1 \\ 0 & -\varepsilon \end{bmatrix}, \quad B = \begin{bmatrix} 0 & 0 \\ 0 & 1 \end{bmatrix}, \quad C = \begin{bmatrix} 1 & 0 \\ 0 & 0 \end{bmatrix}.$$

The function W_ε is the transfer function of the node $\theta_\varepsilon = (A_\varepsilon, B, C; \mathbb{C}^2, \mathbb{C}^2)$. As θ_ε is minimal, the McMillan degree of W_ε is equal to 2. For $\varepsilon \neq 0$ we have the following factorization:

$$W_\varepsilon(\lambda) = \begin{bmatrix} 1 & \frac{1}{2\varepsilon}(\lambda-\varepsilon)^{-1} \\ 0 & 1 \end{bmatrix} \cdot \begin{bmatrix} 1 & \frac{-1}{2\varepsilon}(\lambda+\varepsilon)^{-1} \\ 0 & 1 \end{bmatrix}.$$

By comparing the McMillan degrees of the factors with the McMillan degree of W_ε, we see that this factorization is minimal. On the other hand W_0 does not admit a non-trivial minimal factorization. To prove this note that

$$A_0 = \begin{bmatrix} 0 & 1 \\ 0 & 0 \end{bmatrix}$$

has only one non-trivial invariant subspace, namely the first coordinate space in $\mathbb{C}^2$. But the main operators of θ_0 and $\theta_0^\times$ are equal. It follows that θ_0 has no non-trivial supporting projection, and hence W_0 has no non-trivial minimal factorizations.

Although the first example proves that in general minimal factorizations are not stable, the next theorem shows that in an important case the possibility to factorize in a minimal way is stable under small perturbations. This theorem will appear as a corollary to the main stability theorem to be proved in this chapter.

THEOREM 7.1. <u>Consider the minimal realization</u>

$$W_0(\lambda) = I_n + C_0(\lambda I_\delta - A_0)^{-1}B_0,$$

where $I_n(I_\delta)$ *is the identity on* $\mathbb{C}^n(\mathbb{C}^\delta)$, *and assume that* $W_0(\lambda)$ *admits a (minimal) factorization*:

$$W_0(\lambda) = W_{01}(\lambda)W_{02}(\lambda), \quad W_{0i}(\lambda) = I_n+C_{0i}(\lambda I_{\delta_i}-A_{0i})^{-1}B_{0i},$$

where $\delta = \delta_1+\delta_2$ *and the factors* $W_{01}(\lambda)$ *and* $W_{02}(\lambda)$ *have no common zeros and no common poles. Then, given* $\varepsilon>0$, *there exists* $\omega>0$ *with the following property. If*

$$\|A-A_0\| + \|B-B_0\| + \|C-C_0\| < \omega, \tag{7.2}$$

then the realization $W(\lambda) = I_n+C(\lambda I_j-A)^{-1}B$ *is minimal and* $W(\lambda)$ *admits a (minimal) factorization*:

$$W(\lambda) = W_1(\lambda)W_2(\lambda) \ , \quad W_i(\lambda) = I_n+C_i(\lambda I_{\delta_i}-A_i)^{-1}B_i$$

such that the factors $W_1(\lambda)$ *and* $W_2(\lambda)$ *have no common zeros and no common poles and*

$$\|A_{0i}-A_i\|< \varepsilon \ , \quad \|B_{0i}-B_i\| <\varepsilon \ , \quad \|C_{0i}-C_i\| <\varepsilon$$

for $i = 1,2$.

Later on we shall avoid the ε-ω-language and give more explicit formulas for the relation between the quantity in the left hand side of (7.2) and the perturbation of the factors (see Theorem 7.7). In Section 7.4 it will also be shown that the factors change analytically whenever the operators appearing in the minimal realization of the original function do so (see Theorem 7.8).

The results referred to above will appear as corollaries to infinite dimensional stability theorems for certain divisors of nodes, which deal mainly with the case of spectral factorization (see Section 7.3). In the next chapter the case of stable non-spectral minimal factorizations will be completely described (see Theorem 8.8).

The next section is of preliminary nature; there we describe the relation between angular operators and the minimal and maximal opening between subspaces. In Section 7.5 we employ the method of Section 7.3 to prove stability for certain solutions of the Riccati equation.

7.2 Opening between subspaces and angular operators

From the description of the factors of a node in terms of angular operators (see Theorem 5.6) it is clear that for our purposes it is important to know how the angular operator changes when the operators in the node are perturbed a little. For this reason we study here properties of angular operators in terms of the minimal and maximal opening between certain subspaces.

Let M_1 and M_2 be closed subspaces of the Banach space X. The number

$$\eta(M_1,M_2) = \inf\{\|x+y\| \mid x\in M_1, y\in M_2, \max(\|x\|,\|y\|)=1\}$$

will be called the minimal opening between M_1 and M_2. Note that always $0\leqslant\eta\leqslant 1$ except when both M_1 and M_2 are the zero space in which case $\eta = \infty$. It is well-known (see [29], Lemma 1) that $\eta(M_1,M_2) > 0$ if and only if $M_1 \cap M_2 = (0)$ and $M_1 \oplus M_2$ is closed. If Π is a projection of the space X, then

$$\max\{\|\Pi\|, \|I-\Pi\|\} \leq \frac{1}{\eta(\operatorname{Im}\Pi, \operatorname{Ker}\Pi)} . \tag{7.3}$$

To see this, note that for each $z\in X$

$$\|z\| = \|\Pi z+(I-\Pi)z\| \geqslant \eta(\operatorname{Im}\Pi, \operatorname{Ker}\Pi)\cdot\max(\|\Pi z\|, \|(I-\Pi)z\|).$$

Sometimes it will be convenient to describe $\eta(M_1,M_2)$ in terms of the minimal angle φ_{min} between M_1 and M_2. By definition (cf. [29]) this quantity is given by the following formulas:

$$0 \leq \varphi_{min} \leq \frac{\Pi}{2}, \; \sin \varphi_{min} = \eta(M_1, M_2).$$

Now let us assume that M_1 and M_2 are closed subspaces of a Hilbert space H, and let Q_1 and Q_2 be the orthogonal projections of H onto M_1 and M_2, respectively. Note that for each $x \in M_1$

$$\inf\{\|x+y\| \mid y \in M_2\} = \|x - Q_2 x\|.$$

It follows that

$$\eta(M_1, M_2) = \min\left\{ \inf_{0 \neq x \in M_1} \frac{\|x - Q_2 x\|}{\|x\|}, \inf_{0 \neq y \in M_2} \frac{\|y - Q_1 y\|}{\|y\|} \right\}.$$

If both M_1 and M_2 are non-trivial, then the two infima in the right hand side of the previous identity are equal. This follows from

$$\inf_{0 \neq x \in M_1} \left(\frac{\|x - Q_2 x\|}{\|x\|} \right)^2 = \inf_{0 \neq x \in M_1} \frac{\|x\|^2 - \|Q_2 x\|^2}{\|x\|^2} =$$

$$= 1 - \sup_{0 \neq x \in M_1} \frac{\|Q_2 x\|^2}{\|x\|^2} = 1 - \sup_{\substack{x \in M_1 \\ x \neq 0}} \sup_{\substack{y \in M_2 \\ y \neq 0}} \frac{|(x,y)|^2}{\|x\|^2 \|y\|^2}$$

$$= 1 - \sup_{\substack{y \in M_2 \\ y \neq 0}} \sup_{\substack{x \in M_1 \\ x \neq 0}} \frac{|(x,y)|^2}{\|x\|^2 \|y\|^2} = 1 - \sup_{0 \neq y \in M_2} \frac{\|Q_1 y\|^2}{\|y\|^2}$$

$$= \inf_{0 \neq y \in M_2} \left(\frac{\|y - Q_2 y\|}{\|y\|} \right)^2.$$

From the previous equalities it also follows that

$$(7.4) \qquad 1-\eta(M_1,M_2)^2 = \sup_{0\neq x\in M_1} \frac{\|Q_2x\|^2}{\|x\|^2} = \sup_{0\neq y\in M_2} \frac{\|Q_1y\|^2}{\|y\|^2},$$

provided both M_1 and M_2 contain non-zero elements.

Returning to the Banach space case, put

$$\rho(M_1,M_2) = \sup_{0\neq x\in M_1} \inf_{y\in M_2} \frac{\|x-y\|}{\|x\|}.$$

If $M_1 = (0)$, then $\rho(M_1,M_2) = 0$ by definition. The number

$$\operatorname{gap}(M_1,M_2) = \min\{\rho(M_1,M_2),\rho(M_2,M_1)\}$$

is the so-called <u>gap</u> (or <u>maximal opening</u>) between M_1 and M_2. There exists an extensive literature on this concept, see, e.g. [37] and the references given there.

In the Hilbert space case we have

$$(7.5) \qquad \rho(M_2,M_1^{\perp}) = \sqrt{1-\eta(M_1,M_2)^2} = \cos\varphi_{\min}$$

whenever $M_1 \neq (0)$. To see this, note that for $M_2 \neq (0)$

$$\rho(M_2,M_1^{\perp}) = \sup_{0\neq y\in M_2} \frac{\|y-(I-Q_1)y\|}{\|y\|} = \sup_{0\neq y\in M_2} \frac{\|Q_1y\|}{\|y\|},$$

where Q_1 is the orthogonal projection onto M_1. But then we can use (7.4) to get the formula (7.5). If $M_2 = (0)$, then (7.5) holds trivially.

The next lemma is well-known, but explicit references are difficult to give. For this reason it will be presented with full proof.

LEMMA 7.2. <u>Let</u> Π_0, Π <u>and</u> Π_1 <u>be projections of the Banach space</u> X, <u>and assume that</u> $\operatorname{Ker}\Pi_0 = \operatorname{Ker}\Pi = \operatorname{Ker}\Pi_1$. <u>Let</u> R (R_1) <u>be the angular operator of</u> $\operatorname{Im}\Pi(\operatorname{Im}\Pi_1)$ <u>with respect</u>

to Π_0. *The following statements hold true:*

(i) $\eta(\mathrm{Ker}\ \Pi_0, \mathrm{Im}\ \Pi_0)\rho(\mathrm{Im}\ \Pi_1, \mathrm{Im}\ \Pi) \leq \|R_1 - R\|$;

(ii) *if* $\rho(\mathrm{Im}\ \Pi_1, \mathrm{Im}\ \Pi) < \eta(\mathrm{Ker}\ \Pi, \mathrm{Im}\ \Pi)$, *then*

$$\|R_1 - R\| \leq \frac{\rho(\mathrm{Im}\ \Pi_1, \mathrm{Im}\ \Pi)(1+\|R\|)}{\eta(\mathrm{Ker}\ \Pi, \mathrm{Im}\ \Pi) - \rho(\mathrm{Im}\ \Pi_1, \mathrm{Im}\ \Pi)}.$$

In particular, if $\rho(\mathrm{Im}\ \Pi_1, \mathrm{Im}\ \Pi_0) < \eta(\mathrm{Ker}\ \Pi_0, \mathrm{Im}\ \Pi_0)$, *then*

$$\|R_1\| \leq \frac{\rho(\mathrm{Im}\ \Pi_1, \mathrm{Im}\ \Pi_0)}{\eta(\mathrm{Ker}\ \Pi_0, \mathrm{Im}\ \Pi_0) - \rho(\mathrm{Im}\ \Pi_1, \mathrm{Im}\ \Pi_0)}. \tag{7.6}$$

Finally, if X *is a Hilbert space and* Π_0 *is an orthogonal projection, then* $\|R_1\| = \mathrm{ctg}\ \varphi_{min}$, *where* φ_{min} *is the minimal angle between* $\mathrm{Ker}\ \Pi_0$ *and* $\mathrm{Im}\ \Pi_1$.

PROOF. First we present the proof of the second part of the lemma. We begin with formula (7.6). Put $\rho_0 = \rho(\mathrm{Im}\ \Pi_1, \mathrm{Im}\ \Pi_0)$ and $\eta_0 = \eta(\mathrm{Ker}\ \Pi_0, \mathrm{Im}\ \Pi_0)$. Recall (cf. Proposition 5.1) that

$$R_1 = (\Pi_1 - \Pi_0)\Big|_{\mathrm{Im}\ \Pi_0}. \tag{7.7}$$

For $x \in \mathrm{Im}\ \Pi_1$ and $z \in \mathrm{Im}\ \Pi_0$ we have

$$\|(\Pi_1 - \Pi_0)x\| = \|(I - \Pi_0)x\| = \|(I - \Pi_0)(x - z)\|$$
$$\leq \|I - \Pi_0\|\ \|x - z\|.$$

Taking the infimum over all $z \in \mathrm{Im}\ \Pi_0$ and using inequality (7.3), one sees that

$$\|(\Pi_1 - \Pi_0)x\| \leq \rho_0 \eta_0^{-1} \|x\|, \quad x \in \mathrm{Im}\ \Pi_1. \tag{7.8}$$

Now recall that $R_1y+y \in \operatorname{Im}\Pi_1$ for each $y\in\operatorname{Im}\Pi_0$. As $R_1y\in \operatorname{Ker}\Pi_0 = \operatorname{Ker}\Pi_1$, we see from (7.7)

$$(\Pi_1-\Pi_0)(R_1y+y) = R_1y.$$

So, using (7.8), we obtain

$$\|R_1y\| \leqslant \rho_0\eta_0^{-1}\|R_1y+y\| \quad , \quad y\in\operatorname{Im}\Pi_0.$$

It follows that $(1-\rho_0\eta_0^{-1})\|R_1y\| \leqslant \rho_0\eta_0^{-1}\|y\|$ for each $y\in\operatorname{Im}\Pi_0$, which proves the inequality (7.6).

Next assume that X is a Hilbert space and Π_0 is orthogonal. If $\operatorname{Ker}\Pi_0 = (0)$, then $R_1 = 0$ and $\varphi_{min} = \frac{\pi}{2}$, and hence, in that case, we certainly have $\|R_1\| = \operatorname{ctg}\varphi_{min}$. So we assume that $\operatorname{Ker}\Pi_0 \neq (0)$. Then, by (7.4),

$$\cos^2\varphi_{min} = 1-\eta(\operatorname{Ker}\Pi_0,\operatorname{Im}\Pi_1)^2 = \sup_{0\neq x\in\operatorname{Im}\Pi_1}\left(\frac{\|(I-\Pi_0)x\|}{\|x\|}\right)^2.$$

Given $x\in\operatorname{Im}\Pi_1$, there exists $y\in\operatorname{Im}\Pi_0$ such that $x = R_1y+y$. As $(I-\Pi_0)x = R_1y$, this implies that

$$\cos^2\varphi_{min} = \sup_{0\neq y\in\operatorname{Im}\Pi_0}\frac{\|R_1y\|^2}{\|R_1y+y\|^2}$$

$$= \sup_{0\neq y\in\operatorname{Im}\Pi_0}\frac{\|R_1y\|^2}{\|y\|^2+\|R_1y\|^2} = \frac{\|R_1\|^2}{1+\|R_1\|^2}.$$

Hence, $\|R_1\| = \operatorname{ctg}\varphi_{min}$, and we have proved the second part of the theorem.

Next we prove statement (i). Take an arbitrary $y\in\operatorname{Im}\Pi_1$. Then $y = R_1x+x$ for some $x\in\operatorname{Im}\Pi_0$. Note that $Rx+x\in\operatorname{Im}\Pi$. So

$$\inf_{z\in\operatorname{Im}\Pi}\|y-z\| \leqslant \|y-(Rx+x)\| \leqslant \|R_1-R\|\,\|x\| .$$

Then $\|y\| = \|R_1x+x\| \geq \eta_0\|x\|$, where $\eta_0 = \eta(\mathrm{Ker}\ \Pi_0, \mathrm{Im}\ \Pi_0)$. It follows that $\eta_0 d(y, \mathrm{Im}\ \Pi) \leq \|R_1-R_2\| \cdot \|y\|$. This proves (i).

Finally, we prove statement (ii). Recall that

$$R_1 = (\Pi_1-\Pi_0)\Big|_{\mathrm{Im}\ \Pi_0}, \quad R = (\Pi-\Pi_0)\Big|_{\mathrm{Im}\ \Pi_0}.$$

So $(R_1-R)x = (\Pi_1-\Pi)x$ for each $x \in \mathrm{Im}\ \Pi_0$. Let $\tilde{R}$ be the angular operator of $\mathrm{Im}\ \Pi_1$ with respect to Π. Note that $\tilde{R}y = (\Pi_1-\Pi)y$ for all $y \in \mathrm{Im}\ \Pi$. Take $x \in \mathrm{Im}\ \Pi_0$. As $\mathrm{Im}(I-\Pi) = \mathrm{Ker}\ \Pi = \mathrm{Ker}\ \Pi_1$, we have $(\Pi_1-\Pi)x = (\Pi_1-\Pi)\Pi x = \tilde{R}\Pi x$. Now

$$\|\Pi x\| \leq \|(\Pi-\Pi_0)x\| + \|\Pi_0 x\| \leq (\|R\|+1)\|x\|.$$

It follows that

(7.9) $$\|(R_1-R)x\| \leq \|\tilde{R}\|(\|R\|+1)\|x\|.$$

As $\rho(\mathrm{Im}\ \Pi_1, \mathrm{Im}\ \Pi) < \eta = \eta(\mathrm{Ker}\ \Pi, \mathrm{Im}\ \Pi)$, we can use formula (7.6) for Π instead of Π_0 to show that

$$\|\tilde{R}\| \leq \rho(\mathrm{Im}\ \Pi_1, \mathrm{Im}\ \Pi)[\eta-\rho(\mathrm{Im}\ \Pi_1, \mathrm{Im}\ \Pi)]^{-1}.$$

Substituting this in (7.9) gives the desired inequality.

The following lemma will be most useful in the next section.

LEMMA 7.3. <u>Let</u> P, $P^\times$, Q <u>and</u> $Q^\times$ <u>be projections of the Banach space</u> X, <u>and put</u> $\alpha_0 = \frac{1}{6}\eta(\mathrm{Im}\ P, \mathrm{Im}\ P^\times)(\|P^\times\|+1)^{-1}$. <u>Assume</u> $X = \mathrm{Im}\ P \oplus \mathrm{Im}\ P^\times$ <u>and</u>

(7.10) $$\|P-Q\| + \|P^\times-Q^\times\| < \alpha_0.$$

<u>Then</u> $X = \mathrm{Im}\ Q \oplus \mathrm{Im}\ Q^\times$ <u>and there exists an invertible</u> $S: X \to X$ <u>such that</u>

(i) $S[\mathrm{Im}\ Q] = \mathrm{Im}\ P$, $S[\mathrm{Im}\ Q^\times] = \mathrm{Im}\ P^\times$,

(ii) $\max\{\|S-I\|, \|S^{-1}-I\|\} \leq \beta(\|P-Q\|+\|P^\times-Q^\times\|)$,

<u>where</u> $\beta = 2[\alpha_0\eta(\mathrm{Im}\ P, \mathrm{Im}\ P^\times)]^{-1}$.

PROOF. As $\mathrm{gap}(\mathrm{Im}\,P, \mathrm{Im}\,Q) \leqslant \|P-Q\|$ and $\mathrm{gap}(\mathrm{Im}\,P^{\times}, \mathrm{Im}\,Q^{\times}) \leqslant \|P^{\times}-Q^{\times}\|$, condition (7.10) implies that

$$2\mathrm{gap}(\mathrm{Im}\,P, \mathrm{Im}\,Q) + 2\mathrm{gap}(\mathrm{Im}\,P^{\times}, \mathrm{Im}\,Q^{\times}) < \eta(\mathrm{Im}\,P, \mathrm{Im}\,P^{\times}).$$

But then we may apply Theorem 2 in [29] to show that $X = \mathrm{Im}\,Q \oplus \mathrm{Im}\,Q^{\times}$.

Note that (7.10) implies that $\|P-Q\| < \frac{1}{4}$. Hence $S_1 = I+P-Q$ is invertible, and we can write $S_1^{-1} = I+V$ with $\|V\| \leq \frac{4}{3}\|P-Q\| < \frac{1}{3}$. As $I-P+Q$ is invertible too, we have

$$\text{(7.11)} \qquad \mathrm{Im}\,P = P(I-P+Q)Y = PQY = (I+P-Q)QY = S_1(\mathrm{Im}\,Q).$$

Further

$$S_1Q^{\times}S_1^{-1}-P^{\times} = \{I+P-Q\}Q^{\times}(I+V)-P^{\times}$$

$$= Q^{\times} + (P-Q)Q^{\times} + Q^{\times}V + (P-Q)Q^{\times}V - P^{\times}$$

$$= Q^{\times}-P^{\times} + (P-Q)(Q^{\times}-P^{\times}) + (P-Q)P^{\times} + (Q^{\times}-P^{\times})V +$$

$$+ P^{\times}V + (P-Q)(Q^{\times}-P^{\times})V + (P-Q)P^{\times}V.$$

So $\|S_1Q^{\times}S_1^{-1} - P^{\times}\| \leq 3\|Q^{\times}-P^{\times}\| + 3\|P-Q\|\cdot\|P^{\times}\|$. But then

$$\rho(\mathrm{Im}\,S_1Q^{\times}S_1^{-1}, \mathrm{Im}\,P^{\times}) \leq \|S_1Q^{\times}S_1^{-1} - P^{\times}\|$$

$$\leq 3(\|P-Q\|+\|P^{\times}-Q^{\times}\|)(\|P^{\times}\|+1)$$

$$\leq \frac{1}{2}\,\eta(\mathrm{Im}\,P, \mathrm{Im}\,P^{\times}).$$

Let $\Pi_0(\Pi)$ be the projection of X along $\mathrm{Im}\,P(\mathrm{Im}\,Q)$ onto $\mathrm{Im}\,P^{\times}(\mathrm{Im}\,Q^{\times})$ and put $\tilde{\Pi} = S_1\Pi S_1^{-1}$. Then $\tilde{\Pi}$ is a projection of X and by (7.11) we have $\mathrm{Ker}\,\tilde{\Pi} = \mathrm{Ker}\,\Pi_0$. Further $\mathrm{Im}\,\tilde{\Pi} = \mathrm{Im}\,S_1Q^{\times}S_1^{-1}$, and so we have

$$\rho(\mathrm{Im}\,\tilde{\Pi}, \mathrm{Im}\,\Pi_0) \leq \tfrac{1}{2}\eta(\mathrm{Ker}\,\Pi_0, \mathrm{Im}\,\Pi_0).$$

Hence, if R denotes the angular operator of $\mathrm{Im}\,\tilde{\Pi}$ with respect to Π_0, then because of Lemma 7.2, formula (7.6),

$$\|R\| \leq 2\rho(\mathrm{Im}\,\tilde{\Pi},\mathrm{Im}\,\Pi_0)[\eta(\mathrm{Ker}\,\Pi_0,\mathrm{Im}\,\Pi_0)]^{-1}.$$

As $\rho(\mathrm{Im}\,\tilde{\Pi},\mathrm{Im}\,\Pi_0) \leq 3(\|P-Q\|+\|P^\times-Q^\times\|)(\|P^\times\|+1)$, this implies that

$$\|R\| \leq \frac{1}{\alpha_0}(\|P-Q\|+\|P^\times-Q^\times\|). \tag{7.12}$$

Next, put $S_2 = I-R\Pi_0$, and take $S = S_2S_1$. Clearly, S_2 is invertible, in fact $S_2^{-1} = I+R\Pi_0$. It follows that S is invertible too. From the properties of the angular operator one easily sees that with this choice of S statement (i) holds true. It remains to prove (ii).

To prove (ii) we simplify our notation. Put $d = \|P-Q\| + \|P^\times-Q^\times\|$, and let $\eta = \eta(\mathrm{Im}\,P, \mathrm{Im}\,P^\times)$. From $S = (I-R\Pi_0)(I+P-Q)$ and the fact that $\|P-Q\| < \frac{1}{4}$ one deduces that $\|S-I\| \leq \|P-Q\|+\frac{5}{4}\|R\|\cdot\|\Pi_0\|$. For $\|R\|$ an upper bound is given by (7.12), and from (7.3) we know that $\|\Pi_0\| \leq \eta^{-1}$. It follows that

$$\|S-I\| \leq d + \tfrac{5}{4}d(\alpha_0\eta)^{-1}. \tag{7.13}$$

Finally, we consider S^{-1}. Recall that $S_1^{-1} = I+V$ with $\|V\| \leq \frac{4}{3}\|P-Q\| < \frac{1}{3}$. Hence

$$\begin{aligned}\|S^{-1}-I\| &\leq \|V\| + \|V\|\cdot\|\Pi_0\|\cdot\|R\| + \|R\|\cdot\|\Pi_0\| \\ &\leq \tfrac{4}{3}\|P-Q\| + \tfrac{4}{3}\|R\|\cdot\|\Pi_0\| \\ &\leq \tfrac{4}{3}d + \tfrac{4}{3}d(\alpha_0\eta)^{-1}.\end{aligned}$$

Using the fact that $\alpha_0\eta \leq \frac{1}{6}$, it is easy to derive statement (ii) from (7.13) and the previous inequality.

7.3 Stability of spectral divisors of nodes

To state the main theorem of this section we need the following definition. If $\theta = (A,B,C;X,Y)$ and $\theta_0 = (A_0,B_0,C_0;X,Y)$ are two nodes, then the distance between θ and θ_0 is defined to be

$$\|\theta - \theta_0\| = \|A-A_0\| + \|B-B_0\| + \|C-C_0\| .$$

In particular, we set $\|\theta\| = \|A\| + \|B\| + \|C\|$. If $W(\lambda)$ and $W_0(\lambda)$ are the transfer functions of θ and θ_0, respectively, then

$$\|W(\lambda)-W_0(\lambda)\| \leq \frac{\|\theta-\theta_0\|\|\theta\|\|\theta_0\|}{\|A\|\|A_0\|} ,$$

provided $|\lambda| > 2\max\{\|A\|,\|A_0\|\}$.

THEOREM 7.4. *Let $\theta_0 = (A_0,B_0,C_0;X,Y)$ be a node with a supporting projection Π_0. Assume that*

$$\operatorname{Ker} \Pi_0 = \operatorname{Im} P(A_0;\Gamma),\ \operatorname{Im} \Pi_0 = \operatorname{Im} P(A_0^\times;\Gamma^\times),$$

where $A_0^\times = A_0 - B_0C_0$ and $\Gamma(\Gamma^\times)$ is a Cauchy contour which splits the spectrum of A_0 $(A_0^\times)$. Then there exist positive constants α, β_1 and β_2 such that the following holds. If $\theta=(A,B,C;X,Y)$ is a node such that $\|\theta-\theta_0\| < \alpha$, then Γ splits the spectrum of A, $\Gamma^\times$ splits the spectrum of $A^\times = A-BC$,

$$X = \operatorname{Im} P(A;\Gamma) \oplus \operatorname{Im} P(A^\times;\Gamma^\times),$$

the projection Π of X along $\operatorname{Im} P(A;\Gamma)$ onto $\operatorname{Im} P(A^\times;\Gamma^\times)$ is a supporting projection for θ, and there exists a similarity transformation S such that

$$\|S-I\| \leq \beta_1 \|\theta-\theta_0\| ,$$

*$\Pi_0 = S\Pi S^{-1}$, Π_0 **is** a supporting projection for the node $\hat\theta = (SAS^{-1},SB,CS^{-1};X,Y)$ and for the corresponding divisors we have*

(i) $\|pr_{I-\Pi_0}(\theta_0)-pr_{I-\Pi_0}(\hat{\theta})\| \leq \beta_2\|\theta-\theta_0\|$,

(ii) $\|pr_{\Pi_0}(\theta_0) - pr_{\Pi_0}(\hat{\theta})\| \leq \beta_2\|\theta-\theta_0\|$.

Furthermore, if θ_0 is minimal and the spaces X and Y are finite dimensional, then α can be chosen such that θ is minimal whenever $\|\theta-\theta_0\|<\alpha$.

From the proof of the above theorem it will be clear that in the first part of the theorem we may take for the constant α the following quantity:

$$\alpha = [1+\|\theta_0\|]^{-1}\min\left\{1, \frac{1}{2\gamma}, \frac{\alpha_0\pi}{2\gamma^2\ell}\right\},$$

where ℓ is the maximum of the lengths of the curves Γ and $\Gamma^\times$,

$$\gamma = \max\left\{\max_{\lambda\in\Gamma} \|(\lambda-A_0)^{-1}\|, \max_{\lambda\in\Gamma^\times} \|(\lambda-A_0^\times)^{-1}\|\right\},$$

and $\alpha_0 = \frac{1}{6}\eta(\operatorname{Ker}\Pi_0,\operatorname{Im}\Pi_0)(\|P(A_0^\times;\Gamma)\|+1)^{-1}$. Further we may take

$$\beta_1 = 4(1+\|\theta_0\|)\gamma^2\ell[\pi\alpha_0\eta(\operatorname{Ker}\Pi_0,\operatorname{Im}\Pi_0)]^{-1},$$

$$\beta_2 = \frac{9}{\eta(\operatorname{Ker}\Pi_0,\operatorname{Im}\Pi_0)^3}\left[1 + \frac{2\gamma^2\ell}{\pi\alpha_0}\|\theta_0\|(1+\theta_0)\right].$$

To prove Theorem 7.4 we first prove the following auxiliary theorem

THEOREM 7.5. *Let Π_0 be a supporting projection for the node $\theta_0 = (A_0,B_0,C_0;X,Y)$, and assume that*

$$\operatorname{Ker}\Pi_0 = \operatorname{Im}P, \quad \operatorname{Im}\Pi_0 = \operatorname{Im}P^\times,$$

where P *and* $P^\times$ *are given projections of* X. *Put*

$$\alpha_0 = \frac{1}{6}\eta(\operatorname{Im} P, \operatorname{Im} P^\times)(\|P^\times\|+1)^{-1}.$$

Let $\theta=(A,B,C;X,Y)$ *be another node, and let* Q *and* $Q^\times$ *be projections of* X *such that*

$$A[\operatorname{Im} Q]\subset \operatorname{Im} Q\ ,\ A^\times[\operatorname{Im} Q^\times]\subset \operatorname{Im} Q^\times, \tag{7.14}$$

$$\|P-Q\| + \|P^\times-Q^\times\| < \alpha_0. \tag{7.15}$$

Then $X = \operatorname{Im} Q \oplus \operatorname{Im} Q^\times$, *there exists an invertible operator* $S:X \to X$ *such that* $S^{-1}\Pi_0 S$ *is the projection* Π *of* X *onto* $\operatorname{Im} Q^\times$ *along* Im Q, *the projection* Π_0 *is a supporting projection for the node* $\hat{\theta} = (SAS^{-1}, SB, CS^{-1}; X, Y)$, *while for the corresponding factors we have*

$$\max\{\|pr_{I-\Pi_0}(\theta_0)-pr_{I-\Pi_0}(\hat{\theta})\|, \|pr_{\Pi_0}(\theta)-pr_{\Pi_0}(\hat{\theta})\|\} \leq \tag{7.16}$$

$$\leq \frac{9}{\eta(\operatorname{Im} P, \operatorname{Im} P^\times)^3}[\|\theta-\theta_0\| + \alpha_0^{-1}\|\theta_0\|(\|P-Q\|+\|P^\times-Q^\times\|)].$$

PROOF. From Lemma 7.3 we know that $X = \operatorname{Im} Q \oplus \operatorname{Im} Q^\times$. Let Π be the projection of X along Im Q onto $\operatorname{Im} Q^\times$. Then (7.14) implies that Π is a supporting projection for θ. Take S as in Lemma 7.3. Then we see from statement (i) in Lemma 7.3 that $S\Pi S^{-1} = \Pi_0$. But then it is clear that Π_0 is a supporting projection for $\hat{\theta}$.

Let θ_{01} and $\hat{\theta}_1$ be the left factors of θ_0 and $\hat{\theta}$ associated with Π_0, and let θ_{02} and $\hat{\theta}_2$ be the corresponding right factors. From the definition of the factors (see Section 1.1) it is clear that

$$\|\theta_{01}-\hat{\theta}_1\| \leq \|I-\Pi_0\|\|A_0-\hat{A}\| + \|I-\Pi_0\|\|B_0-\hat{B}\| + \|C_0-\hat{C}\|.$$

It follows that $\|\theta_{01}-\hat{\theta}_1\| \leq \|I-\Pi_0\|\|\theta_0-\hat{\theta}\|$. Similarly, $\|\theta_{02}-\hat{\theta}_2\| \leq \|\Pi_0\|\|\theta_0-\hat{\theta}\|$. Using (7.3) we obtain

$$\max_{i=1,2} \|\theta_{0i}-\hat{\theta}_i\| \leq \|\theta_0-\hat{\theta}\| \, [\eta(\operatorname{Im} P,\operatorname{Im} P^{\times})]^{-1}. \tag{7.17}$$

As $\|\theta_0-\hat{\theta}\| \leq \|\theta_0-\theta\| + \|\theta-\hat{\theta}\|$, it remains to compute a suitable upper bound for $\|\theta-\hat{\theta}\|$.

Put $S = I+V$ and $S^{-1} = I+W$. Note that

$$\|\theta-\hat{\theta}\| = \|A-SAS^{-1}\| + \|B-SB\| + \|C-CS^{-1}\|$$

$$\leq \|A\|(\|V\|+\|W\|+\|V\|\|W\|) + \|B\|\|V\| + \|C\|\|W\|.$$

By Lemma 7.3 (ii) we have $\max\{\|V\|,\|W\|\} \leq 2d\{\alpha_0\eta\}^{-1}$, where $d = \|P-Q\|+\|P^{\times}-Q^{\times}\|$ and $\eta = \eta(\operatorname{Im} P,\operatorname{Im} P^{\times})$. It follows that

$$\|\theta-\hat{\theta}\| \leq \frac{4d}{\alpha_0\eta}\left(1+\frac{d}{\alpha_0\eta}\right)\|\theta\|. \tag{7.18}$$

Since $d\alpha_0^{-1} < 1$ and $\eta \leq 1$, we can use (7.18) to show that

$$\|\theta_0-\hat{\theta}\| \leq \|\theta_0-\theta\| + \frac{8d}{\alpha_0\eta^2}\|\theta\|$$

$$\leq \|\theta_0-\theta\| + \frac{8d}{\alpha_0\eta^2}\|\theta-\theta_0\| + \frac{8d}{\alpha_0\eta^2}\|\theta_0\|$$

$$\leq \frac{9}{\eta^2}\|\theta-\theta_0\| + \frac{8d}{\alpha_0\eta^2}\|\theta_0\|$$

$$\leq \frac{9}{\eta^2}\left\{\|\theta-\theta_0\| + \frac{d}{\alpha_0}\|\theta_0\|\right\}.$$

By using this in (7.17) we obtain the desired inequality (7.16)

PROOF OF THEOREM 7.4. Take γ, ℓ, α_0 and α as in the first paragraph after Theorem 7.4, and take $\|\theta-\theta_0\| < \alpha$. In particular, we have $\|\theta-\theta_0\| < 1$. Note that

$$\|A^\times - A_0^\times\| \leq \|A-A_0\| + \|B-B_0\|\cdot\|C-C_0\| + \|B_0\|\cdot\|C-C_0\|$$

$$+ \|C_0\|\cdot\|B-B_0\|$$

$$\leq \|\theta-\theta_0\| \ (1+\|\theta_0\|).$$

It follows that

$$\max\{\|A-A_0\|, \|A^\times-A_0^\times\|\} \leq \|\theta-\theta_0\| (1+\|\theta_0\|) = \frac{\nu}{2\gamma}, \tag{7.19}$$

where $0 \leq \nu < 1$. Using elementary spectral theory, we may conclude from (7.19) that $\Gamma(\Gamma^\times)$ splits the spectrum of $A(A^\times)$, while further

$$\|(\lambda-A)^{-1} - (\lambda-A_0)^{-1}\| \leq 2\gamma^2\|\theta-\theta_0\|(1+\|\theta_0\|), \ \lambda\in\Gamma,$$

$$\|(\lambda-A^\times)^{-1} - (\lambda-A_0^\times)^{-1}\| \leq 2\gamma^2\|\theta-\theta_0\|(1+\|\theta_0\|), \ \lambda\in\Gamma^\times.$$

Hence for the corresponding Riesz projections we have,

$$\|P(A;\Gamma)-P(A_0;\Gamma)\| + \|P(A^\times;\Gamma^\times)-P(A_0^\times;\Gamma^\times)\| \leq \tag{7.20}$$

$$\leq 2\gamma^2\|\theta-\theta_0\|\cdot(1+\|\theta_0\|)\ell\pi^{-1} < \alpha_0.$$

So, if $P = P(A_0;\Gamma)$, $P^\times = P(A_0^\times;\Gamma^\times)$, $Q = P(A;\Gamma)$ and $Q^\times = P(A^\times;\Gamma^\times)$, then conditions (7.10) and (7.15) are both satisfied. Hence we may apply Lemma 7.3 and Theorem 7.5 to the four projections $P, P^\times, Q$ and $Q^\times$.

It follows that $X = \operatorname{Im} P(A;\Gamma) \oplus \operatorname{Im} P(A^\times;\Gamma^\times)$. Further, if Π is the projection of X along $\operatorname{Im} P(A;\Gamma)$ onto $\operatorname{Im} P(A^\times;\Gamma^\times)$, then Π is a supporting projection for the node θ. Also there exists a similarity transformation S such that $\Pi_0 = S\Pi S^{-1}$ and Π_0 is a supporting projection for the node $\hat{\theta} = (SAS^{-1}, SB, CS^{-1}; X, Y)$. Finally, by virtue of Lemma 7.3 (ii) and formulas (7.16) and (7.20), we have $\|S-I\| \leq \beta_1\|\theta-\theta_0\|$ and

$$\max\{\| pr_{I-\Pi_0}(\theta_0)-pr_{I-\Pi_0}(\hat\theta)\|, \| pr_{\Pi_0}(\theta_0)-pr_{\Pi_0}(\hat\theta)\|\}$$

$$\leq \beta_2\|\theta-\theta_0\|,$$

where β_1 and β_2 are as in the paragraph after Theorem 7.4.

Now suppose θ_0 is minimal and X and Y are finite dimensional. The minimality of θ_0 and the fact that X is finite dimensional imply that for some ℓ the operator $\mathrm{col}(C_0A_0^j)_{j=0}^{\ell}$ is injective and the operator $\mathrm{row}(A_0^jB_0)_{j=0}^{\ell}$ is surjective. As Y is finite dimensional too, it follows that for

$$\|\theta-\theta_0\| = \|A-A_0\| + \|B-B_0\| + \|C-C_0\|$$

sufficiently small the operator $\mathrm{col}(CA^j)_{j=0}^{\ell}$ will be injective and the operator $\mathrm{row}(A^jB)_{j=0}^{\ell}$ will be surjective. This implies that θ will be minimal whenever $\|\theta-\theta_0\|$ is sufficiently small. This completes the proof of Theorem 7.4.

THEOREM 7.6. _Let_ $\theta_\varepsilon = (A_\varepsilon, B_\varepsilon, C_\varepsilon; X, Y)$ _be a node, and assume that the operators_ A_ε, B_ε _and_ C_ε _depend analytically on_ ε _in a neighbourhood of_ $\varepsilon = 0$. _Let_ Π_0 _be a supporting projection of_ θ_0, _and assume that_

$$\mathrm{Ker}\,\Pi_0 = \mathrm{Im}\,P(A_0;\Gamma), \quad \mathrm{Im}\,\Pi_0 = \mathrm{Im}\,P(A_0^\times;\Gamma^\times),$$

where $A_0^\times = A_0-B_0C_0$ _and_ $\Gamma(\Gamma^\times)$ _is a Cauchy contour that splits the spectrum of_ $A_0(A_0^\times)$. _Then for_ $|\varepsilon|$ _sufficiently small, there exists a similarity transformation_ S_ε, _which depends analytically on_ ε, _such that_ $S_0 = I$ _and the projection_ Π_0 _is a supporting projection for the node_

$$\hat\theta_\varepsilon = (S_\varepsilon A_\varepsilon S_\varepsilon^{-1}, S_\varepsilon B_\varepsilon, C_\varepsilon S_\varepsilon^{-1}; X, Y).$$

In particular, if

$$pr_{I-\Pi_0}(\hat{\theta}_\varepsilon) = (\hat{A}_{1\varepsilon},\hat{B}_{1\varepsilon},\hat{C}_{1\varepsilon};\text{Ker }\Pi_0,Y),$$

$$pr_{\Pi_0}(\hat{\theta}_\varepsilon) = (\hat{A}_{2\varepsilon},\hat{B}_{2\varepsilon},\hat{C}_{2\varepsilon};\text{Im }\Pi_0,Y),$$

then the operators $\hat{A}_{1\varepsilon},\hat{A}_{2\varepsilon},\hat{B}_{1\varepsilon},\hat{B}_{2\varepsilon},\hat{C}_{1\varepsilon}$ *and* $\hat{C}_{2\varepsilon}$ *depend analytically on* ε.

PROOF. We know already that for $|\varepsilon|$ sufficiently small the Cauchy contour Γ $(\Gamma^\times)$ splits the spectrum of $A_\varepsilon(A_\varepsilon^\times)$. Put

$$P_\varepsilon = P(A_\varepsilon;\Gamma),\ P_\varepsilon^\times = P(A_\varepsilon^\times\ \Gamma^\times).$$

From the Cauchy integral formula for the Riesz projections P_ε and $P_\varepsilon^\times$ it follows that P_ε and $P_\varepsilon^\times$ depend analytically on ε.

Now we proceed as in the proof of Lemma 7.3. Put $S_{1\varepsilon}=I+P_0-P_\varepsilon$. Then $S_{1\varepsilon}$ depends analytically on ε, the operator $S_{10} = I$, and hence $S_{1\varepsilon}$ is invertible for $|\varepsilon|$ sufficiently small.

Let Π_ε be the projection of X along $\text{Im } P_\varepsilon$ onto $\text{Im } P_\varepsilon^\times$. As both P_ε and $P_\varepsilon^\times$ are analytic functions of ε, the same is true for Π_ε (cf. [46]). It follows that $\tilde{\Pi}_\varepsilon = S_{1\varepsilon}\Pi_\varepsilon S_{1\varepsilon}^{-1}$ is analytic in ε also. Note that $\tilde{\Pi}_0 = \Pi_0$.

Next, we consider the angular operator R_ε of $\text{Im }\tilde{\Pi}_\varepsilon$ with respect to Π_0. Recall (see Section 5.1) that

$$R_\varepsilon = (\tilde{\Pi}_\varepsilon-\Pi_0)\Big|_{\text{Im }\Pi_0}.$$

It follows that R_ε depends analytically on ε and R_0 is the zero operator. So the operator $S_{2\varepsilon} = I-R_\varepsilon\Pi_0$ is analytic in ε and $S_{20} = I$. In particular we see that $S_{2\varepsilon}$ is invertible for $|\varepsilon|$ sufficiently small. Now put $S_\varepsilon = S_{2\varepsilon}S_{1\varepsilon}$. Then for $|\varepsilon|$ sufficiently small S_ε has all the desired properties.

7.4 Applications to transfer functions

In this section we shall prove Theorem 7.1. We begin with its infinite dimensional analogue. Throughout this section X and Y are Banach spaces.

THEOREM 7.7. *Consider the transfer function*

$$W_0(\lambda) = I_Y + C_0(\lambda I_X - A_0)^{-1}B_0, \tag{7.21}$$

and assume that $W_0(\lambda)$ *admits a factorization:*

$$W_0(\lambda) = W_{01}(\lambda)W_{02}(\lambda),\ W_{0i}(\lambda) = I_Y + C_{0i}(\lambda I_{X_i} - A_{0i})^{-1}B_{0i}$$

such that

$$\bigcap_{i=1}^{2} \sigma(A_{0i}) = \phi\ ,\ \bigcap_{i=1}^{2} \sigma(A_{0i} - B_{0i}C_{0i}) = \phi, \tag{7.22}$$

and assume that the node $\theta_0 = (A_0, B_0, C_0; X, Y)$ *is similar to the product* $\theta_{01}\theta_{02}$, *where* $\theta_{0i} = (A_{0i}, B_{0i}, C_{0i}; X_i, Y)$, $i = 1,2$. *Then there exist positive constants* α_0 *and* β_0 *such that the following holds. If*

$$\| A - A_0\| + \| B - B_0\| + \| C - C_0\| < \alpha_0, \tag{7.23}$$

then the transfer function $W(\lambda) = I_Y + C(\lambda I_X - A)^{-1}B$ *admits a factorization*

$$W(\lambda) = W_1(\lambda)W_2(\lambda),\ W_i(\lambda) = I_Y + C_i(\lambda I_{X_i} - A_i)^{-1}B_i \tag{7.24}$$

such that

$$\bigcap_{i=1}^{2} \sigma(A_i) = \phi,\ \bigcap_{i=1}^{2} \sigma(A_i - B_iC_i) = \phi \tag{7.25}$$

and for $i = 1,2$ *one has*

$$\| A_i - A_{0i}\| + \| B_i - B_{0i}\| + \| C_i - C_{0i}\| \leq \tag{7.26}$$

$$\leq \beta_0(\| A-A_0\| + \| B-B_0\| + \| C-C_0\|).$$

PROOF. Let $T:X \to X_1 \oplus X_2$ be a node similarity between θ_0 and $\theta_{01}\theta_{02}$. Assume that (7.23) holds, and put

$$\overline{\theta} = (TAT^{-1}, TB, CT^{-1}; X_1\oplus X_2, Y).$$

Note that for the node distance $\| \theta_{01}\theta_{02}-\overline{\theta}\|$ we have:

$$\| \theta_{01}\theta_{22}-\overline{\theta}\| = \| TA_0T^{-1}-TAT^{-1}\| + \| TB_0-TB\| + \| C_0T^{-1}-CT^{-1}\| \leq$$

$$\leq (\| A_0-A\| + \| B_0-B\| + \| C-C_0\|)(\| T\| \| T^{-1}\| + \| T\| + \| T^{-1}\|).$$

With respect to the direct sum $X_1\oplus X_2$ the main operator of the node $\overline{\theta}_0 = \theta_{01}\theta_{02}$ and the associated main operator (respectively) have the following form

$$\overline{A}_0 = \begin{bmatrix} A_{01} & * \\ 0 & A_{02} \end{bmatrix}, \quad \overline{A}_0^{\times} = \begin{bmatrix} A_{01}-B_{01}C_{01} & 0 \\ * & A_{02}-B_{02}C_{02} \end{bmatrix}.$$

Put a Cauchy contour Γ around $\sigma(A_{01})$ that separates the spectrum $\sigma(A_{01})$ from $\sigma(A_{02})$. Similarly, put a Cauchy contour $\Gamma^{\times}$ around $\sigma(A_{02}-B_{02}C_{02})$ such that $\Gamma^{\times}$ separates $\sigma(A_{02}-B_{02}C_{02})$ from $\sigma(A_{01}-B_{01}C_{01})$. Then we can apply Lemma 1.4 to show that

$$X_1 = \operatorname{Im} P(\overline{A}_0,\Gamma) , \quad X_2 = \operatorname{Im} P(\overline{A}_0^{\times};\Gamma^{\times}).$$

It follows that we may apply Theorem 7.4 to the node $\overline{\theta}_0=\theta_{01}\theta_{02}$.

Let α and β_2 be the positive numbers that according to Theorem 7.4 correspond to the node $\overline{\theta}_0$. Put

$$\alpha_0 = \alpha[\| T\| \cdot \| T^{-1}\| + \| T\| + \| T^{-1}\|]^{-1}.$$

Now assume that (7.23) holds.

Then $\|\bar{\theta}_0-\bar{\theta}\|<\alpha$. So by Theorem 7.4 there exists a similarity transformation S such that for the node

$$\tilde{\theta} = (STAT^{-1}S^{-1}, STB, CT^{-1}S^{-1}; X_1 \oplus X_2, Y)$$

the projection Π_0 of $X_1 \oplus X_2$ along X_1 onto X_2 is a supporting projection. This shows that $W(\lambda)$ admits a factorization of the form (7.24). Moreover we know that

$$\|pr_{I-\Pi_0}(\bar{\theta}_0)-pr_{I-\Pi_0}(\tilde{\theta})\| \leq \beta_2 \|\bar{\theta}_0-\bar{\theta}\|,$$

$$\|pr_{\Pi_0}(\bar{\theta}) - pr_{\Pi_0}(\tilde{\theta})\| \leq \beta_2 \|\bar{\theta}_0-\bar{\theta}\|.$$

But this is the same as

$$\| A_{0i}-A_i\| + \|B_{0i}-B_i\| + \|C_{0i}-C_i\| \leq \beta_2 \|\bar{\theta}_0-\bar{\theta}\|$$

for i = 1,2. So, if we take

$$\beta_0 = \beta_2[\|T\| \cdot \|T^{-1}\| + \|T\| + \|T^{-1}\|],$$

then (7.26) holds true.

Let $\bar{A}$ be the main operator of $\bar{\theta}$, and let $\bar{A}^{\times}$ be the main operator of the associated node $\bar{\theta}^{\times}$. As $\|\bar{\theta}_0-\bar{\theta}\|<\alpha$, we can apply Theorem 7.4 to show that $\Gamma(\Gamma^{\times})$ splits the spectrum of $\bar{A}(\bar{A}^{\times})$ and

$$X_1 \oplus X_2 = \operatorname{Im} P(\bar{A};\Gamma) \oplus \operatorname{Im} P(\bar{A}^{\times};\Gamma^{\times}).$$

Let Π be the projection of $X_1 \oplus X_2$ along $\operatorname{Im} P(\bar{A};\Gamma)$ onto $\operatorname{Im} P(\bar{A}^{\times};\Gamma^{\times})$. Then $\Pi_0 = S\Pi S^{-1}$. It follows that $\sigma(A_1)$ is inside the contour Γ and $\sigma(A_2)$ is outside the contour Γ. Similarly, $\sigma(A_2-B_2C_2)$ is inside $\Gamma^{\times}$ and $\sigma(A_1-B_1C_1)$ is outside $\Gamma^{\times}$. In particular, we see that (7.25) holds true. This completes the proof of the theorem.

To prove Theorem 7.1, we shall show that Theorem 7.1 appears as a corollary of Theorem 7.7. To do this, let us assume that X and Y are finite dimensional. Further, let us assume that the realization (7.21) is minimal. Applying the last paragraph of Theorem 7.4, we see that in Theorem 7.7 the positive number α_0 may be chosen such that (7.23) implies that the realization $W(\lambda) = I_Y + C(\lambda I_X - A)^{-1}B$ is also minimal. Next we observe that the assumption in Theorem 7.7 that θ_0 is similar to the product $\theta_{01}\theta_{02}$ may be replaced by

$$\dim X = \dim X_1 + \dim X_2, \tag{7.27}$$

because we have assumed that θ_0 is minimal. Further, again because of minimality, the condition (7.22) is equivalent to the requirement that the factors $W_{01}(\lambda)$ and $W_{02}(\lambda)$ have no common zeros and no common poles, and, similarly, (7.25) is equivalent to the statement that the factors $W_1(\lambda)$ and $W_2(\lambda)$ have no common zeros and no common poles. By virtue of (7.27), the minimality of the realizations of $W_0(\lambda)$ and $W(\lambda)$ implies that $W_0(\lambda) = W_{01}(\lambda)W_{02}(\lambda)$ and $W(\lambda) = W_1(\lambda)W_2(\lambda)$ are minimal factorizations (cf. Section 4.3). Using the above remarks it is simple to obtain Theorem 7.1 as a corollary of Theorem 7.7.

Using Theorem 7.6 in the same way as Theorem 7.4 has been used in the proof of Theorem 7.7, one can see that the following analytic version of Theorem 7.7 holds true.

THEOREM 7.8. _Consider the transfer function_

$$W_\varepsilon(\lambda) = I_Y + C_\varepsilon(\lambda I_X - A_\varepsilon)^{-1}B_\varepsilon,$$

and assume that the operators $A_\varepsilon, B_\varepsilon$ _and_ C_ε _depend analytically on_ ε _in a neighbourhood of_ $\varepsilon=0$. _Assume that_

$$W_0(\lambda) = W_{01}(\lambda)W_{02}(\lambda), \quad W_{0i}(\lambda) = I_Y + C_{0i}(\lambda I_{X_i} - A_{0i})^{-1}B_{0i}$$

such that

$$\bigcap_{i=1}^{2} \sigma(A_{0i}) = \phi, \quad \bigcap_{i=1}^{2} \sigma(A_{0i}-B_{0i}C_{0i}) = \phi,$$

and assume that the node $\theta_0 = (A_0,B_0,C_0;X,Y)$ *is similar to the product* $\theta_{01}\theta_{02}$, *where* $\theta_{0i} = (A_{0i},B_{0i},C_{0i};X_i,Y)$, $i=1,2$. *Then for* $|\varepsilon|$ *sufficiently small*

$$W_\varepsilon(\lambda) = W_{1\varepsilon}(\lambda)W_{2\varepsilon}(\lambda), W_{i\varepsilon}(\lambda) = I_Y+C_i^\varepsilon(\lambda I_{X_i}-A_i^\varepsilon)^{-1}B_i^\varepsilon$$

such that

$$\bigcap_{i=1}^{2} \sigma(A_i^\varepsilon) = \phi, \quad \bigcap_{i=1}^{2} \sigma(A_i^\varepsilon-B_i^\varepsilon C_i^\varepsilon) = \phi,$$

the operators $A_1^\varepsilon,A_2^\varepsilon,B_1^\varepsilon,B_2^\varepsilon,C_1^\varepsilon$ *and* C_2^ε *are analytic in* ε, *and for* $\varepsilon=0$ *they are equal to* $A_{01},A_{02},B_{01},B_{02},C_{01}$ *and* C_{02}, *respectively*.

7.5 Applications to Riccati equation

In this section we show that the method of Section 7.3 also can be used to prove stability theorems for certain solutions of the Riccati equation. Throughout this section X_1 and X_2 are Banach spaces, and we use the symbol $L(X_j,X_i)$ to denote the space of all bounded linear operators from X_j into X_i.

THEOREM 7.9. *Let* $T_{ij} \in L(X_j,X_i)$, $1\leq i,j\leq 2$, *and let* $R \in L(X_2,X_1)$ *be a solution of*

$$RT_{21}R + RT_{22} - T_{11}R - T_{12} = 0. \tag{7.28}$$

Assume that $\sigma(T_{11}-RT_{21})\cap\sigma(T_{22}+T_{21}R) = \phi$, *and let* Γ *be a Cauchy contour with* $\sigma(T_{22}+T_{21}R)$ *in the inner domain of* Γ *and* $\sigma(T_{11}-RT_{21})$ *in the outer domain. Then there exist positive constants* α *and* β *such that the following holds. If* $S_{ij}\in L(X_j,X_i)$, $1\leq i,j\leq 2$ *and*

$$\|S_{ij}-T_{ij}\| <\alpha \ , \quad (1\leq i,j\leq 2) \tag{7.29}$$

then the equation

$$QS_{21}Q + QS_{22} - S_{11}Q - S_{12} = 0 \tag{7.30}$$

has a solution $Q \in L(X_2, X_1)$ *such that* $\sigma(S_{22}+S_{21}Q)$ *lies in the inner domain of* Γ, $\sigma(S_{11}-QS_{21})$ *lies in the outer domain of* Γ *and*

$$\| R-Q \| \leq \beta \max_{1 \leq i,j \leq 2} \| T_{ij}-S_{ij} \| . \tag{7.31}$$

PROOF. Consider the operators

$$T = \begin{bmatrix} T_{11} & T_{12} \\ T_{21} & T_{22} \end{bmatrix} , \quad S = \begin{bmatrix} S_{11} & S_{12} \\ S_{21} & S_{22} \end{bmatrix}$$

on $X = X_1 \oplus X_2$. Assume that X is endowed with the norm $\| (x_1, x_2) \| = \| x_1 \| + \| x_2 \|$. Then

$$\| T-S \| \leq 2 \max_{1 \leq i,j \leq 2} \| T_{ij}-S_{ij} \| . \tag{7.32}$$

As the Riccati equation (7.28) has a solution R such that $\sigma(T_{11}-RT_{21}) \cap \sigma(T_{22}+T_{21}R) = \phi$, we know from Section 5.3 that the space

$$N_R = \{(Rz, z) \mid z \in X_2\}$$

is a spectral subspace for T. In fact, if Γ is as in the statement of the theorem, then Γ splits the spectrum of T and $N_R = \operatorname{Im} P(T;\Gamma)$.

Let ℓ be the length of Γ, and put $\gamma = \max_{\lambda \in \Gamma} \| (\lambda - T)^{-1} \|$. Take $\| T-S \| < \frac{1}{2\gamma}$. By elementary spectral theory this implies that Γ splits the spectrum of S and

$$\| (\lambda-T)^{-1} - (\lambda-S)^{-1} \| \leq 2\gamma^2 \| S-T \| , \quad \lambda \in \Gamma .$$

But then $\| P(T;\Gamma)-P(S;\Gamma)\| \leq \pi^{-1}\gamma^2\ell\| S-T\|$.

As $X = X_1 \oplus N_R$, the number $\eta(X_1,N_R)$ is positive. Put

$$\alpha = \min\left\{\frac{1}{4\gamma}, \frac{\pi}{4\gamma^2\ell}\eta(X_1,N_R)\right\},$$

and assume that (7.29) holds true. By (7.32) this implies that $\| T-S\| < 2\alpha \leq (2\gamma)^{-1}$, and we can apply the result of the previous paragraph to show that

$$\| P(T;\Gamma)-P(S;\Gamma)\| < \tfrac{1}{2}\eta(X_1,N_R).$$

In particular we see that

$$\text{gap}(N_R, \text{Im } P(S;\Gamma)) < \tfrac{1}{2}\eta(X_1,N_R). \tag{7.33}$$

By Theorem 2 in [29] this implies that

$$X = X_1 \oplus \text{Im } P(S;\Gamma).$$

It follows that there exists $Q \in L(X_2,X_1)$ such that

$$N_Q = \{(Qz,z) \mid z \in X_2\} = \text{Im } P(S;\Gamma).$$

By Proposition 5.10, this operator Q is a solution of equation (7.30), the spectrum $\sigma(S_{22}+S_{21}Q)$ is in the inner domain of Γ and $\sigma(S_{11}- QS_{21})$ is in the outer domain of Γ.

By (7.33), we have $\text{gap}(N_R,N_Q) < \tfrac{1}{2}\eta(X_1,N_R)$. So we can apply Lemma 7.2 (ii) to show that

$$\| R-Q\| \leq \frac{2(1+\| R\|)}{\eta(X_1,N_R)}\,\text{gap}(N_R,N_Q). \tag{7.34}$$

But

$$\begin{aligned} \text{gap}(N_R,N_Q) &\leq \| P(T,\Gamma)-P(S;\Gamma)\| \\ &\leq \frac{\gamma^2\ell}{\pi}\| T-S\| \end{aligned} \tag{7.35}$$

$$\leq 2\,\frac{\gamma^2 \ell}{\pi} \max_{1\leq i,j\leq 2} \|T_{ij}-S_{ij}\| .$$

Put

$$\beta = 4(1+\|R\|)\,\frac{\gamma^2 \ell}{\pi\eta(X_1 N_R)} .$$

Then we see from (7.34) and (7.35) that (7.31) holds true. This completes the proof of the theorem.

Using arguments similar to the ones employed in the proof of Theorem 7.6, one can see that the following analytic analogue of the previous theorem holds true.

THEOREM 7.10. _Let_ $T_{ij}(\varepsilon) : X_j \to X_i$, $1\leq i,j\leq 2$, _be bounded linear operators which depend analytically on_ ε _in a neighbourhood of_ $\varepsilon = 0$. _Let_ $R\in L(X_2,X_1)$ _be a solution of_

$$RT_{21}(0)R + RT_{22}(0) - T_{11}(0)R-T_{12}(0) = 0,$$

and assume that $\sigma(T_{11}(0)-RT_{21}(0))\cap\sigma(T_{22}(0)+T_{21}(0)R) = \phi$. _Then for_ $|\varepsilon|$ _sufficiently small, there exists an operator_ $R(\varepsilon)\in L(X_2,X_1)$, _which depends analytically on_ ε, _such that_ $R(0)=R$,

$$R(\varepsilon)T_{21}(\varepsilon)R(\varepsilon)+R(\varepsilon)T_{22}(\varepsilon)-T_{11}(\varepsilon)R(\varepsilon)-T_{12}(\varepsilon) = 0$$

and $\sigma(T_{11}(\varepsilon)-R(\varepsilon)T_{21}(\varepsilon))\cap\sigma(T_{22}(\varepsilon)+T_{21}(\varepsilon)R(\varepsilon)) = \phi$.

CHAPTER VIII

STABILITY OF DIVISORS

In this chapter we shall prove that there exist stable factorizations which are not spectral factorizations. In fact, for the finite dimensional case we shall give a complete description of all possible stable minimal factorizations.

8.1 Stable invariant subspaces

In the previous chapter we have implicitly been dealing with invariant subspaces which have a certain stability property. In this section we shall investigate this matter more explicitly.

Let T be a bounded linear operator on a Banach space X. A closed T-invariant subspace N of X is called *stable* if, given $\varepsilon>0$, there exists $\delta>0$ such that the following statement holds true: If S is a bounded linear operator on X and $\|S-T\|<\delta$, then S has a closed invariant subspace M such that $\text{gap}(M,N)<\varepsilon$.

If N is the image of a Riesz projection corresponding to T, then N is clearly a stable invariant subspace for T. In general, not every stable T-invariant subspace is of this form. For the finite dimensional case we shall give a complete description.

Let A be a $k\times k$ matrix. As usual we identify A with its canonical action on $\mathbb{C}^k$. The generalized eigenspace $\text{Ker}(\lambda_0-A)^k$ of A corresponding to the eigenvalue λ_0 will be denoted by $N(\lambda_0)$.

THEOREM 8.1. *Let $\lambda_1,\ldots,\lambda_r$ be the different eigenvalues of the $k\times k$ matrix A. A subspace N of $\mathbb{C}^k$ is A-invariant and stable if and only if $N = N_1 \oplus\ldots\oplus N_r$, where for each j the space N_j is an arbitrary A-invariant subspace of $N(\lambda_j)$ whenever $\dim \text{Ker}(\lambda_j-A) = 1$, while otherwise $N_j = (0)$ or $N_j=N(\lambda_j)$.*

The proof of Theorem 8.1 will be based on a series of lemmas and an auxiliary theorem which is of some interest in itself.

To state the latter theorem we need the following notion. A chain $M_1 \subset M_2 \subset \ldots \subset M_{k-1}$ of A-invariant subspaces is said to be *complete* if $\dim M_j = j$ for $j = 1,\ldots,k-1$.

THEOREM 8.2. *Given* $\varepsilon>0$, *there exists* $\delta>0$ *such that the following holds true: If* B *is a* $k\times k$ *matrix with* $\| B-A \| < \delta$ *and* $\{M_j\}$ *is a complete chain of* B-*invariant subspaces, then there exists a complete chain* $\{N_j\}$ *of* A-*invariant subspaces such that* $\operatorname{gap}(N_j, M_j)<\varepsilon$ *for* $j = 1,\ldots,k-1$.

In general the chain $\{N_j\}$ for A will depend on the choice of B. To see this, consider

$$A = \begin{bmatrix} 0 & 0 \\ 0 & 0 \end{bmatrix}, \quad B_\nu = \begin{bmatrix} 0 & 0 \\ \nu & 0 \end{bmatrix}, \quad B'_\nu = \begin{bmatrix} 0 & \nu \\ 0 & 0 \end{bmatrix},$$

where $\nu\in\mathbb{C}$. Observe that for $\nu\neq 0$ the only one dimensional invariant subspace of B_ν is $(0) \oplus \mathbb{C}$ and for B_ν, $\nu\neq 0$, the only one-dimensional invariant subspace is $\mathbb{C} \oplus (0)$.

PROOF. Assume that the conclusion of the theorem is not correct. Then there exists $\varepsilon>0$ with the property that for every positive integer m there exists a $k\times k$ matrix B_m satisfying $\| B_m-A \| < \frac{1}{m}$ and a complete chain $\{M_{mj}\}$ of B_m-invariant subspaces such that for every complete chain $\{N_j\}$ of A-invariant subspaces

$$(8.1) \qquad \max_{1\leq j\leq k-1} \operatorname{gap}(M_j, M_{mj}) \geq \varepsilon \ , \quad m = 1,2,\ldots \ .$$

Denote by P_{mj} the orthogonal projection of $\mathbb{C}^k$ onto M_{mj}. Since $\mathbb{C}^k$ is finite-dimensional and all P_{mj} are in the unit ball of $L(\mathbb{C}^k)$, there exist a subsequence $\{m_i\}$ of the sequence of positive integers and operators $P_1,\ldots,P_{k-1}$ on $\mathbb{C}^k$ such that

$$\lim_{i\to\infty} P_{m_i j} = P_j, \quad j = 1,\ldots,k-1.$$

Note that $P_1,\dots,P_{k-1}$ are orthogonal projections and that $N_j = \operatorname{Im} P_j$ has dimension j. By passing to the limits it follows from $B_m P_{mj} = P_{mj} B_m P_{mj}$ that $AP_j = P_j A P_j$. Hence N_j is A-invariant. Since $P_{mj} = P_{m,j+1} P_{mj}$ we have $P_j = P_{j+1} P_j$, and thus $N_j \subset N_{j+1}$. It follows that N_j is a complete chain of A-invariant subspaces. Finally $\operatorname{gap}(N_j, M_{m_i j}) = \| P_j - P_{m_i j} \| \to 0$. But this contradicts (8.1), and the proof is complete.

COROLLARY 8.3. <u>If</u> A <u>has only one eigenvalue,</u> λ_0 <u>say, and if</u> $\dim \operatorname{Ker}(\lambda_0 - A) = 1$, <u>then each invariant subspace of</u> A <u>is stable.</u>

PROOF. The conditions on A are equivalent to the requirement that for each $1 \leq j \leq k-1$ the operator A has only one j-dimensional invariant subspace and the non-trivial invariant subspaces form a complete chain. So we may apply the previous theorem to get the desired result.

LEMMA 8.4. <u>If</u> A <u>has only one eigenvalue,</u> λ_0 <u>say, and if</u> $\dim \operatorname{Ker}(\lambda_0 - A) \geq 2$, <u>then the only stable</u> A-<u>invariant subspaces are</u> (0) <u>and</u> $\mathbb{C}^k$.

PROOF. Let $J = \operatorname{diag}(J_1,\dots,J_s)$ be a Jordan matrix for A. Here J_i is a simple Jordan block with λ_0 on the main diagonal and of size κ_i, say. As $\dim \operatorname{Ker}(\lambda_0 - A) \geq 2$ we have $s \geq 2$. By similarity, it suffices to prove that J has no non-trivial stable invariant subspace.

Let $e_1,\dots,e_k$ be the standard basis for $\mathbb{C}^k$. Define on $\mathbb{C}^k$ the operator T_ε by setting $T_\varepsilon e_i = \varepsilon e_{i-1}$ if $i = \kappa_1 + \dots + \kappa_j + 1$, $j = 1,\dots,s-1$ and $T_\varepsilon e_i = 0$ otherwise. Put $B_\varepsilon = J + T_\varepsilon$. Then $B_\varepsilon \to J$ as $\varepsilon \to 0$. For $\varepsilon \neq 0$ the operator B_ε has exactly one j-dimensional invariant subspace namely, $N_j = \operatorname{sp}\{e_1,\dots,e_j\}$. Here $1 \leq j \leq k-1$. It follows that N_j is the only candidate for a stable J-invariant subspace of dimension j.

Now consider $\tilde{J} = \operatorname{diag}(J_s,\dots,J_1)$. Repeating the argument of the previous paragraph for $\tilde{J}$ instead of J, we see that N_j

is the only candidate for a stable $\tilde{J}$-invariant subspace of dimension j. But $J = S\tilde{J}S^{-1}$, where S is the similarity transformation that reverses the order of the blocks in J. It follows that SN_j is the only candidate for a stable J-invariant subspace of dimension j. However, as $s \geq 2$, we have $SN_j \neq N_j$ for $1 \leq j \leq k-1$, and the proof is complete.

Corollary 8.3 and Lemma 8.4 together prove Theorem 8.1 for the case when A has one eigenvalue only. The next two lemmas will show that the general version of the theorem may be proved by reduction to the case of a single eigenvalue.

In the remainder of this section $\mathbf{X}$ will be a complex Banach space and T will be a bounded linear operator on X.

LEMMA 5. <u>Let</u> Γ <u>be a Cauchy contour that splits the spectrum of</u> T, <u>let</u> T_0 <u>be the restriction of</u> T <u>to</u> $\operatorname{Im} P(T;\Gamma)$ <u>and let</u> N <u>be a closed subspace of</u> $\operatorname{Im} P(T;\Gamma)$. <u>Then</u> N <u>is a stable invariant subspace for</u> T <u>if and only if</u> N <u>is a stable invariant subspace for</u> T_0.

PROOF. Suppose N is a stable invariant subspace for T_0, but not for T. Then one can find $\varepsilon>0$ such that for every positive integer m there exists $S_m \in L(Y)$ satisfying

$$\|S_m - T\| < \frac{1}{m} \tag{8.2}$$

and

$$\operatorname{gap}(N,M) \geqq \varepsilon, \quad M \in \Omega_m. \tag{8.3}$$

Here Ω_m denotes the collection of all closed invariant subspaces for S_m. From (8.2) it is clear that $S_m \to T$. By assumption Γ splits the spectrum of T. Thus, for m sufficiently large, the contour Γ will split the spectrum of S_m too. Moreover, $P(S_m;\Gamma) \to P(T;\Gamma)$ and hence $\operatorname{Im} P(S_m;\Gamma)$ tends to $\operatorname{Im} P(T;\Gamma)$ in the gap topology. But then, for m sufficiently large,

$$\operatorname{Ker} P(T;\Gamma) \oplus \operatorname{Im} P(S_m;\Gamma) = X$$

(cf [29], Theorem 2).

Let R_m be the angular operator of $\operatorname{Im} P(S_m;\Gamma)$ with respect to $P(T;\Gamma)$. Here, as in the sequel, m is supposed to be sufficiently large. As $P(S_m;\Gamma) \to P(T;\Gamma)$, we have $R_m \to 0$. Put

$$E_m = \begin{bmatrix} I & R_m \\ 0 & I \end{bmatrix},$$

where the matrix representation corresponds to the decomposition

$$X = \operatorname{Ker} P(T;\Gamma) \oplus \operatorname{Im} P(T;\Gamma). \tag{8.4}$$

Then E_m is invertible with inverse

$$E_m^{-1} = \begin{bmatrix} I & -R_m \\ 0 & I \end{bmatrix},$$

$E_m \operatorname{Im} P(T;\Gamma) = \operatorname{Im} P(S_m;\Gamma)$ and $E_m \to I$.

Put $T_m = E_m^{-1} S_m E_m$. Then $T_m \operatorname{Im} P(T;\Gamma) \subset \operatorname{Im} P(T;\Gamma)$ and $T_m \to T$. Let T_{m0} be the restriction of T_m to $\operatorname{Im} P(T;\Gamma)$. Then $T_{m0} \to T_0$. As N is a stable invariant subspace for T_0 there exists a sequence $\{N_m\}$ of closed subspaces of $\operatorname{Im} P(T;\Gamma)$ such that N_m is T_{m0}-invariant and $\operatorname{gap}(N_m,N) \to 0$. Note that N_m is also T_m-invariant.

Now put $M_m = E_m N_m$. Then M_m is a closed invariant subspace for S_m. Thus $M_m \in \Omega_m$. From $E_m \to I$ one can easily deduce that $\operatorname{gap}(M_m,N_m) \to 0$. Together with $\operatorname{gap}(N_m,N) \to 0$ this gives $\operatorname{gap}(M_m,N) \to 0$, which contradicts (8.3).

Next assume that N is a stable invariant subspace for T, but not for T_0. Then one can find $\varepsilon>0$ such that for every positive integer m there exists a bounded linear operator S_{m0}

on $\text{Im } P(T;\Gamma)$ satisfying

(8.5) $$\| S_{m0}-T_0 \| < \frac{1}{m}$$

and

(8.6) $$\text{gap}(N,M) \geq \varepsilon \ , \ M\in\Omega_{m0}.$$

Here Ω_{m0} denotes the collection of all closed invariant subspaces of S_{m0}. Let T_1 be the restriction of T to $\text{Ker } P(T;\Gamma)$ and write

$$S_m = \begin{pmatrix} T_1 & 0 \\ 0 & S_{m0} \end{pmatrix},$$

where the matrix representation corresponds to the decomposition (8.4). From (8.5) it is clear that $S_m \to T$. Hence, as N is a stable invariant subspace for T, there exists a sequence $\{N_m\}$ of closed subspaces of X such that N_m is S_m-invariant and $\text{gap}(N_m,N) \to 0$. Put $M_m = P(T;\Gamma)N_m$. Since $P(T;\Gamma)$ commutes with S_m, we have that M_m is an invariant subspace for S_{m0}. As N is a closed subspace of $\text{Im} P(T;\Gamma)$, the minimal opening $\eta = \eta(N,\text{Ker } P(T;\Gamma))$ is strictly positive. From [29], Lemma 2 we know that $\text{gap}(N_m,N) \to 0$ implies that $\eta(N_m ,\text{Ker } P(T;\Gamma))\to\eta$.

So, for m sufficiently large, $\eta(N_m,\text{Ker } P(T;\Gamma)) \geq \frac{1}{2}\eta > 0$. It follows that $N_m + \text{Ker } P(T;\Gamma)$ is closed. But then M_m is also closed by [32], Lemma IV.2.9. Hence M_m is a closed invariant subspace for S_{m0}. In other words $M_m\in\Omega_{m0}$. We shall now prove that $\text{gap}(M_m,N) \to 0$, thus obtaining a contradiction to (8.6).

Take $y\in M_m$ with $\|y\| \leq 1$. Then $y = P(T;\Gamma)x$ for some $x\in M_m$. As

$$\|y\| = \|P(T;\Gamma)x\| \geq \inf\{\|x-u\| \mid u\in\text{Ker } P(T;\Gamma)\}$$

$$\geq \eta(N_m, \text{Ker } P(T;\Gamma)).\| x \|,$$

we see that $\|y\| \geq \frac{1}{2}\eta\|x\|$ for m sufficiently large. Using this it is not difficult to deduce that

$$\operatorname{gap}(M_m,N) \leq (1+\frac{2}{\eta})\|P(T;\Gamma)\|\cdot\operatorname{gap}(N_m,N)$$

for m sufficiently large. We conclude that $\operatorname{gap}(N_m,N) \to 0$, and the proof is complete.

LEMMA 8.6. _Let_ N _be a complemented invariant subspace for_ T, _and assume that the Cauchy contour_ Γ _splits the spectrum of_ T _and the spectrum of the restriction operator_ $T|_N$. _If_ N _is stable for_ T, _then_ $P(T;\Gamma)N$ _is a stable closed invariant subspace for the restriction_ T_0 _of_ T _to_ $\operatorname{Im} P(T;\Gamma)$.

PROOF. It is clear that $M = P(T;\Gamma)N$ is T_0-invariant. Since $(\lambda-T|_N)^{-1} = (\lambda-T)^{-1}|_N$ for all $\lambda\in\Gamma$, we have $M = P(T;\Gamma)N = \operatorname{Im} P(T|_N;\Gamma) \subset N$, and it follows that M is closed.

Assume that M is not stable for T_0. Then M is neither stable for T by Lemma 8.5. Hence there exist $\varepsilon>0$ and a sequence $\{S_m\}$ such that $S_m \to T$ and

$$\operatorname{gap}(L,M) \geq \varepsilon\ , \quad L\in\Omega_m;\quad m=1,2,\dots\ , \tag{8.7}$$

where Ω_m denotes the set of all closed invariant subspaces of S_m.

As N is stable for T, one can find a sequence of closed subspace $\{N_m\}$ such that $S_mN_m \subset N_m$ and $\operatorname{gap}(N_m,N) \to 0$. Further, since Γ splits the spectrum of T and $S_m \to T$, the contour Γ will split the spectrum of S_m for m sufficiently large. But then, without loss of generality, we may assume that Γ splits the spectrum of each S_m. Again using $S_m \to T$, it follows that $P(S_m;\Gamma) \to P(T;\Gamma)$.

Let Z be a closed complement of N in X, i.e., $X = Z \oplus N$. As $\operatorname{gap}(N_m,N) \to 0$, we have $X = Z \oplus N_m$ for m sufficiently large. So, without loss of generality, we may assume that $X = Z \oplus N_m$ for each m. Let R_m be the angular operator of N_m with respect to the projection of X along Z onto N, and put

$$E_m = \begin{pmatrix} I & R_m \\ 0 & I \end{pmatrix},$$

where the matrix corresponds to the decomposition $X = Z \oplus N$. Note that $T_m = E_m^{-1} S_m E_m$ leaves invariant N. Because $R_m \to 0$ we have $E_m \to I$, and so $T_m \to T$.

By assumption Γ splits the spectrum of $T|_N$. As $T_m \to T$ and N is invariant under T_m, the contour Γ will split the spectrum of $T_m|_N$ too, provided m is sufficiently large. But then we may assume that this happens for all m. Also, we have

$$\lim_{m\to\infty} P(T_m|_N;\Gamma) \to P(T|_N;\Gamma).$$

Hence $M_m = \operatorname{Im} P(T_m|_N;\Gamma) \to \operatorname{Im} P(T|_N;\Gamma) = M$ in the gap topology.

Now consider $L_m = E_m M_m$. Then L_m is a closed S_m-invariant subspace of X. In other words $L_m \in \Omega_m$. From $E_m \to I$ it follows that $\operatorname{gap}(L_m, M_m) \to 0$. This, together with $\operatorname{gap}(M_m, M) \to 0$, gives $\operatorname{gap}(L_m, M) \to 0$. So we arrive at a contradiction to (8.7) and the proof is complete.

PROOF OF THEOREM 8.1. Suppose N is a stable invariant subspace for A. Put $N_j = P_j N$, where P_j is the Riesz projection corresponding to A and λ_j. Then $N = N_1 \oplus \ldots \oplus N_r$. By Lemma 8.6 the space N_j is a stable invariant subspace for the restriction A_j of A to $N(\lambda_j)$. But A_j has one eigenvalue only, namely λ_j. So we may apply Lemma 8.4 to prove that N_j has the desired form.

Conversely, assume that each N_j has the desired form, and let us prove that $N = N_1 \oplus \ldots \oplus N_r$ is a stable invariant subspace for A. By Corollary 8.3 the space N_j is a stable invariant subspace for the restriction A_j of A to $\operatorname{Im} P_j$. Hence we may apply Lemma 8.5 to show that each N_j is a stable invariant subspace for A. But then the same is true for the direct sum

$N = N_1 \oplus \ldots \oplus N_r$.

For shortness sake, the proofs of Lemmas 8.5 and 8.6 were given by reductio ad absurdum. It is of some practical interest to note that they could have been given in a more constructive way.

The next theorem indicates the way in which Theorem 8.1 will be applied in the context of minimal factorization theory.

THEOREM 8.7. _Let_ X_1 _and_ X_2 _be finite-dimensional spaces and let_

$$A = \begin{pmatrix} A_1 & A_0 \\ 0 & A_2 \end{pmatrix}$$

be a linear operator acting on $X = X_1 \oplus X_2$. _Then_ X_1 _is a stable invariant subspace for_ A _if an only if each common eigenvalue of_ A_1 _and_ A_2 _is an eigenvalue of_ A _of geometric multiplicity one_.

PROOF. It is clear that X_1 is an invariant subspace for A. We know from Theorem 8.1 that X_1 is stable if and only if for each Riesz projection P of A corresponding to an eigenvalue λ_0 with $\dim \operatorname{Ker}(\lambda_0 - A) \geq 2$, we have $PX_1 = 0$ or $PX_1 = \operatorname{Im} P$.

Let P be a Riesz projection of A corresponding to an arbitrary complex number λ_0. Also for $i = 1,2$ let P_i be the Riesz projection associated with A_i and λ_0. Then P has the form

$$P = \begin{pmatrix} P_1 & P_1Q_1 + Q_2P_2 \\ 0 & P_2 \end{pmatrix},$$

where Q_1 and Q_2 are certain linear operators acting from X_2 into X_1 (cf. the proof of Theorem 4.2). It follows that $(0) \neq PX_1 \neq \operatorname{Im} P$ if and only if λ_0 is a common eigenvalue of A_1 and A_2. This proves the theorem.

Let T be a bounded linear operator on a complex Banach space X. A closed invariant subspace of T is called _isolated_ if there exists $\varepsilon>0$ such that each invariant subspace M of T different from N satisfies $\mathrm{gap}(M,N) \geqq \varepsilon$. When X is finite-dimensional, an invariant subspace N of T is isolated if and only if it is stable. This appears from Theorem 8.1 above and Theorem 9 in [16] (cf. Section 9.3). This fact has also been proved by S. Campbell and J. Daughtry in [12] (see also [13]). Their main theorem also contains the characterization given in Theorem 8.1.

8.2 Stable minimal factorizations of rational matrix functions

Throughout this section W_0, W_{01} and W_{02} are rational $k\times k$ matrix functions that are analytic at ∞ with value I_k, the $k\times k$ identity matrix. We assume that $W_0 = W_{01}W_{02}$ and that this factorization is minimal. In view of Theorems 7.1 and 7.7 the following definition is natural. Let

$$W_0(\lambda) = I_k + C_0(\lambda I_\delta - A_0)^{-1}B_0, \tag{8.8}$$

$$W_{0i}(\lambda) = I_k + C_{0i}(\lambda I_{\delta_i} - A_{0i})^{-1}B_{0i}, \quad i = 1,2, \tag{8.9}$$

be minimal realizations of W_0, W_{01} and W_{02}. The factorization $W_0 = W_{01}W_{02}$ is called <u>stable</u> if for each $\varepsilon>0$ there exists $\omega>0$ such that $\|A-A_0\|+\|B-B_0\|+\|C-C_0\| < \omega$ implies that the realization

$$W(\lambda) = I_k + C(\lambda I_\delta - A)^{-1}B$$

is minimal and W admits a minimal factorization $W = W_1W_2$,

$$W_i(\lambda) = I_k + C_i(\lambda I_{\delta_i} - A_i)^{-1}B_i, \quad i = 1,2,$$

with the extra property that $\|A_i-A_{0i}\| + \|B_i-B_{0i}\| + \|C_i-C_{0i}\| < \varepsilon$. Since in the finite-dimensional case all minimal realizations of a given transfer function are mutually similar, this definition does not depend on the choice of the minimal realizations (8.8) and (8.9).

From Theorem 7.1 we see that a sufficient condition for the factorization $W_0 = W_{01}W_{02}$ to be stable is that W_{01} and W_{02} have no common poles and no common zeros. The next theorem characterizes stability of minimal factorization in terms of spectral data.

THEOREM 8.8. *Suppose* $W_0 = W_{01}W_{02}$ *is a minimal factorization. This factorization is stable if and only if each common pole (zero) of* W_{01} *and* W_{02} *is a pole (zero) of* W_0 *of geometric multiplicity one.*

The proof of this theorem will be given in a number of steps. Recall that there is a one-one correspondence between minimal factorizations and supporting projections of minimal realizations (see Theorem 4.8). Therefore we begin by characterizing stability of minimal factorizations in terms of supporting projections. This leads to the notion of a stable supporting projection.

Let Π_0 be a supporting projection for the node $\theta_0=(A_0,B_0,C_0;X,Y)$. We call Π_0 *stable* if, given $\varepsilon>0$, there exists $\omega>0$ such that the following is true: If $\theta=(A,B,C;X,Y)$ is a node satisfying $\|\theta-\theta_0\|<\omega$, then θ has a supporting projection Π such that $\|\Pi-\Pi_0\|<\varepsilon$.

LEMMA 8.9. *Let* $W_0(\lambda) = I_k + C_0(\lambda I_\delta - A_0)^{-1}B_0$ *be a minimal realization for* W_0, *and let* Π_0 *be the supporting projection for the node* $\theta_0 = (A_0,B_0,C_0;\mathbb{C}^\delta,\mathbb{C}^k)$ *corresponding to the minimal factorization* $W_0 = W_{01}W_{02}$. *This factorization is stable if and only if* Π_0 *is stable.*

PROOF. We know already that for $\|A-A_0\|+\|B-B_0\|+\|C-C_0\|$ sufficiently small the realization $W(\lambda) = I_k+C(\lambda I_\delta-A)^{-1}B$ will be minimal. So, if Π_0 is stable, we can apply Theorem 7.5 to show that the factorization $W_0 = W_{01}W_{02}$ is stable too.

Conversely, let the factorization $W_0 = W_{01}W_{02}$ be stable and assume Π_0 is not stable. Then there exist $\varepsilon>0$ and a sequence $\{\theta_n\}$ of nodes such that $\|\theta_n-\theta_0\| \to 0$ and $\|\Pi-\Pi_0\| \geq \varepsilon$ for each supporting projection Π of θ_n $(n=1,2,\dots)$. Since

θ_0 is minimal and $\|\theta_n-\theta_0\|\to 0$, we may assume that θ_n is minimal for all n. Also we may assume that for each n the transfer function $W_n = W_{\theta_n}$ admits a minimal factorization $W_n=W_{n1}W_{n2}$,

$$W_{ni}(\lambda) = I_k + C_{ni}(\lambda I_{\delta_i}-A_{ni})^{-1}B_{ni}$$

such that for $i = 1,2$ and $n\to\infty$, we have

$$A_{ni} \to A_{0i}\ ,\ B_{ni} \to B_{0i}\ ,\ C_{ni} \to C_{0i}. \tag{8.10}$$

Here $I_k + C_{0i}(\lambda I_{\delta_i}-A_{0i})^{-1}B_{0i}$ is a minimal realization for W_{0i} $(i=1,2)$.

Let Π_n be the supporting projection for θ_n corresponding to the minimal factorization $W_n = W_{n1}W_{n2}$. Write $\theta_{ni}=(A_{ni},B_{ni},C_{ni};\mathbb{C}^{\delta_i},\mathbb{C}^k)$. Then $\theta_{n1}\theta_{n2}$ and θ_n are similar, say with node similarity $S_n:\mathbb{C}^{\delta_1}\oplus\mathbb{C}^{\delta_2} \to \mathbb{C}^{\delta}$. For $n = 0,1,2,\dots$, we have $\Pi_n = S_nPS_n^{-1}$, where P is the projection of $\mathbb{C}^{\delta_1}\oplus\mathbb{C}^{\delta_2}$ along $\mathbb{C}^{\delta_1}$ onto $\mathbb{C}^{\delta_2}$. From Theorem 3.1 we know how S_n can be described explicitly. This description, together with formula (8.10) and $\|\theta_n-\theta_0\| \to 0$, gives $S_n\to S_0$. So $\Pi_n\to\Pi_0$, which contradicts the fact that $\|\Pi_n-\Pi_0\|\geq\varepsilon$ for all n. We conclude that Π_0 must be stable.

Next we make the connection with stable invariant subspaces.

LEMMA 8.10. <u>Let Π_0 be a supporting projection for the node $\theta_0 = (A_0,B_0,C_0;X,Y)$. Then Π_0 is stable if and only if Ker Π_0 and Im Π_0 are stable invariant subspaces for A_0 and $A_0^\times = A_0-B_0C_0$, respectively</u>.

PROOF. Let Ker Π_0 and Im Π_0 be stable invariant subspaces for A_0 and $A_0^\times$, respectively. Assume Π_0 is not stable. Then there exist $\varepsilon>0$ and a sequence $\{\theta_n\}$ of nodes such that $\|\theta_n-\theta_0\|\to 0$ and $\|\Pi-\Pi_0\|\geq\varepsilon$ for every supporting projection Π of θ_n $(n=1,2,\dots)$. Write $\theta_n = (A_n,B_n,C_n;X,Y)$. Then clearly $A_n\to A_0$ and $A_n^\times = A_n-B_nC_n \to A_0-B_0C_0 = A_0^\times$. But then our hypothesis ensures the existence of two sequences $\{M_n\}$ and $\{M_n^\times\}$ of closed subspaces of X such that $A_nM_n\subset M_n$, $A_n^\times M_n^\times\subset M_n^\times$ $(n=1,2,\ldots)$ and

$$\text{(8.11)}\qquad \operatorname{gap}(M_n,\operatorname{Ker}\Pi_0)\to 0,\ \operatorname{gap}(M_n^\times,\operatorname{Im}\Pi_0)\to 0.$$

By [29], Theorem 2 we may assume that $X = M_n\oplus M_n^\times$ for all n. Let Π_n be the projection of X along M_n onto $M_n^\times$. Then Π_n is a supporting projection for θ_n. Moreover it follows from (8.11) that $\Pi_n\to\Pi_0$. This contradicts the fact that $\|\Pi_n-\Pi_0\|\geq\varepsilon$ for all n. So Π_0 must be stable.

Now conversely. Let Π_0 be a stable supporting projection for θ_0 and assume $\operatorname{Ker}\Pi_0$ is not stable for A_0. Then there exist $\varepsilon>0$ and a sequence $\{A_n\}$ of bounded linear operators on X such that $A_n\to A_0$ and $\operatorname{gap}(M,\operatorname{Ker}\Pi_0)\geq\varepsilon$ for each closed invariant subspace of A_n $(n=1,2,\ldots)$. Put $\theta_n = (A_n,B_0,C_0;X,Y)$. Then $\|\theta_n-\theta_0\|\to 0$. So we can find a sequence $\{\Pi_n\}$ of projections such that Π_n is a supporting projection for θ_n $(n=1,2,\ldots)$ and $\Pi_n\to\Pi_0$. Hence $\operatorname{Ker}\Pi_n$ is a closed invariant subspace for A_n and gap $(\operatorname{Ker}\Pi_n,\operatorname{Ker}\Pi_0)\to 0$. But this contradicts the fact that $\operatorname{gap}(\operatorname{Ker}\Pi_n,\operatorname{Ker}\Pi_0)\geq\varepsilon$ for all n. So $\operatorname{Ker}\Pi_0$ must be stable for A_0. In a similar way one can prove that $\operatorname{Im}\Pi_0$ is a stable invariant subspace for $A_0^\times$.

We now come to the proof Theorem 8.8. Recall that W_0, W_{01} and W_{02} are rational $k\times k$ matrix functions that are analytic at ∞ with value I_k. Moreover $W_0 = W_{01}W_{02}$ and this factorization is minimal.

PROOF OF THEOREM 8.8. Let $W_0(\lambda) = I_k + C_0(\lambda I_\delta-A_0)^{-1}B_0$ be a minimal realization for W_0, and let Π_0 be the supporting projection for the node $\theta_0=(A_0,B_0,C_0;\mathbb{C}^\delta,\mathbb{C}^k)$ corresponding to the minimal factorization $W_0 = W_{01}W_{02}$. From Lemma 8.9 we know that this factorization is stable if and only if Π_0 is stable.

With respect to the decomposition $\mathbb{C}^\delta = \operatorname{Ker}\Pi_0\oplus\operatorname{Im}\Pi_0$, we write

$$A_0 = \begin{pmatrix} A_1 & * \\ 0 & A_2 \end{pmatrix}.$$

Applying Theorem 8.7 we see that Ker Π_0 is a stable invariant subspace for A_0 if and only if each common eigenvalue of A_1 and A_2 is an eigenvalue of A_0 of geometric multiplicity one. Thus, by Lemma 4.7, Ker Π_0 is stable for A_0 if and only if each common eigenvalue of A_1 and A_2 is a pole of W_0 of geometric multiplicity one. Observe now that A_1 and A_2 are the main operators in the nodes $\mathrm{pr}_{\Pi_0}(\theta)$ and $\mathrm{pr}_{I_\delta - \Pi_0}(\theta)$, respectively. Since these nodes are minimal, we have that $\sigma(A_1)$ and $\sigma(A_2)$ coincide with the sets of poles of W_{01} and W_{02}, respectively. Hence Ker Π_0 is stable for A_0 if and only if each common pole of W_{01} and W_{02} is a pole of W_0 of geometric multiplicity one. In the same way one can prove that Im Π_0 is stable for $A_0^\times$ if and only if each common zero of W_{01} and W_{02} is a zero of W_0 of geometric multiplicity one. The desired result is now immediate from Lemma 8.10.

8.3 Stable factorizations of monic matrix polynomials

Throughout this section k will be a fixed positive integer. Given a positive integer m, we denote the set of all monic $k\times k$ matrix polynomials by M_m. If L_1 and L_2 are in M_m, say

$$L_i(\lambda) = \lambda^m I + \sum_{j=0}^{m-1} \lambda^j A_{ij}, \quad i = 1,2,$$

we put

$$\| L_1 - L_2 \| = \sum_{j=0}^{m-1} \| A_{1j} - A_{2j} \|.$$

This defines a metric on M_m.

Suppose L, L_1 and L_2 are monic $k\times k$ matrix polynomials of degree p, q and r, respectively. So $L\in M_p$, $L_1\in M_q$ and $L_2 \in M_r$.

Assume $L = L_2L_1$. We say that this factorization is <u>stable</u> if, given $\varepsilon>0$, there exists $\delta>0$ with the following property: If $L'\in M_p$ and $\|L-L'\|<\delta$, then L' admits a factorization $L' = L_2'L_1'$ with $L_1'\in M_q$, $L_2'\in M_r$ and

$$\|L_i'-L_i\| < \varepsilon, \quad i = 1,2.$$

The aim of this section is to characterize stability of a factorization in terms of spectral data. We begin by making the connection with stable invariant subspaces. This will be done via the notion of a supporting subspace discussed in Subsection 1.4.3. Supporting subspaces will always be taken with respect to first companion nodes (see formula 1.25). For briefness sake we shall simply speak about supporting subspaces (of the first companion operator) of L. Recall that there is a one-one correspondence between the supporting subspaces of L and the factorizations of L into monic operator polynomials.

LEMMA 8.11. *Let L, L_1 and L_2 be monic $k\times k$ matrix polynomials and assume $L = L_2L_1$. This factorization is stable if and only if the corresponding supporting subspace is stable for the first companion operator of* L.

PROOF. It is possible to give a rather quick proof based on [27], Theorem 3. We prefer however to present a more direct argument.

For convenience we put $L_0 = L$ and $L_{0i} = L_i (i=1,2)$. The degree of L_0 will be denoted by p and that of L_{01} by q. The first companion operator of L_0 is indicated by C_0, the supporting subspace of L_0 corresponding to the factorization $L_0 = L_{02}L_{01}$ by M_0.

Suppose the factorization is stable. In order to prove that M_0 is a stable invariant subspace for C_0 we consider a sequence $\{C_n\}_{n=1}^{\infty}$ of operators converging to C_0. Put

$$Q = \mathrm{row}(\delta_{i1}I)_{i=1}^{p}, \quad S_n = \mathrm{col}\,(QC_n^i)_{i=0}^{p-1}, \quad n = 0,1,\ldots .$$

Then $\{S_n\}$ converges to S_0 which is equal to the identity operator on $\mathbb{C}^{kp}$. So, passing if necessary to a subsequence, we may assume that S_n is invertible for all n. Write $S_n^{-1}=\mathrm{row}(U_{ni})_{i=1}^{p}$. Then

$$U_{ni} \to \mathrm{col}(\delta_{ji}I)_{j=1}^{p}, \quad i=1,2,\dots,p. \tag{8.12}$$

A straightforward calculation shows that $S_nC_nS_n^{-1}$ is the first companion operator associated with the monic operator polynomial

$$L_n(\lambda) = \lambda^p I - \sum_{i=1}^{p} \lambda^{i-1} QC_n^p U_{ni}.$$

From (8.12) and the fact that $C_n \to C$ it follows that $\|L_n-L_0\| \to 0$. But then we may assume that for all n the polynomial L_n admits a factorization $L_n = L_{n2}L_{n1}$ with $L_{n1}\in M_q$, $L_{n2}\in M_r$, $r=p-q$, and

$$\| L_{ni}-L_{0i} \| \to 0 \ , \ i = 1,2.$$

Let M_n be the supporting subspace corresponding to the factorization $L_n = L_{n2}L_{n1}$. We shall show that $M_n \to M_0$ in the gap topology. In order to do this we describe M_n as follows. Let D_n be the first companion operator of L_{n1}. Then M_n is the image of the operator

$$\mathrm{col}(QD_n^i)_{i=0}^{p-1} : \mathbb{C}^{kr} \to \mathbb{C}^{kp}$$

(see Subsection 1.4.3). Define $P : \mathbb{C}^{kp} = \mathbb{C}^{kr}\oplus\mathbb{C}^{k(p-r)}\to\mathbb{C}^{kr}$ by $P=[I\ 0]$. Since P is surjective, we have $M_n = \mathrm{Im}\, P_n$, where $P_n = [\mathrm{col}(QD_n^i)_{i=0}^{p-1}]P$ has the form

$$P_n = \begin{pmatrix} I & 0 \\ F_n & 0 \end{pmatrix} : \mathbb{C}^{kr} \oplus \mathbb{C}^{k(p-r)} \to \mathbb{C}^{kr} + \mathbb{C}^{k(p-r)}.$$

Observe that P_n is a projection. Now $\| L_{n1}-L_{01} \| \to 0$ implies that $F_n \to F_0$. Hence $P_n \to P_0$. But $\mathrm{gap}(M_n, M_0) = \mathrm{gap}(\mathrm{Im}\, P_k, \mathrm{Im}\, P_0) \leq \|P_n - P_0\|$, and so $\mathrm{gap}(M_n, M_0) \to 0$.

Put $V_n = S_n^{-1} M_n$. Then V_n is an invariant subspace for C_n. Moreover, it follows from $S_n \to I$ that $\mathrm{gap}(V_n, M_n) \to 0$. But then $\mathrm{gap}(V_n, M) \to 0$, and the first part of the proof is complete.

Next assume that M_0 is a stable invariant subspace of C_0, and let $\{L_n\}_{n=1}^{\infty}$ be a sequence in M_p converging to L_0. Denote the first companion operator of L_n by C_n. Then $C_n \to C_0$, and hence there exists a C_n-invariant subspace M_n of $\mathbb{C}^{kp}$ such that $\mathrm{gap}(M_n, M_0) \to 0$. Recall now that $\mathbb{C}^{kp} = M_0 \oplus N_q$, where

(8.13) $$N_q = \{x = (x_1, \ldots, x_p) \in \mathbb{C}^{kp} \mid x_1 = \ldots = x_q = 0\}.$$

So, passing if necessary to a subsequence, we may assume that

(8.14) $$\mathbb{C}^{kp} = M_n \oplus N_q, \quad n = 0, 1, 2, \ldots .$$

This means that M_n is a supporting subspace for L_n. Let $L_n = L_{n2} L_{n1}$ be the corresponding factorization. We need to show that $\|L_{n1} - L_{01}\| \to 0$ and $\|L_{n2} - L_{02}\| \to 0$.

With respect to the decomposition (8.13) we write

$$C_n = \begin{pmatrix} C_{n1} & C_{n0} \\ 0 & C_{n2} \end{pmatrix}, \quad Q_n = [Q_{n1} \; Q_{n2}].$$

The polynomial L_{n1} can be explicitly expressed in terms of C_{n1} and Q_{n1} (cf. Subsection 1.4.3). A complication here is that the decomposition (8.14) depends on n. This difficulty however can be easily overcome by the usual angular operator argument. From the expression for L_{n1} one then sees that $\|L_{n1} - L_{01}\| \to 0$. In the same way one shows that $\|L_{n2} - L_{02}\| \to 0$, and the proof is complete.

Recall that a complex number λ_0 is an eigenvalue of the matrix polynomial L if $L(\lambda_0)$ is not invertible. In that case

Ker $L(\lambda_0)$ is non-trivial and its dimension is the geometric multiplicity of λ_0 as an eigenvalue of L. This number is also equal to the geometric multiplicity of λ_0 as an eigenvalue of the first companion operator of L.

THEOREM 8.12 . *Let L, L_1 and L_2 be monic $k\times k$ matrix polynomials and assume $L = L_2L_1$. This factorization is stable if and only if each common eigenvalue of L_1 and L_2 is an eigenvalue of L of geometric multiplicity one.*

PROOF. Let M be the supporting subspace of L corresponding to the factorization $L = L_2L_1$. From Lemma 8.1 we know that this factorization is stable if and only if M is a stable invariant subspace for the first companion operator C of L. Let p be the degree of L, let q be the degree of L_1 and let N_q be as in (8.13). Then $\mathbb{C}^{kp} = M \oplus N_q$. With respect to this decomposition we write

$$C = \begin{pmatrix} C_1 & C_0 \\ 0 & C_2 \end{pmatrix}.$$

Then it is known (cf. Subsection 1.4.3 and the end of Section 2.4) that a complex number is an eigenvalue of C_i if and only if it is an eigenvalue of L_i $(i=1,2)$. The desired result is now obtained by applying Theorem 8.7.

8.4 Stable solutions of the operator Riccati equation

Consider the operator Riccati equation

$$XT_{21}X + XT_{22} - T_{11}X - T_{12} = 0. \tag{8.15}$$

Here for $i,j = 1,2$, the symbol T_{ij} denotes a linear operator from Y_j into Y_i. The spaces Y_1 and Y_2 are assumed to be finite-dimensional. A solution $R: Y_2 \longrightarrow Y_1$ of (8.15) is said to be <u>stable</u> if for each $\varepsilon>0$ there exists $\delta>0$ such that $\max_{i,j=1,2} \|S_{ij}-T_{ij}\| <\delta$ implies that the Riccati equation

$$XS_{21}X + XS_{22} - S_{11}X - S_{12} = 0$$

has a solution $Q: Y_2 \to Y_1$ for which $\|Q-R\|<\varepsilon$.

THEOREM 8.13. *A solution R of the Riccati equation (8.15) is stable if and only if each common eigenvalue of $T_{11}-RT_{21}$ and $T_{22} + T_{21}R$ is an eigenvalue of the operator*

$$T = \begin{pmatrix} T_{11} & T_{12} \\ T_{21} & T_{22} \end{pmatrix} : Y_1 \oplus Y_2 \to Y_1 \oplus Y_2$$

of geometric multiplicity one.

PROOF. Put $N = \{(Rz,z) \mid z \in Y_2\}$. Then $Y_1 \oplus N = Y_1 \oplus Y_2$ and R is the angular operator for N with respect to the projection of $Y_1 \oplus Y_2$ along Y_1 onto Y_2. By Proposition 5.9, the hypothesis that R is a solution of (8.15) is equivalent to the assumption that N is an invariant subspace for T. It is not difficult to prove that R is a stable solution of (8.15) if and only if N is a stable invariant subspace for T. The latter is the case if and only if Y_2 is a stable invariant subspace for the operator given by the right hand side of (5.11). The desired result is now an immediate consequence of Theorem 8.7.

8.5 Stability of stable factorizations

Let X be a finite dimensional Banach space, and let T be a bounded linear operator on X. If N is a stable invariant subspace for T, then by definition for each $\varepsilon>0$, there exists $\delta > 0$ such that $\|S-T\|<\delta$ implies that S has an invariant subspace M with gap$(M,N)<\varepsilon$. On the basis of Theorem 8.7 one can prove that for an appropriate choice of δ the space M may always be chosen to be stable for S. This is the contents of the next theorem.

THEOREM 8.14. Let N be a stable invariant subspace for a linear operator T acting on a finite-dimensional space X. Then, given $\varepsilon > 0$, there exists $\delta > 0$ such that $\|S-T\| < \delta$ implies that S has a stable invariant subspace M such that gap$(M,N)<\varepsilon$.

PROOF. Suppose not. Then there exist $\varepsilon > 0$ and a sequence $\{S_m\}$ of linear operators on X converging to T such that

$$\text{gap}(M,N) \geq \varepsilon, \quad M \in \Omega_m;\ m = 1,2,\ldots .$$

Here Ω_m denotes the collection of all stable invariant subspaces for S_m. Since N is stable for T and $S_m \to T$ there exists a sequence $\{N_m\}$ of subspaces of X with $S_m N_m \subset N_m$ and gap$(N_m,N) \to 0$. For m sufficiently large, we have gap$(N_m,N)<\varepsilon$ and hence $N_m \notin \Omega_m$. So, passing if necessary to a subsequence, we may assume that for all m the S_m-invariant subspace N_m is not stable.

Let Z be an algebraic complement of N in X. Since N_m converges to N in the gap topology, we may assume that $Z \oplus N_m = Z \oplus N = X$ for all m. Let R_m be the angular operator of N_m with respect to the projection of X onto N along Z. Then $R_m \to 0$. Write

$$E_m = \begin{bmatrix} I & R_m \\ 0 & I \end{bmatrix},$$

where the matrix representation is taken with respect to the decomposition $X = Z \oplus N$. Then E_m is invertible, $E_m N = N_m$ and $E_m \to I$. Put $T_m = E_m^{-1} S_m E_m$. Obviously, $T_m \to T$ and $T_m N \subset N$. Note that N is not stable for T_m.

With respect to the decomposition $X = N \oplus Z$, we write

$$T = \begin{pmatrix} U & V \\ 0 & W \end{pmatrix}, \quad T_m = \begin{pmatrix} U_m & V_m \\ 0 & W_m \end{pmatrix}.$$

Then $U_m \to U$ and $W_m \to W$. Since N is not stable for T_m, Theorem 8.7 ensures the existence of a common eigenvalue λ_m of U_m and W_m such that

(8.16) $$\dim \operatorname{Ker}(\lambda_m I - T_m) \geqq 2, \quad m = 1,2,\ldots .$$

Now $|\lambda_m| \leq \|U_m\|$ and $\{U_m\}$ converges to U. Hence, the sequence $\{\lambda_m\}$ is bounded. Passing, if necessary, to a subsequence, we may assume that $\lambda_m \to \lambda_0$ for some $\lambda_0 \in \mathbb{C}$. But then $\lambda_m I - U_m \to \lambda_0 I - U$ and $\lambda_m I - W_m \to \lambda_0 I - W$. It follows that λ_0 is a common eigenvalue of U and W. Again applying Theorem 8.7, we see that λ_0 is an eigenvalue of T of geometric multiplicity one. But this cannot be true in view of (8.16) and the fact that $\{\lambda_m I - T_m\}$ converges to $\lambda_0 I - T$.

With the help of Theorem 8.14 one can sharpen Theorem 8.8 as follows.

THEOREM 8.15. Suppose $W_0 = W_{01}W_{02}$ is a stable minimal factorization involving rational $k\times k$ matrix functions that are analytic at ∞ with value I_k. Let

$$W_0(\lambda) = I_k + C_0(\lambda I_\delta - A_0)^{-1}B_0,$$

$$W_{0i}(\lambda) = I_k + C_{0i}(\lambda I_{\delta_i} - A_{0i})^{-1}B_{0i}, \quad i = 1,2,$$

be minimal realizations for W_0, W_{01} and W_{02}. Then for each $\varepsilon>0$ there exists $\omega>0$ with the following property: If $\|A-A_0\|+\|B-B_0\|+\|C-C_0\|<\omega$, then $W(\lambda) = I_k+C(\lambda I_\delta - A)^{-1}B$ is a minimal realization and W admits a stable minimal factorization $W = W_1W_2$,

$$W_i(\lambda) = I_k + C_i(\lambda I_{\delta_i} - A_i)^{-1}B_i \ , \ i = 1,2,$$

<u>with the extra property that</u> $\| A_i - A_{0i} \| + \| B_i - B_{0i} \| + \| C_i - C_{0i} \| < \varepsilon$.

Note that each common pole (zero) of W_1 and W_2 is a pole (zero) of W of geometric multiplicity one. So Theorem 8.15 extends Theorem 7.1. Similar refinements can be formulated for Theorems 8.12 and 8.13. For the exact formulation, see [3], Theorems 4.2 and 4.3

We conclude this chapter with a remark. At the end of Section 8.1 we briefly discussed the notion of an isolated invariant subspace. It is of course also possible to introduce the concepts of an isolated minimal factorization of a rational matrix function, of an isolated factorization of a monic matrix polynomial and of an isolated solution of the operator Riccati equation. By way of example we give the complete definition of the latter. A solution R of the Riccati equation (8.15) is called <u>isolated</u> if there exists $\varepsilon>0$ such that each solution Q of (8.15) different from R satisfies $\| Q-R \| \geq \varepsilon$. The other definitions are similar. Using the fact, mentioned in Section 8.1, that in the finite dimensional case the isolated invariant subspaces are the same as the stable invariant subspaces, one can easily see that Theorems 8.8, 8.12 and 8.13 remain valid if "stable" is replaced by "isolated". In the case when the underlying scalar field is $\mathbb{R}$ instead of $\mathbb{C}$, the situation is different. Then stable invariant subspaces (factorizations, solutions of the Riccati equation) are isolated, but the converse is no longer true. For details, we refer to the next chapter.

Chapter IX

FACTORIZATION OF REAL MATRIX FUNCTIONS

In this chapter we review the factorization theory for the case of real matrix functions with respect to real divisors. As in the complex case the minimal factorizations are completely determined by the supporting projections of a given realization, but of course in this case one has the additional requirement that all linear transformations must be representable by matrices with real entries. Due to the difference between the real and complex Jordan canonical form the structure of the stable real minimal factorizations is somewhat more complicated than in the complex case. This phenomenon is also reflected by the fact that for real matrices there is a difference between the stable and isolated invariant subspaces.

9.1 Real rational matrix functions

We begin by introducing some notation and terminology. Let $x = (x_1,\dots,x_n)$ be a vector in $\mathbb{C}^n$. Then $\bar{x} = (\bar{x}_1,\dots,\bar{x}_n)$ is called the conjugate of x. We say that x is real if $x = \bar{x}$. So the real vectors in $\mathbb{C}^n$ are just the elements of $\mathbb{R}^n$.

Let M be a subspace of $\mathbb{C}^n$. Then by definition $\bar{M}=\{\bar{x} \mid x\in M\}$. Observe that $\bar{M}$ is also a subspace of $\mathbb{C}^n$. We call M selfconjugate if $M = \bar{M}$. This notion will be used in Sections 9.2 and 9.3. It is easy to see that M is selfconjugate if and only if there exists a (unique) subspace N of the real vector space $\mathbb{R}^n$ such that $M = \{x+iy \mid x,y\in N\}$.

Suppose $A = (a_{jk})_{j=1,k=1}^{n\ \ m}$ is a complex matrix. By the conjugate $\bar{A}$ of A, we mean the matrix

$$\bar{A} = \{\bar{a}_{jk}\}_{j=1,k=1}^{n\ \ m}.$$

The matrix A is called real if $A = \bar{A}$. In other words, A is real if and only if all its entries are real numbers. Now specify bases $e_1,\dots,e_m$ of $\mathbb{C}^m$ and $f_1,\dots,f_n$ of $\mathbb{C}^n$ consisting of real vectors. Then A defines a linear operator from $\mathbb{C}^m$ into $\mathbb{C}^n$. Note that A is a real matrix if and only if this operator maps real vectors in $\mathbb{C}^n$ into real vectors in $\mathbb{C}^n$.

Let W be a rational $k\times k$ matrix function. We say that W is <u>real</u> if $W(\lambda)$ is a real matrix for all real λ (in the domain of W). A realization

$$W(\lambda) = D + C(\lambda I_\delta - A)^{-1}B \tag{9.1}$$

is called a <u>(minimal)</u> <u>real</u> <u>realization</u> of W if (it is minimal in the sense of Section 3.1 and) A, B, C and D are real matrices. Clearly, if W admits a real realization, then W is a real matrix function. The converse of this is also true; in fact, one can always make a minimal real realization (cf. [51], Lemma 1).

THEOREM 9.1. *Let W be a rational $k\times k$ matrix function. Suppose W is analytic at ∞ and real. Then W admits a minimal real realization.*

PROOF. Let δ be the McMillan degree of W. Then W admits a minimal realization of the form (9.1), where A, B, C and D are complex matrices of appropriate sizes. Define the rational $k\times k$ matrix function $\overline{W}$ by $\overline{W}(\lambda) = \overline{W(\overline{\lambda})}$. Then clearly $\overline{W}(\lambda) = \overline{D} + \overline{C}(\lambda - \overline{A})^{-1}\overline{B}$ is a minimal realization for $\overline{W}$. For all real λ (in the domain of W), we have $\overline{W}(\lambda) = W(\lambda)$. It follows that $\overline{W} = W$, and hence $W(\lambda) = \overline{D} + \overline{C}(\lambda - \overline{A})^{-1}\overline{B}$ is a minimal realization for W. So the nodes $(A,B,C,D;\mathbb{C}^\delta,\mathbb{C}^k)$ and $(\overline{A},\overline{B},\overline{C},\overline{D};\mathbb{C}^\delta,\mathbb{C}^k)$ are similar. In particular $D = \overline{D}$, and thus D is a real matrix.

Let U be an invertible complex matrix such that

$$U^{-1}AU = \overline{A}\ ,\ U^{-1}B = \overline{B}\ ,\ CU = \overline{C}. \tag{9.2}$$

Put $\Omega = \mathrm{col}(CA^{j-1})_{j=1}^{\delta}$. Then $\overline{\Omega} = \mathrm{col}(\overline{C}\overline{A}^{j-1})_{j=1}^{\delta}$, and so $\Omega U = \overline{\Omega}$.

Due to the minimality, the matrix Ω has rank δ. Now we construct a special left inverse $\Omega^{(-1)}$ of Ω and an invertible $\delta\times\delta$ matrix S such that

$$\Omega^{(-1)}\bar{\Omega} = S^{-1}\bar{S}.$$

Write $\Omega = (\omega_{ij})_{i=1,j=1}^{k\delta\ \ \delta}$. Choose $1\leqslant i_1<i_2<\ldots<i_\delta\leqslant k\delta$ such that

$$S = (\omega_{i_\alpha\beta})_{\alpha,\beta=1}^{\delta}$$

is invertible. Define $\Omega^{(-1)}$ to be the $\delta\times k\delta$ matrix all of whose columns are zero except those with index $i_1,\ldots,i_\delta$, while together the latter form the inverse of S. Then Ω and S have the desired properties, and hence

$$U = \Omega^{(-1)}\bar{\Omega} = S^{-1}\bar{S}.$$

Using this in (9.2), we get

$$S^{-1}AS = \overline{SAS^{-1}},\ SB = \overline{SB}\ ,\ CS^{-1} = \overline{CS^{-1}}.$$

Thus SAS^{-1}, SB and CS^{-1} are real matrices. But then

$$W(\lambda) = D + CS^{-1}(\lambda I_\delta - SAS^{-1})^{-1}SB$$

is clearly a minimal real realization for W. This completes the proof.

Let W be a rational $k\times k$ matrix function, and write

$$W(\lambda) = (w_{ij}(\lambda))_{i,j=1}^{k}.$$

If the functions w_{ij} may be written as quotients of (scalar) polynomials having real coefficients, then obviously W is real. The converse is also true. For the special case when W is analytic at ∞, this is an easy consequence of Theorem 9.1. For arbitrary real rational $k\times k$ matrix functions, not necessarily analytic at ∞, the result follows by applying a suitable Möbius transformation mapping the extended real line onto itself.

Next we study real factorizations of rational matrix functions. Let W, W_1 and W_2 be rational $k\times k$ matrix functions, and suppose that $W = W_1W_2$. We say that this factorization is a (*minimal*) *real factorization* if (it is minimal and) the factors W_1 and W_2 are real. We shall characterize minimal real factorizations in terms of supporting projections. For convenience we restrict ourselves to the case where the functions W, W_1 and W_2 are analytic at ∞ with value I_k.

THEOREM 9.2. *Suppose* $W(\lambda) = I_k + C(\lambda I_\delta - A)^{-1}B$ *is a minimal real realization. Let* Π *be a supporting projection of the node* $\theta = (A,B,C;\mathbb{C}^\delta,\mathbb{C}^n)$, *and let* $W = W_1W_2$ *be the corresponding (minimal) factorization of* W. *This factorization is real if and only if* Π *is a real matrix*.

PROOF. One checks without difficulty that $\bar{\Pi}$ is also a supporting projection of the node θ. The corresponding (minimal) factorization is $W = \bar{W}_1\bar{W}_2$, where

$$\overline{W_j}(\lambda) = \overline{W_j(\bar{\lambda})} \qquad (j=1,2).$$

The desired result is now immediate from Theorem 4.8.

Let us remark that it may happen that W has plenty of minimal factorizations with non-real factors, but no minimal real factorizations. For example, let W be the real rational 3×3 matrix function given by

$$W(\lambda)=\begin{pmatrix} \dfrac{\lambda^3+2\lambda^2+1}{\lambda(\lambda^2+1)} & \dfrac{3\lambda^2+1}{\lambda(\lambda^2+1)} \\[2ex] \dfrac{-2\lambda^2-1}{\lambda(\lambda^2+1)} & \dfrac{\lambda^3-2\lambda^2-1}{\lambda(\lambda^2+1)} \end{pmatrix}.$$

Put

$$A = \begin{bmatrix} 0 & 1 & 0 \\ -1 & 0 & 0 \\ 0 & 0 & 0 \end{bmatrix}, \quad B = \begin{bmatrix} 1 & 1 \\ 0 & 1 \\ 1 & 1 \end{bmatrix}, \quad C = \begin{bmatrix} 1 & 1 & 1 \\ -1 & 0 & -1 \end{bmatrix}.$$

Then $W(\lambda) = I_2 + C(\lambda I_3 - A)^{-1}B$ is a minimal real realization for W. Observe that

$$A^{\times} = A - BC = \begin{bmatrix} 0 & 0 & 0 \\ 0 & 0 & 1 \\ 0 & -1 & 0 \end{bmatrix}.$$

The non-trivial invariant subspaces of A, considered as an operator on $\mathbb{R}^3$, are $\mathbb{R}\oplus\mathbb{R}\oplus(0)$ and $(0)\oplus(0)\oplus\mathbb{R}$. The non-trivial invariant subspaces of $A^{\times}$, considered as an operator on $\mathbb{R}^3$, are $\mathbb{R}\oplus(0)+(0)$ and $(0)\oplus\mathbb{R}\oplus\mathbb{R}$. From this it is clear that the node $\theta = (A,B,C;\mathbb{C}^3,\mathbb{C}^2)$ has no real supporting projections. But then the function W does not admit any minimal real factorization at all. On the other hand, as W has simple poles only, we know from Theorem 3.4 that W can be written as a product of three factors each of which has degree one, and therefore it admits non-real minimal factorizations. In fact, one such non-real minimal factorization is given by

$$W(\lambda) = \begin{bmatrix} \frac{\lambda+1}{\lambda} & \frac{1-i}{\lambda} \\ \frac{-1}{\lambda} & \frac{\lambda-1+i}{\lambda} \end{bmatrix} \cdot \begin{bmatrix} 1 & \frac{1+2i}{\lambda+i} \\ 0 & \frac{\lambda-i}{\lambda+i} \end{bmatrix} \cdot \begin{bmatrix} \frac{\lambda-i+1}{\lambda-1} & \frac{1-i}{\lambda-i} \\ \frac{-1}{\lambda-i} & \frac{\lambda-1}{\lambda-i} \end{bmatrix}.$$

Observe that from this example it also follows that without further conditions Theorem 3.4 does not hold for real rational functions (cf. [48]).

9.2 Real monic matrix polynomials

Throughout this section L will be a monic $k\times k$ matrix polynomial. We say that L is real if $L(\lambda)$ is a real matrix for all $\lambda \in \mathbb{R}$. An equivalent requirement is that all coefficients of L are real matrices.

Let ℓ be the degree of L. If there exists a monic node $\theta = (T,R,Q,0;\mathbb{C}^{k\ell},\mathbb{C}^{k})$ such that the transfer function of θ is L^{-1} and T,R and Q are real matrices, then clearly L is real. The converse is also true. To see this, just take the first companion node (1.25) corresponding to L. This characterization of real monic matrix polynomial could also have been obtained from Theorem 9.1.

Assume that $L = L_2L_1$, where L_1 and L_2 are monic $k\times k$ matrix polynomials. We say that the factorization $L = L_2L_1$ is real if the factors L_1 and L_2 (and therefore also L) are real. The next theorem is the analogue of Theorem 9.2.

THEOREM 9.3. *Suppose $\theta = (T,R,Q,0;\mathbb{C}^{k\ell},\mathbb{C}^{k})$ is a monic node such that the transfer function of θ is L^{-1} and T, R and Q are real matrices. Let M be a supporting subspace for θ, and let $L = L_2L_1$ be the corresponding factorization of L. This factorization is real if and only if M is selfconjugate.*

PROOF. Write $\bar{M} = \{\bar{x} \mid x \in M\}$. Then $\bar{M}$ is also a supporting subspace for θ and the corresponding factorization of L is $L = \bar{L}_2\bar{L}_1$, where

$$\bar{L}_j(\lambda) = \overline{L_j(\bar{\lambda})} \qquad (j=1,2).$$

This implies the desired result.

9.3 Stable and isolated invariant subspaces

In this section we study stable invariant subspaces and isolated invariant subspaces of operators acting on finite dimensional real spaces. We refrain from giving the explicit definitions of these notions because they are formally the same as those presented in Section 8.1. Recall that in the complex case each stable invariant subspace is isolated and conversely. When the underlying scalar field is the real line, this is no longer true.

We shall begin our investigation by considering some simple special cases. But first we introduce some notation and terminology.

Let E be a real Banach space. The complexification of E will be denoted by E^c. As a set, E^c consists of all pairs (x,y) with x and y in E. Instead of (x,y) we shall write $x+iy$. If $\eta = x+iy$ belongs to E^c, then $\bar{\eta} = x-iy$ is called the <u>conjugate</u> of η. We call $\eta = x+iy$ <u>real</u> if $\eta=\bar{\eta}$ or, equivalently, $y=0$. The real vectors are identified with those of E in the usual way.

If N is a subspace of E, then N^c is a subspace of E^c. Let M be a subspace of E^c. Then $\bar{M} = \{\bar{\eta} \mid \eta \in M\}$ is also a subspace of E^c. We call M <u>selfconjugate</u> if $M=\bar{M}$. Observe that M is selfconjugate if and only if there exists a subspace N of E such that $M = N^c$.

Suppose T is a (bounded) linear operator from E into F. Here E and F are real Banach spaces. Define $T^c:E^c \to F^c$ by $T^c(x+iy) = Tx+iTy$. Then T^c is a (bounded) linear operator which is called the <u>complexification</u> of T. For an arbitrary (bounded) linear operator $S:E^c \to F^c$, we define the <u>conjugate</u> $\bar{S} : E^c \to F^c$ by $\bar{S}(\eta) = \overline{S(\bar{\eta})}$. Observe that $\bar{S}$ is a (bounded) linear operator. We call S <u>real</u> if $S = \bar{S}$. One checks without difficulty that S is real if and only if $S = T^c$ for some (bounded) linear operator $T:E \to F$. Also, S is real if and only if S maps real vectors in E into real vectors in F.

Assume now that E and F are finite dimensional real spaces with bases $e_1,\dots,e_m$ and $f_1,\dots,f_n$, respectively. Note that $e_1,\dots,e_m$ and $f_1,\dots,f_n$ form bases of E^c and F^c, respectively. With respect to these bases a linear operator $S:E^c \to F^c$ can be represented by a matrix, say

$$S = (s_{ij})_{i=1,j=1}^{n\quad m}.$$

A straightforward calculation shows that $\bar{S}$ is then given by

$$\bar{S} = (\bar{s}_{ij})_{i=1,j=1}^{n\quad m} .$$

Thus S is real if and only if all entries s_{ij} in the matrix representation for S are real. So, after specification of bases consisting of real vectors, real operators between complexifications of finite dimensional real spaces can be identified with real matrices.

Let T be a linear operator acting on a finite dimensional real space E. The <u>spectrum</u> of T is by definition the spectrum of T^c. It is denoted by $\sigma(T)$. Since the characteristic polynomial of T^c has real coefficients, the spectrum of T is symmetric with respect to the real line. The points of $\sigma(T)$ are called the <u>eigenvalues</u> of T. By the <u>geometric</u> (<u>algebraic</u>) <u>multiplicity</u> of an eigenvalue λ_0 of T we mean the geometric (algebraic) multiplicity of λ_0 as an eigenvalue of T^c. If λ_0 is a real eigenvalue of T, the geometric and algebraic multiplicity of λ_0 are equal to $\dim \operatorname{Ker}(\lambda_0 - T)$ and $\dim \operatorname{Ker}(\lambda_0 - T)^n$, respectively. Here $n = \dim E$.

LEMMA 9.4. *Suppose* $\dim E$ *is odd and* $\sigma(T)$ *consists of exactly one real eigenvalue of geometric multiplicity one. Then each invariant subspace of* T *is both stable and isolated.*

PROOF. The hypothesis on T implies that T is unicellular. Hence each invariant subspace of T is isolated.

Let N be an invariant subspace of T. Put $k = \dim N$. Since $\dim E$ is odd each operator S on E has an invariant subspace of dimension k. To see this, observe that $\sigma(S)$ contains at least one real point and use the real Jordan normal form for S (see [39], 36.2). The proof that N is stable is now similar to that of Theorem 8.2 (see also the proof of Corollary 8.3).

LEMMA 9.5. *Suppose* $\dim E$ *is even and* $\sigma(T)$ *consists of exactly one real eigenvalue of geometric multiplicity one. Then the even dimensional invariant subspaces of* T *are stable and the odd dimensional invariant subspaces of* T *are not stable. All invariant subspaces of* T *are isolated.*

PROOF. The last statement of the theorem is clear from the fact that T is unicellular.

Let N be an invariant subspace of T, and put $k=\dim N$. Assume k is even. Then each operator S on E has an invariant subspace of dimension k. This follows from the hypothesis that dim E is even and the real Jordan normal form of S. Using the same method as in the proof of lemma 9.4 we can now show that N is stable.

Next assume that k is odd. In order to prove that N is not stable, we may suppose that $\sigma(T) = \{0\}$. With respect to a suitable basis of E, the matrix representation of T has the form

$$T = (t_{\mu\nu})_{\mu,\nu=1}^{n},$$

where $n = \dim E$, $t_{\mu\nu} = 1$ for $(\mu,\nu) = (1,2), (2,3),\dots,(n-1,n)$ and $t_{\mu\nu} = 0$ otherwise. For $\varepsilon>0$ put $T_\varepsilon = T+S_\varepsilon$ with

$$S_\varepsilon = (S_{\mu\nu}(\varepsilon))_{\mu,\nu=1}^{n},$$

where $S_{\mu\nu}(\varepsilon) = -\varepsilon^2$ whenever (μ,ν) is one of the pairs $(2,1),(4,3),\dots(n-2,n-3),(n,n-1)$ and $S_{\mu\nu}(\varepsilon) = 0$ otherwise. Then $T_\varepsilon \to T$ as $\varepsilon \downarrow 0$. One checks without difficulty that $\sigma(T_\varepsilon) = \{i\varepsilon,-i\varepsilon\}$. So $\sigma(T_\varepsilon) \cap \mathbb{R} = \phi$. But then T_ε has no invariant subspaces of odd dimension. This completes the proof.

From Lemma 9.5 it is already clear that not every isolated invariant subspace will be stable.

LEMMA 9.6. *Suppose* $\sigma(T)$ *consists of exactly one real eigenvalue of geometric multiplicity at least two. Then* T *has neither stable nor isolated non-trivial invariant subspaces.*

PROOF. Let N be a non-trivial invariant subspace of T. The proof that N is not stable is almost word for word the same as that of Lemma 8.4.

To prove that N is also not isolated, we assume (without loss of generality) that $\sigma(T) = \{0\}$. First consider the case when $N = \operatorname{Ker} T^p$ for some positive integer p. Let

$$(9.3) \qquad \{x_{jk}\}_{j=1,k=1}^{q \quad r_j}$$

be a basis of E such that the corresponding matrix representation for T has Jordan form. In other words, for $j=1,\dots,q$, we have

$$(9.4) \qquad Tx_{j0} = 0, \quad Tx_{jk} = x_{j,k-1} \quad (k=1,\dots,r_j).$$

For convenience we assume that $r_1 \geqq r_2 \geqq \dots \geqq r_q$. Observe that $\operatorname{Ker} T^p$ is the span of

$$(9.5) \qquad \{x_{jk}\}_{j=1,k=0}^{q \quad r_j \wedge (p-1)}.$$

Now $r_1 \geqq p$, for if not, then $N = \operatorname{Ker} T^p$ would be all of E. For $\varepsilon > 0$, let N_ε be the span of

$$\{x_{jk}\}_{j=1,k=0}^{q-1 \quad r_j \wedge (p-1)} \cup \{x_{qk}\}_{k=0}^{(r_q-1)\wedge(p-2)} \cup$$

$$\cup \{x_{q,r_q \wedge (p-1)} + \varepsilon x_{1p}\}.$$

Since $q = \dim \operatorname{Ker} T \geq 2$, we have that N_ε is an invariant subspace of T. Moreover $\operatorname{gap}(N_\varepsilon, N) \to 0$ as $\varepsilon \downarrow 0$. As all N_ε are different from N, it follows that N is not isolated.

Next assume that N is not of the form $\operatorname{Ker} T^m$. Since $\operatorname{Ker} T^m = E$ for m sufficiently large and $N \neq E$, there exists a unique non-negative integer p such that

$$\operatorname{Ker} T^p \subset N, \quad \operatorname{Ker} T^{p+1} \not\subset N.$$

Consider the restriction T_0 of T to N. The spectrum of T_0

consists of zero only. Let (9.3) now denote a basis of N such that the corresponding matrix representation for T_0 has Jordan form. This means that (9.3) is a basis of N for which (9.4) holds. Again we assume that $r_1 \geqq r_2 \geqq \cdots \geqq r_q$. Now $\operatorname{Ker} T^p = \operatorname{Ker} T_0^p$ is the span of (9.5). Since $N \neq \operatorname{Ker} T^p$, it follows that $r_1 \geqq p$. Choose $u \in \operatorname{Ker} T^{p+1} \setminus N$, and put

$$u_k = T^{p-k}u \quad (k=0,\ldots,p) .$$

Then clearly

$$Tu_0 = 0 , \quad Tu_k = u_{k-1} \quad (k=1,\ldots,p).$$

Moreover $u_p = u \notin N$. For $\varepsilon > 0$, we now define N_ε to be the span of

$$\{x_{jk}\}_{j=2,k=0}^{q \quad r_j} \cup \{x_{1k}\}_{k=0}^{r_1-p-1} \cup$$

$$\cup \{x_{1,r_1-p+k}+\varepsilon u_k\}_{k=0}^{p} .$$

Then N_ε is well-defined for $r_1 \geq p$. Observe that N_ε is T-invariant and $\operatorname{gap}(N_\varepsilon,N) \to 0$ as $\varepsilon \downarrow 0$. Since all N_ε are different from N, it follows that N is not isolated, and the proof is complete.

From Lemmas 9.4-9.6, the following is clear. If $\sigma(T)$ consists of exactly one real eigenvalue of geometric multiplicity one (at least two), then each (no non-trivial) invariant subspace of T is isolated. The arguments used to prove this also work in the complex case when the spectrum of the operator in question consists of exactly one possibly non-real eigenvalue. This can be used to give a quick elementary proof of [16], Theorem 9.

LEMMA 9.7. _Suppose_ $\sigma(T)$ _consists of two non-real eigenvalues of geometric multiplicity one. Then each invariant subspace of_ T _is both stable and isolated._

PROOF. First of all, note that T is unicellular. Hence each invariant subspace of T is isolated. Next observe that all invariant subspaces of T are even dimensional. In particular the dimension of E is even. The rest of the argument is now similar to that presented in the second paragraph of the proof of Lemma 9.5.

LEMMA 9.8. <u>Suppose $\sigma(T)$ consists of two non-real eigenvalues of geometric multiplicity at least two. Then T has neither stable nor isolated non-trivial invariant subspaces.</u>

PROOF. Let N be a non-trivial invariant subspace of T. The proof that N is not stable is analogous to that of Lemma 8.4. In order to prove that N is also not isolated, we argue as follows.

Consider $N^c = \{x+iy \mid x,y \in N\}$. Observe that N^c is a non-trivial invariant subspace for T^c. The spectrum of T^c consists of two non-real eigenvalues of geometric multiplicity at least two. Denote these eigenvalues by $\alpha+i\beta$ and $\alpha-i\beta$, and let $N_\pm$ be the generalized eigenspace corresponding to T^c and $\alpha\pm i\beta$. The only non-trivial stable invariant subspaces of T^c are N_+ and N_-. In the complex case, however, the notion of a stable and that of an isolated invariant subspace coincide. So the only non-trivial isolated invariant subspaces of T^c are N_+ and N_-. Now $N_- = \{\bar{\eta} \mid \eta \in N_+\}$ and $E^c = N_+ \oplus N_-$. From this it is clear that $N_- \neq N^c \neq N_+$. It follows that the T^c-invariant subspace N^c is not isolated.

Let $M_1, M_2, \ldots$ be a sequence of T^c-invariant subspaces, all different from N^c, such that $\text{gap}(M_k, N^c) \to 0$. For $k=1,2,\ldots$ we put

$$M_k^+ = M_k \cap N_+ \;,\; M_k^- = M_k \cap N_- .$$

Then $M_k = M_k^+ \oplus M_k^-$, $\text{gap}(M_k^+, N^c \cap N_+) \to 0$ and $\text{gap}(M_k^-, N^c \cap N_-) \to 0$. From $M_k \neq N^c$ and

$$N^c = [N^c \cap N_+] \oplus [N^c \cap N_-],$$

we see that either $M_k^+ \neq N^c \cap N_+$ or $M_k^- \neq N^c \cap N_-$. Assume, for instance, that $M_k^+ \neq N^c \cap N_+$ for infinitely many k. Then, by passing to a subsequence, we may assume that $M_k^+ \neq N^c \cap N_+$ for all k. Put

$$L_k = M_k^+ \oplus \{\bar{\eta} \mid \eta \in M_k^+\}.$$

Then L_k is T^c-invariant. Moreover L_k is selfconjugate and hence $L_k = N_k^c = \{x+iy \mid x,y \in N_k\}$ for some T-invariant subspace N_k of E.

Observe that

$$N_k^c = [N_k^c \cap N_+] \oplus [N_k^c \cap N_-],$$

where $N_k^c \cap N_+ = M_k^+$ and $N_k^c \cap N_- = \{\bar{\eta} \mid \eta \in M_k^+\}$. So

$$\text{gap}(N_k^c \cap N_+, N^c \cap N_+) \to 0 \ , \quad \text{gap}(N_k^c \cap N_-, N^c \cap N_-) \to 0.$$

It follows that $\text{gap}(N_k^c, N^c) \to 0$. But then $\text{gap}(N_k, N) \to 0$ too. Since $N_k^c \cap N_+ = M_k^+ \neq N^c \cap N_+$, we have that $N_k \neq N$ for all k. We conclude that N is not isolated, and the proof is complete.

In order to deal with an arbitrary linear operator T on a finite dimensional real space E, we introduce some more notation and terminology. Let λ_0 be a real eigenvalue of T. Recall that the algebraic multiplicity of λ_0 is equal to dim Ker $(\lambda_0 - T)^n$, where n=dim E. The space $\text{Ker}(\lambda_0 - T)^n$ can be described as follows. Consider the spectral projection of T^c corresponding to λ_0. It is easy to see that this spectral projection is a real operator. Hence it is of the form $P(T;\lambda_0)^c$ for some projection $P(T;\lambda_0)$ of E. We call $P(T;\lambda_0)$ the _spectral projection_ of T corresponding to λ_0. The image of $P(T;\lambda_0)$ is $\text{Ker}(\lambda_0 - T)^n$; it is called the _generalized eigenspace_ corresponding to T and λ_0.

Next let $\alpha + i\beta$ be a non-real eigenvalue of T. Then also $\alpha - i\beta$ is an eigenvalue of T and the geometric (algebraic) multiplicities of $\alpha + i\beta$ and $\alpha - i\beta$ are the same. The spectral projections of T^c corresponding to $\alpha + i\beta$ and $\alpha - i\beta$ are non-real. However, their sum is real. In other words, there exists a projection $P(T;\alpha,\beta)$ of E such that $P(T;\alpha,\beta)^c$ is the spectral projection corresponding to T and the spectral set $\{\alpha+i\beta,\alpha-i\beta\}$. We call $P(T;\alpha,\beta)$ the <u>spectral projection</u> corresponding to $\alpha\pm i\beta$. Note that

$$[\operatorname{Im} P(T;\alpha,\beta)]^c = \operatorname{Ker}(\alpha+i\beta-T^c)^n \oplus \operatorname{Ker}(\alpha-i\beta-T^c)^n.$$

The image $\operatorname{Im} P(T;\alpha,\beta)$ of $P(T;\alpha,\beta)$ is called the <u>generalized eigenspace</u> corresponding to T and $\alpha\pm i\beta$; its dimension is two times the algebraic multiplicity of $\alpha\pm i\beta$ as an eigenvalue of T^c.

Write

$$\sigma(T) = \{\lambda_j\}_{j=1}^{r} \cup \{\alpha_k\pm i\beta_k\}_{k=1}^{s},$$

where $\lambda_1,\ldots,\lambda_r$ are the different real eigenvalues of T and $\alpha_1+i\beta_1,\ldots,\alpha_s+i\beta_s$ are the different eigenvalues of T lying in the upper half plane. Put

$$P(\lambda_j) = P(T;\lambda_j), \quad P(\alpha_k,\beta_k) = P(T;\alpha_k,\beta_k),$$

$$N(\lambda_j) = \operatorname{Im} P(T;\lambda_j), \quad N(\alpha_k,\beta_k) = \operatorname{Im} P(T;\alpha_k,\beta_k).$$

So $N(\lambda_1),\ldots,N(\lambda_r)$, $N(\alpha_1,\beta_1),\ldots,N(\alpha_s,\beta_s)$ are the different generalized eigenspaces of T. Note that the projections $P(\lambda_1),\ldots,P(\lambda_r)$, $P(\alpha_1,\beta_1),\ldots,P(\alpha_s,\beta_s)$ are mutually disjoint and add up to the identity. Hence

$$E = N(\lambda_1)\oplus\ldots\oplus N(\lambda_r)\oplus N(\alpha_1,\beta_1)\oplus\ldots\oplus N(\alpha_s,\beta_s).$$

The invariant subspaces for T are the subspaces of E of the form

$$N = N_1\oplus\ldots\oplus N_r\oplus\tilde{N}_1\oplus\ldots\oplus\tilde{N}_s, \tag{9.6}$$

where, for $j=1,\ldots,r$, the space N_j is a T-invariant subspace of $N(\lambda_j)$ and, for $k=1,\ldots,s$, the space $\tilde{N}_k$ is a T-invariant subspace of $N(\alpha_k,\beta_k)$.

THEOREM 9.9. *A subspace* N *of* E *is* T-*invariant and stable if and only if* N *is of the form* (9.6), *where, for* $j=1,\ldots,r$ *and* $k=1,\ldots,s$,

(i) N_j *is an arbitrary even dimensional* T-*invariant subspace of* $N(\lambda_j)$ *whenever the algebraic multiplicity of* λ_j *is even and the geometric multiplicity of* λ_j *is one*;

(ii) N_j *is an arbitrary* T-*invariant subspace of* $N(\lambda_j)$ *whenever the algebraic multiplicity of* λ_j *is odd and the geometric multiplicity of* λ_j *is one*;

(iii) $N_j = (0)$ *or* $N_j = N(\lambda_j)$ *whenever* λ_j *has geometric multiplicity at least two*;

(iv) $\tilde{N}_k$ *is an arbitrary* T-*invariant subspace of* $N(\alpha_k,\beta_k)$ *whenever* $\alpha_k+i\beta_k$ *and* $\alpha_k-i\beta_k$ *have geometric multiplicity one*;

(v) $\tilde{N}_k = (0)$ *or* $\tilde{N}_k = N(\alpha_k,\beta_k)$ *whenever* $\alpha_k+i\beta_k$ *and* $\alpha_k-i\beta_k$ *have geometric multiplicity at least two*.

Also, N *is an isolated invariant subspace of* T *if and only if* N *is of the form* (9.6), *where for* $j=1,\ldots,r$ *and* $k=1,\ldots,s$ *the conditions* (iii), (iv), (v) *and*

(vi) N_j *is an arbitrary* T-*invariant subspace of* $N(\lambda_j)$ *whenever the geometric multiplicity of* λ_j *is one*

are satisfied.

PROOF. Let N be an invariant subspace of T, and write N in the form (9.6), where $N_j = P(\lambda_j)N$ $(j=1,\ldots,r)$ and $\tilde{N}_k = P(\alpha_k,\beta_k)N$ $(k=1,\ldots,s)$. For $j = 1,\ldots,r$, let T_j be the restriction of T to $N(\lambda_j)$, and for $k=1,\ldots,s$, let $\tilde{T}_k$ be the restriction of T to $N(\alpha_k,\beta_k)$. It is easy to see that N is isolated if and only if, for $j = 1,\ldots,r$, the space N_j is an isolated invariant subspace of T_j and, for $k = 1,\ldots,s$, the space $\tilde{N}_k$ is an isolated invariant subspace of $\tilde{T}_k$. This statement remains true if isolated is replaced by stable. The proof of this involves the analogues for the real case of Lemmas

8.5 and 8.6. Observe now that $\sigma(T_j) = \{\lambda_j\}$ and $\sigma(\tilde{T}_k) = \{\alpha_k+i\beta_k, \alpha_k-i\beta_k\}$. Here $j = 1,\dots,r$ and $k = 1,\dots,s$. The desired result is now immediate from Lemmas 9.5-9.9.

Theorem 9.9 implies that every stable invariant subspace is also isolated. As we already observed, the converse of this is not correct. The next theorem is a reformulation of Theorem 9.9.

THEOREM 9.10. *Let* N *be an invariant subspace for* T. *Then* N *is stable if and only if* N *meets the following requirements:*

(i) *If* $(0) \neq P(\lambda_j)N \neq N(\lambda_j)$, *then the geometric multiplicity of* λ_j *is one* $(j=1,\dots,r)$;

(ii) *If* $\dim P(\lambda_j)N$ *is odd, then the algebraic multiplicity of* λ_j *is odd too* $(j=1,\dots,r)$;

(iii) *If* $(0) \neq P(\alpha_k,\beta_k)N \neq N(\alpha_k,\beta_k)$, *then the geometric multiplicity of* $\alpha_k \pm i\beta_k$ *is one* $(k=1,\dots,s)$.

Also N *is isolated if and only if* (i) *and* (iii) *are satisfied.*

In the next section we shall deal with stable and isolated real factorizations of rational matrix functions and monic matrix polynomials, and also with stable and isolated solutions of the real operator Riccati equation. The version of Theorem 9.9 most fitted for studying these notions reads as follows.

THEOREM 9.11. *Let* E_1 *and* E_2 *be finite dimensional real spaces, and let*

$$T = \begin{bmatrix} T_1 & T_0 \\ 0 & T_2 \end{bmatrix}$$

be a linear operator acting on $E = E_1 \oplus E_2$. *Then* E_1 *is a stable invariant subspace for* T *if and only if the following conditions are satisfied:*

(i) *each common eigenvalue of* T_1 *and* T_2 *is an eigenvalue of* T *of geometric multiplicity one;*

(ii) <u>each common real eigenvalue of T_1 and T_2 whose algebraic multiplicity with respect to T_1 is odd, has odd algebraic multiplicity with respect to</u> T.

<u>Also</u>, E_1 <u>is an isolated invariant subspace for</u> T <u>if and only if</u> (i) <u>is satisfied</u>.

PROOF. The proof is similar to that of Theorem 8.7. Use Theorem 9.10 instead of Theorem 8.1.

9.4 Stable and isolated real factorizations

In this section we discuss stable and isolated real factorizations of rational matrix functions and monic matrix polynomials. Also we deal with stable and isolated solutions of the real operator Riccati equation. We begin by considering real rational matrix functions.

Suppose

$$W_0 = W_{01}W_{02} \tag{9.7}$$

is a minimal real factorization. Here W_0, W_{01} and W_{02} are real rational $k\times k$ matrix functions, analytic at ∞ with value I_k. For $j = 1,2$, let

$$W_{0j}(\lambda) = I_k + C_{0j}(\lambda I_{\delta_j} - A_{0j})^{-1}B_{0j} \tag{9.8}$$

be a minimal real realization for W_{0j}. We say that the factorization (9.7) is <u>isolated</u> (<u>with respect to real perturbations</u>) if there exists $\varepsilon > 0$ with the following property. If $W_0 = W_1W_2$, where W_1 and W_2 admit minimal real realizations

$$W_j(\lambda) = I_k + C_j(\lambda I_{\delta_j} - A_j)^{-1}B_j \quad (j=1,2)$$

such that

$$\| A_j - A_{0j}\| + \| B_j - B_{0j}\| + \| C_j - C_{0j}\| < \varepsilon \quad (j=1,2),$$

then $W_1 = W_{01}$ and $W_2 = W_{02}$. By Theorem 3.1, this definition does not depend on the choice of the minimal realization (9.8).

The definition of the notion of a factorization that is <u>stable (with respect to real perturbations)</u> is analogous to that of a stable minimal factorization given in Section 8.2. The only difference is that now all (minimal) realizations are required to be real. We omit the details.

Closely related to the concepts introduced in the preceding paragraph are those of an isolated and of a stable real supporting projection. Let A_0, B_0 and C_0 be real matrices of appropriate sizes, and consider the node $\theta_0 = (A_0, B_0, C_0; \mathbb{C}^\delta, \mathbb{C}^k)$. Here the matrices A_0, B_0 and C_0 are of course identified with their canonical actions. Suppose Π_0 is a real $\delta\times\delta$ matrix whose canonical action on $\mathbb{C}^\delta$ is a supporting projection for θ_0. In other words Π_0 is a real supporting projection for θ_0. We say that Π_0 is <u>isolated (with respect to real perturbations)</u> if there exists $\varepsilon > 0$ such that each real supporting projection Π for θ_0 different from Π_0 satisfies $\|\Pi-\Pi_0\| \geq \varepsilon$. Similarly, we call Π_0 <u>stable (with respect to real perturbations)</u> if, given $\varepsilon > 0$, there exists $\omega > 0$ such that the following is true: If $\theta = (A,B,C;\mathbb{C}^\delta,\mathbb{C}^k)$ is a node with real matrices A,B,C and $\|\theta-\theta_0\|<\omega$, then θ has a real supporting projection Π such that $\|\Pi-\Pi_0\|<\varepsilon$.

In the next theorem W_0, W_{01} and W_{02} are real rational $k\times k$ matrix functions, analytic at ∞ with value I_k.

THEOREM 9.12. <u>Suppose</u> $W_0 = W_{01}W_{02}$ <u>is a minimal real factorization. This factorization is stable with respect to real perturbations if and only if the following conditions are satisfied:</u>

(i) <u>each common pole (zero) of</u> W_{01} <u>and</u> W_{02} <u>is a pole (zero) of</u> W_0 <u>of geometric multiplicity one;</u>

(ii) <u>each common real pole of</u> W_{01} <u>and</u> W_{02} <u>whose order with respect to</u> W_{01} <u>is odd has odd order as a pole of</u> W_0;

(iii) <u>each common real pole of</u> W_{01}^{-1} <u>and</u> W_{02}^{-1} <u>whose order with respect to</u> W_{02}^{-1} <u>is odd has odd order as a pole of</u> W_0^{-1}.

<u>Also,</u> $W_0 = W_{01}W_{02}$ <u>is isolated with respect to real perturbation</u>

if and only if condition (i) *is satisfied*.

PROOF. We only present an outline of the proof. Let

$$W(\lambda) = I_k + C_0(\lambda I_\delta - A_0)^{-1}B_0$$

be a minimal real realization of W. Denote the supporting projection for $\theta_0 = (A_0,B_0,C_0;\mathbb{C}^\delta,\mathbb{C}^k)$ corresponding to the factorization (9.7) by Π_0. From Theorem 9.3 we know that Π_0 is real. Using the techniques of Section 8.2, one can show that (9.7) is stable (isolated) with respect to real perturbations if and only if the same is true for Π_0. Consider the matrices A_0,B_0,C_0 and Π_0 now as operators from $\mathbb{R}^\delta$ into $\mathbb{R}^\delta$, from $\mathbb{R}^k$ into $\mathbb{R}^\delta$, from $\mathbb{R}^\delta$ into $\mathbb{R}^k$ and from $\mathbb{R}^\delta$ into $\mathbb{R}^\delta$, respectively. Then Π_0 is stable (isolated) with respect to real perturbations if and only if $\operatorname{Ker}\Pi_0$ and $\operatorname{Im}\Pi_0$ are stable (isolated) invariant subspaces for A_0 and $A_0-B_0C_0$, respectively. From Theorem 9.11 we conclude that Theorem 9.12 is correct if (ii) and (iii) are replaced by

(ii)' each common real pole (zero) of W_{01} and W_{02} whose pole (zero) multiplicity with respect to $W_{01}(W_{02})$ is odd, is a pole (zero) of W_0 of odd pole (zero) multiplicity.

Note that a pole of W_0 has geometric multiplicity one if and only if its order and pole-multiplicity are the same (cf. Section 2.1). The desired result is now immediate from the fact that if λ_0 is a pole of W_0 of geometric multiplicity one, then the geometric multiplicity of λ_0 with respect to W_{01} does not exceed one.

In Theorems 8.8 and 9.12 poles of geometric multiplicity one play an important role. If λ_0 is a pole of a rational matrix function W_0 of (positive) order p, then always $p \le \delta(W_0;\lambda_0)$, where $\delta(W_0;\lambda_0)$ is the local degree (pole-multiplicity) of W_0 at λ_0; equality occurs if and only if the geometric multiplicity of λ_0 is one. This fact was used in the proof of Theorem 9.12. It is also useful in dealing with specific examples.

Consider the case where

$$W_0(\lambda) = \begin{bmatrix} 1 & \frac{1}{\lambda}+\frac{1}{\lambda^2} \\ 0 & 1+\frac{1}{\lambda} \end{bmatrix}, \quad W_{01}(\lambda) = \begin{bmatrix} 1 & \frac{1}{\lambda} \\ 0 & 1 \end{bmatrix},$$

$$W_{02}(\lambda) = \begin{bmatrix} 1 & 0 \\ 0 & 1+\frac{1}{\lambda} \end{bmatrix}.$$

Then $W_0 = W_{01}W_{02}$ and this factorization is minimal. Indeed, $\delta(W_0) = \delta(W_0;0) = 2$ and $\delta(W_{01}) = \delta(W_{01};0) = \delta(W_{02}) = \delta(W_{02};0) = 1$. The (only) common pole of W_{01} and W_{02} is 0 and the order of 0 as a pole of W_0 is equal to $\delta(W_0;0)$, namely 2. Moreover, W_{01} and W_{02} have no common zeros. So the factorization $W_0 = W_{01}W_{02}$ is isolated with respect to real perturbations. It is clear that (ii) is not satisfied, so the factorization is not stable with respect to real perturbations. Note that it is a stable factorization in the sense of Section 8.3.

Next we consider factorizations of real monic matrix polynomials that are _stable_ or _isolated_ (_with respect to real perturbations_). The definition of these notions is straightforward (cf. Sections 8.3 and 8.5) and we therefore omit the details. The crucial point is that now all factorizations are required to be real. The proof of the next theorem may be based on Theorem 9.4 and involves the techniques of Section 8.3.

THEOREM 9.13. _Let L, L_1 and L_2 be real monic $k\times k$ matrix polynomials, and suppose that $L = L_2L_1$. This factorization is stable with respect to real perturbations if and only if the following conditions are satisfied:_

(i) _each common eigenvalue of L_1 and L_2 is an eigenvalue of L of geometric multiplicity one;_
(ii) _each common real eigenvalue of L_1 and L_2 whose zero-multiplicity with respect to L_1 is odd, is an_

eigenvalue of L *with odd zero-multiplicity.*

Also, $L = L_2L_1$ *is isolated with respect to real perturbations if and only if condition* (i) *is satisfied.*

Note that the zero-multiplicity of an eigenvalue λ_0 of a monic matrix polynomial L is equal to the order of λ_0 as a zero of the scalar polynomial det $L(\lambda)$. Using this one can easily construct examples showing that an isolated factorization of a real monic matrix polynomial need not be stable (with respect to real perturbations).

Finally, we consider the real operator Riccati equation

$$XT_{21}X + XT_{22} - T_{11}X - T_{12} = 0. \tag{9.9}$$

Here, for $j,k = 1,2$, the symbol T_{jk} denotes a linear operator from the finite dimensional real space E_k into the finite dimensional real space E_j. The definition of a *stable* (*isolated*) solution of (9.9) is formally the same as that given in Section 8.4 (Section 8.5). The only difference is that here the underlying spaces are real instead of complex.

THEOREM 9.14. *Let* R *be a solution of the Riccati equation* (9.9), *and put*

$$T = \begin{bmatrix} T_{11} & T_{12} \\ T_{21} & T_{22} \end{bmatrix} : E_1 \oplus E_2 \to E_1 \oplus E_2.$$

Then R *is stable if and only if the following conditions are satisfied:*

(i) *each common eigenvalue of* $T_{11}-RT_{21}$ *and* $T_{22}+T_{21}R$ *is an eigenvalue of* T *of geometric multiplicity one;*

(ii) *each common real eigenvalue of* $T_{11}-RT_{21}$ *and* $T_{22}+T_{21}R$ *for which the algebraic multiplicity with respect to* $T_{22}+T_{21}R$ *is odd, is an eigenvalue of odd algebraic multiplicity of* T.

9.5 Stability of stable real factorizations

In order to simplify the following discussion we introduce some terminology. Let T be a linear operator on a finite dimensional real space E. An invariant subspace N of T is called *perfectly stable* if for each $\varepsilon>0$ there exists $\delta>0$ such that $\|S-T\|<\delta$ implies that S has a stable invariant subspace M with gap $(M,N) < \varepsilon$. This terminology will be only of temporary use because we shall show that the notion of a stable and that of a perfectly stable invariant subspace coincide. It is clear that perfect stability implies stability.

LEMMA 9.15. *Suppose that all eigenvalues of T have geometric multiplicity one. Put $n = \dim E$. If n is odd, then for each integer k between 0 and n, the operator T has a stable invariant subspace of dimension k. If n is even, then for each even integer m between 0 and n, the operator T has a stable invariant subspace of dimension m.*

PROOF. Consider the real Jordan normal form of S (cf. [39], 36.2) and apply Theorem 9.9.

From Lemmas 9.4, 9.5 and 9.7 we recall the following facts. If $\sigma(T)$ consists of one real eigenvalue of geometric multplicity one and dim E is even, then an invariant subspace for T is stable if and only if it has even dimension. If either $\sigma(T)$ consists of one real eigenvalue of geometric multiplicity one and dim E is odd, or $\sigma(T)$ consists of two non-real eigenvalues of geometric multiplicity one, then each invariant subspace for T is stable. Also note that if T has no real eigenvalue, then each T-invariant subspace (so in particular E itself) has even dimension.

LEMMA 9.16. *Suppose that either $\sigma(T)$ consists of exactly one real eigenvalue of geometric multiplicity one, or $\sigma(T)$ consists of two non-real eigenvalues of geometric multiplicity one. Then each stable invariant subspace of T is perfectly stable.*

PROOF. Let N be a stable invariant subspace for T, and put $k = \dim N$. Since T is unicellular, N is the only T-invariant subspace of dimension k. Let (T_n) be a sequence of operators on E converging to T. A simple rank argument (cf. the proof of Theorem 8.14) shows that for n sufficiently large all eigenvalues of T_n have geometric multiplicity one. But then Lemma 9.15 guarantees that for n sufficiently large the operator T_n has a stable invariant subspace M_n of dimension k. The method used to prove Theorem 8.2 can now be employed to show that there exists a subsequence of (M_n) converging in the gap topology to a k-dimensional invariant subspace M for T. Since M must be equal to N, the proof is complete.

THEOREM 9.17. _Let_ N _be a stable invariant subspace for a linear operator_ T _acting on a finite dimensional space_ E. _Then, given_ $\varepsilon>0$, _there exists_ $\delta>0$ _such that_ $\|S-T\|<\delta$ _implies that_ S _has a stable invariant subspace_ M _satisfying_ $\text{gap}(M,N)<\varepsilon$.

PROOF. It must be shown that N is perfectly stable. We only present an outline of the proof.

Let us adopt the notation of Section 9.3. Write N in the form (9.6), where $N_j = P(\lambda_j)N$ $(j=1,\dots,r)$ and $\tilde{N}_k=P(\alpha_k,\beta_k)N$ $(k=1,\dots,s)$. For $j = 1,\dots,r$, let T_j be the restriction of T to $N(\lambda_j)$, and for $k=1,\dots,s$, let $\tilde{T}_k$ be the restriction of T to $N(\alpha_k,\beta_k)$. From (the proof of) Theorem 9.9 and Lemma 9.16 it follows that N_j is a perfectly stable invariant subspace for T_j $(j=1,\dots,r)$ and $\tilde{N}_k$ is a perfectly stable invariant subspace for $\tilde{T}_k$ $(k=1,\dots,s)$.

Fix j between 1 and r, and let (S_m) be a sequence of operators on E converging to T. Further, let Γ be a circle centered at λ_j such that all eigenvalues of T different from λ_j are outside Γ. For m sufficiently large, the circle Γ will split the spectrum of S_m. Moreover

$$\lim_{m\to\infty} P(S_m^c;\Gamma) = P(T^c;\Gamma) = P(\lambda_j)^c.$$

Observe that $P(S_m^c;\Gamma)$ is a real operator, so $P(S_m^c;\Gamma) = P_m^c$ for some projection P_m of E. We obviously have

$$\lim_{m\to\infty} P_m = P(\lambda_j).$$

Put $F_m = P(\lambda_j)P_m + [I-P(\lambda_j)]\cdot[I-P_m]$. Then $F_m \to I$. By passing to a subsequence (if necessary) we may assume that F_m is invertible for all m. It is clear that $F_m P_m = P(\lambda_j)F_m$, so

$$P(\lambda_j) = F_m P_m F_m^{-1} \qquad (m=1,2,\ldots).$$

Set $T_m = F_m S_m F_m^{-1}$. Then $T_m \to T$. Moreover

$$P(\lambda_j)^c = P(T_m^c;\Gamma) \qquad (m=1,2\ldots).$$

Let T_{mj} be the restriction of T_m to $N(\lambda_j) = \operatorname{Im}P(\lambda_j)$. Then $T_{mj}\to T_j$ as $m\to\infty$. Since N_j is a perfectly stable invariant subspace for T_j, there exists a sequence (L_m) of subspaces of $N(\lambda_j)$ such that L_m is a stable T_{mj}-invariant subspace and $\operatorname{gap}(L_m,N_j) \to 0$ as $m \to \infty$. Observe now that L_m is also a stable invariant subspace for T_m. This we know from the real analogue of Lemma 8.5. Put $M_m = F_m^{-1}L_m$. Then M_m is a stable invariant subspace for S_m. From $F_m \to I$ one gets that $\operatorname{gap}(M_m,L_m) \to 0$. Together with $\operatorname{gap}(L_m,N_j) \to 0$, this gives that $\operatorname{gap}(M_m,N_j) \to 0$ as $m \to \infty$.

We have now proved that the spaces N_j are perfectly stable invariant subspaces for T. In the same way one can show that the spaces $\tilde{N}_k$ are of this type. Since N has the form (9.6), it follows that N is a perfectly stable invariant subspace for T, and the proof is complete.

One might think that Theorem 9.17 could be proved in the same way as Theorem 8.14, using Theorem 9.11 instead of Theorem

8.7. This method of proof however does not work.

With the help of Theorem 9.17 one can sharpen Theorems 9.12, 9.13, 9.14. By way of example, we present the details concerning the extension of Theorem 9.14 (see also Theorem 8.15 and [4], Theorems 4.2 and 4.3).

THEOREM 9.18. Let R be a stable solution of the Riccati equation (9.9). Then, given $\varepsilon>0$, there exists $\delta>0$ such that $\max \|S_{ij}-T_{ij}\|<\delta$ implies that the Riccati equation

$$XS_{21}X + XS_{22} - S_{11}X - S_{12} = 0$$

admits a stable solution Q for which $\|Q-R\|<\varepsilon$.

We emphasize that the solution Q is stable. This can also be expressed as follows. Each common eigenvalue of $S_{11}-QS_{21}$ and $S_{22}+S_{21}Q$ is an eigenvalue of

$$S = \begin{pmatrix} S_{11} & S_{12} \\ S_{21} & S_{22} \end{pmatrix}$$

of geometric multiplicity one, and each common real eigenvalue of $S_{11}-QS_{21}$ and $S_{22}+S_{21}Q$ for which the algebraic multiplicity with respect to $S_{22}+S_{21}Q$ is odd, is an eigenvalue of odd algebraic multiplicity of S.

REFERENCES

1. S. Barnett: Introduction to mathematical control theory. Oxford, Clarendon Press, 1975.

2. H. Bart, I. Gohberg, M.A. Kaashoek: A new characteristic operator function connected with operator polynomials. Wiskundig Seminarium der Vrije Universiteit, Amsterdam Rapport nr 62, 1977.

3. H. Bart, I. Gohberg, M.A. Kaashoek: Operator polynomials as inverses of characteristic functions. Integral Equations and Operator Theory 1(1978), 1-12.

4. H. Bart, I. Gohberg, M.A. Kaashoek: Stable factorizations of monic matrix polynomials and stable invariant subspaces. Integral Equations and Operator Theory 1(1978), 496-517.

5. H. Bart, I. Gohberg, M.A. Kaashoek, P. Van Dooren: Factorizations of transfer functions. Wiskundig Seminarium der Vrije Universiteit, Amsterdam, Rapport nr. 107, 1979.

6. V. Belevitch: Classical Network Theory. San Francisco - Cambridge - Amsterdam, Holden Day, 1968.

7. B. den Boer: Linearization of operator function on arbitrary open sets. Integral Equations and Operator Theory 1(1978), 19-27.

8. M.S. Brodskii: Triangular and Jordan representations of linear operators. Transl. Math. Monographs, Vol. 32, Providence, R.I., Amer. Math. Soc., 1970.

9. M.S. Brodskii: Unitary operator nodes and their characteristic functions. Uspehi Mat. Nauk 33(4) (1978), 141-168 [Russian].

10. V.M. Brodskii: Some theorems on knots and their characteristic functions. Functional Analysis and Applications 4(3) (1970), 250-251.

11. V.M. Brodskii, I.C. Gohberg, M.G. Krein: On characteristic functions of an invertible operator. Acta.Sci. Math. (Szeged) 32(1971), 141-164.

12. S. Campbell, J. Daughtry: The stable solutions of quadratic matrix equations. Proc. Amer. Math. Soc. 74 (1979), 19-23.

13. J. Daughtry: Isolated solutions of quadratic matrix equations. J. Lin. Alg. Appl. 21 (1978), 89-94.

14. P. Dewilde: Cascade scattering matrix synthesis. Tech. Rep. 6560-21. Information Systems Lab., Stanford University, Stanford, 1970.

15. P. Dewilde, J. Vandewalle: On the factorization of a non-singular rational matrix. IEEE Trans. Circuits and Systems, vol CAS-22 (8) (1975), 387-401.

16. R.G. Douglas, C. Pearcy: On a topology for invariant subspaces. J. Funct. Anal. 2(1968), 323-341.

17. I.A. Feldman: Wiener-Hopf operator equation and its application to the transport equation. Mat. Issled. 6(3) (1971), 115-132 [Russian].

18. I.C. Gohberg: The problem of factorization of operator functions. Izvestija Akad. Nauk SSSR, Series Math. 28 (1964), 1055-1082 [Russian].

19. I.C. Gohberg, I.A. Feldman: Convolution equations and projection methods for their solution. Transl. Math. Monographs, Vol. 41, Providence, R.I., Amer. Math. Soc., 1974.

20. I. Gohberg, M.A. Kaashoek, D.C. Lay: Equivalence linearization and decompositions of holomorphic operator functions. J. Funct. Anal. 28(1978), 102-144.

21. I. Gohberg, M.A. Kaashoek, L. Lerer, L. Rodman: Common multiples and common divisors of matrix polynomials, I. Spectral method.

22. I. Gohberg, M.A. Kaashoek, L. Rodman: Spectral analysis of families of operator polynomials and a generalized Vandermonde matrix, I. The finite dimensional case. Topics in Functional Analysis (I. Gohberg, M. Kac, eds), Advances in Mathematics Supplementary Studies, Vol. 3, New York, Academic Press (1978), 91-128.

23. I.C. Gohberg, M.G. Krein: Systems of integral equations on a half line with kernels depending on the difference of arguments. Uspehi Mat. Nauk 13(1958), no. 2 (80), 3-72 [Russian] = Amer. Math. Soc. Transl. (2)14 (1960), 217-287.

24. I. Gohberg, P. Lancaster, L. Rodman: Spectral analysis of matrix polynomials. I. Canonical forms and divisors. Linear Algebra Appl. 20 (1978), 1-44.

25. I. Gohberg, P. Lancaster, L. Rodman: Spectral analysis of matrix polynomials. II. The resolvent form and spectral divisors. Linear Algebra Appl. 21 (1978), 65-88.

26. I. Gohberg, P. Lancaster, L. Rodman: Representations and divisibility of operator polynomials. Can. J. Math. 30(1978), 1045-1069.

27. I. Gohberg, P. Lancaster, L. Rodman: Perturbation theory for divisors of operator polynomials. Siam J. Analysis.

28. I.C. Gohberg, J. Leiterer: Factorization of operator functions relative to a contour. III. Factorization and algebras. Math. Nachr. 55(1973), 33-61 [Russian].

29. I.C. Gohberg, A.S. Markus: Two theorems on the gap between subspaces of a Banach space. Uspehi Mat. Nauk 14(1959), 135-140 [Russian].

30. I. Gohberg, L. Rodman: On spectral analysis of non-monic matrix and operator polynomials, I. Reduction to monic polynomials. Israel J. Math. 30(1978), 133-151.

31. I.C. Gohberg, E.I. Sigal: An operator generalization of the logarithmic residue theorem and the theorem of Rouché. Mat. Sbornik 84(126) (1971), 607-629 [Russian]= Math. USSR, Sbornik 13(1971), 603-625.

32. S. Goldberg: Unbounded linear operators. New York, McGraw-Hill, 1966.

33. R.J. Hangelbroek: A functional analytic approach to the linear transport equation. Thesis Universiteit Groningen, 1973.

34. R.J. Hangelbroek: The linear transport equation in a medium with anisotropic scattering (degenerate scattering function).

35. R.J. Hangelbroek, C.G. Lekkerkerker: Decompositions of a Hilbert space and factorization of a W-A determinant. Siam J. Math. Analysis 8(1977), 459-472.

36. J.W. Helton: Systems with infinite-dimensional state space: the Hilbert space approach. Proc. IEEE 64(1) (1976), 145-160.

37. T. Kato: Perturbation theory for linear operators. Springer, Berlin-Heidelberg-New York, 1966.

38. N.M. Kostenko: Necessary and sufficient condition for factorization of rational matrix functions. Functional Analysis and Applications 12(1978), 87-88 [Russian].

39. H-J. Kowalsky: Lineare Algebra. Berlin, Walter de Gruyter, 1967.

40. M.G. Krein: Introduction to the geometry of indefinite J-spaces and to the theory of operators in these spaces. Amer. Math. Soc. Transl. (2) 93 (1970), 103-176.

41. H. Kwakernaak, R. Sivan: Linear optimal control systems. Wiley-Interscience, New York, 1972.

42. C.G. Lekkerkerker: On eigendistributions in linear trans-

port theory. Proc. Royal Soc. Edinburgh, to appear.

43. C. van der Mee: Realization and linearization. Wiskundig Seminarium der Vrije Universiteit, Amsterdam, Rapport nr 109, 1979.

44. B. Mitiagin: Linearization of holomorphic operator functions. I, II. Integral equations and operator theory 1(1978), 114-131 and 226-249.

45. L.A. Sahnovic: On the factorization of an operator-valued transfer function. Soviet Math. Dokl. 17(1976), 203-207.

46. M.A. Shubin: On holomorphic families of subspaces of a Banach space. Mat. Issled. 5(1970), 153-165; Letter to the editors, Mat. Issled. 6(1971), 180 [Russian].

47. B. Sz-Nagy, C. Foiaş: Analyse harmonique des opérateur de l'espace de Hilbert. Paris, Masson and Akad. Kiado, Budapest, 1967.

48. J. Vandewalle, P. Dewilde: On the irreducible cascade synthesis of a system with a real rational transfer matrix. IEEE Trans. Circuits and Systems, vol CAS-24 (9)(1977), 481-494.

49. J. Vandewalle, P. Dewilde: A local i/o structure theory for multivariable systems and its application to minimal cascade realization. IEEE Trans. Circuits and Systems, vol. CAS-25 (5)(1978), 279-289.

50. D.C. Youla, P. Tissi: An explicit formula for the degree of a rational matrix, Electrophysics Memo, PIBM RI-1273-65, Polytechnic Institute of Brooklyn, Electrophysics Department, 1965.

51. D.C. Youla, P. Tissi: n-Port synthesis via reactance extraction. Part 1. IEEE Int. Con. Rec. Pt 7, vol. 14 (1966), 183-208.

SUBJECT INDEX

angular operator, 110
angular subspace, 110
associate main operator, 7

canonical Jordan triple, 48
canonical system of Jordan chains, 46
canonical Wiener-Hopf factorization, 125
characteristic operator function
  Krein characteristic operator function, 21
  Livsic-Brodskii characteristic operator function, 20

degree
  of monic node, 25
  of monic supporting projection, 26
  local degree, 77
  McMillan degree, 83
distance between nodes, 154

eigenvalue
  of operator on real space, 198
  of rational matrix function, 44, 48
eigenvector of rational matrix function, 45, 48
  rank of, 45
equation
  discrete Wiener-Hopf equation, 100
  Riccatti equation, 118
  singular integral equation, 105
  transport equation, 122
  Wiener-Hopf integral equation, 93
equivalence of operator functions, 56
extension, 56
external operator, 5

factorization
canonical Wiener-Hopf factorization, 125
isolated factorization, 190, 207, 210
left canonical factorization, 13
left spectral factorization, 13
minimal factorization, 84, 85
minimal real factorization, 194
real factorization, 194
right canonical factorization, 13
right spectral factorization, 13
stable factorization of monic matrix polynomials, 183, 210
stable factorization of rational matrix functions, 178, 208
Wiener-Hopf factorization, 124

gap, 148

Hautus test, 82

input space, 5
invariant subspace
isolated invariant subspace, 177, 196
perfectly stable invariant subspace, 212
stable invariant subspace, 169, 196

Jordan chain, 45
canonical system of Jordan chains, 46
length of, 45
Jordan pair, 46
dual Jordan pair, 47
Jordan triple
canonical Jordan triple, 48

linearization, 56
local degree, 77

main operator, 5
maximal opening, 148
McMillan degree, 83
minimal
    angle, 146
    factorization, 84, 85
    node, 63
    opening, 146
    real factorization, 194
    realization, 63
    real realization, 192
Möbius transformation of nodes, 35
multiplicity
    algebraic multiplicity, 198
    geometric multiplicity, 198
    geometric multiplicity of pole, 50
    geometric multiplicity of zero, 45
    partial pole-multiplicities, 50
    partial zero-multiplicities, 46, 48
    pole-multiplicity, 50
    zero-multiplicity, 46

node, 5
    associate node, 7
    biminimal node, 72
    Brodskii J-node, 20
    comonic polynomial node, 29
    companion node, 25
    controllable node, 63
    first companion node, 25
    Krein J-node, 22
    minimal node, 63
    monic node, 25
    node similarity, 5
    observable node, 63

polynomial node, 29
product of nodes, 6
projection of nodes, 10

operator, 4
angular operator, 110
associate main operator, 7
conjugate of operator, 197
external operator, 5
main operator, 5
real operator, 197
state space operator, 5

partial indices, 124
pole-vector, 49
pole-zero cancellation, 86
product of nodes, 6
projection
of monic node, 27
Riesz projection, 11
spectral projection, 203
stable supporting projection, 179, 208
supporting projection, 9

rank
of eigenvector, 45
of pole-vector, 50
realization, 6
controllable realization, 63
minimal realization, 63
minimal real realization, 192
observable realization, 63
real realization, 192
Riccati equation, 118
isolated solution of Riccati equation, 190, 211

stable solution of Riccati equation, 187, 211
Riesz projection, 11

selfconjugate, 191, 197
similarity of nodes, 5
spectral subspace, 12
spectrum of operator on real space, 198
stable factorization
of monic matrix polynomials, 183, 210
of rational matrix functions, 178, 208
stable invariant subspace, 169, 196
perfectly stable invariant subspace, 212
stable solution of Riccati equation, 187, 211
state space, 5
state space operator, 5
supporting projection, 9
isolated supporting projection, 208
stable supporting projection, 179, 208
monic supporting projection, 26
supporting subspace, 29
symbol, 94, 101, 124

transfer function, 5

zero of rational matrix function, 44, 48

Volume 1

OPERATOR THEORY: ADVANCES AND APPLICATIONS

H. Bart
Vrije Universiteit, Amsterdam

I. Gohberg
Tel-Aviv University, Ramat-Aviv

M. A. Kaashoek
Vrije Universiteit, Amsterdam

Minimal Factorization of Matrix and Operator Functions

Birkhäuser Verlag
Basel · Boston · Stuttgart

Printed in Switzerland

Library of Congress Cataloging in Publication Data

Bart, Harm.
Minimal factorization of matrix and operator functions.
(Operator theory, advances and applications; 1)
Bibliography: p.
Includes index.
1. Operator theory. 2. Matrices. 3. Integral equations – Numerical solutions. I. Gokhberg, Izrail' Tsudikovich, joint author. II. Kaashoek, M. A., joint author. III. Title. IV. Series.
QA329.B37 515.7'24 79–28096
ISBN 3–7643–1139–8

CIP-Kurztitelaufnahme der Deutschen Bibliothek

Bart, Harm:
Minimal factorization of matrix and operator functions / by H. Bart; I. Gohberg; M. A. Kaashoek. – Basel, Boston, Stuttgart: Birkhäuser, 1979.
(Operator theory; 1)
ISBN 3–7643–1139–8
NE: Gochberg, Izrail' C.; Kaashoek, Marinus A.

ISBN 3–7643–1139–8